Listen
Closely

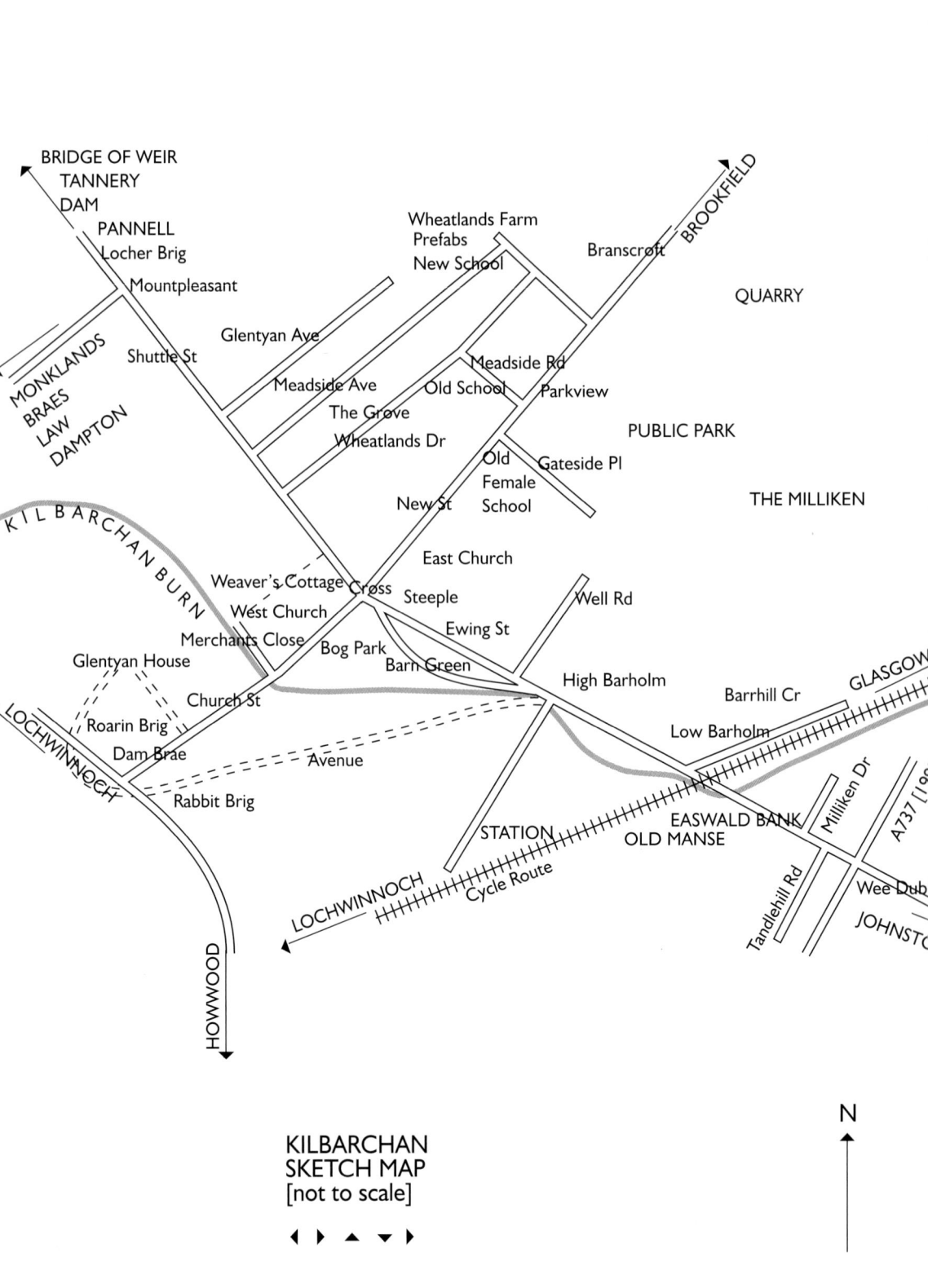

Listen Closely

an oral history of Kilbarchan 1900 – 2000

COLIN CAMPBELL
CHRISTINE MACLEOD

ARGYLL✥PUBLISHING

© Colin Campbell and Christine MacLeod 2020
© photos as credited

Argyll Publishing
an imprint of Thirsty Books
www.thirstybooks.com

The rights of the authors have been asserted by them in accordance with the Copyright, Designs and Patents Act 1988.

British Library Cataloguing-in-Publication Data.
A catalogue record for this book is available from the British Library.

ISBN 978-1-9161112-1-9

Printing & Binding
Bell & Bain Ltd, Glasgow

To the people of Kilbarchan

Stand close and touch this way marker;
listen closely to what it is telling you;
Even the longest winters have an end.

from 'Clochoderick Stone'
Jim Carruth
Black Cart (Polygon, 2019)

The Clochoderick Stone – A glacial deposit, a rocking stone. For many generations a popular destination for childhood expeditions. 'One of the boys fell off and broke his leg.'

Contents

	Foreword	9
1	Country Life	13
2	Farming life	23
3	Kilbarchan – a place like no other	33
4	Interloupers	45
5	Three Rs	58
6	Homes	63
7	New Houses from Old	73
8	Keeping a Roof Over Your Head	81
9	Schools	87
10	World War I	109
11	World War II	125
12	The Kilbarchan Churches	146
13	Organisations	157
14	More Organisations	169
15	Football	177
16	Athletics	189
17	Dancing and 'the dancin'	196
18	Hatches, Matches and Despatches	203
19	Gardens	211
20	Pigeons	218
21	By Road and Rail	227
22	Work	237
23	Shops	253
24	Childhood Memories	265

The Cross at the start of the twentieth century, looking towards the Steeple, along Steeple Street. Nothing but horse drawn vehicles. Meikle's shop on the corner. The building was demolished in the 1960s, to widen the roads for increased traffic

Looking down narrow Church Street from the Cross. The blank gable end belonged to a café, since demolished, as was the next building. The men on the steps of what became the Weaver's Cottage are risking a soaking from Miss Christie. Kilbarchan's roofs were not red. They have been wrongly coloured by the German printers, who were not familiar with slate roofs!

Foreword

IN 2018, sharing interests in both national and local history, the decision was made to interview people who live, or had lived, in the village. A comprehensive history, covering every twentieth century event and interest in Kilbarchan, was not intended. There was a draft outline, but it was much modified by villagers' collective reminiscences.

No one was intimidated by the presence of the digital recorder. It was explained that anything that was said might appear in print!

The recordings began in May 2018 and ended in December 2019. Conversations with each individual were relaxed, as all were villagers. Formal barriers had been broken years ago! Work on the content began in January 2020. It was severely curtailed by the lockdown in March, which made e-mail and telephone contact mandatory, but the impetus was maintained.

Normal access to old newspaper files was impossible. Fortunately a thirty years old summary of *Renfrewshire Gazette* Kilbarchan headlines was available, which covered 1900 to 1920, and a forty years old tape recording of a First World War veteran. These and the internet supplemented the content of the interviews.

As history began a second ago, it was clear, as the book progressed, that it encompassed a very long time! The oldest person interviewed was born in 1924. To the young, that's an unimaginable age ago, but to older folk, whose lifetime memories are fresh, it is almost yesterday. The fundamentals of life, birth, death, love, joy and sorrow are timeless. The background to these is a kaleidoscope of never ending change and adaptation.

The Second World War was a watershed which separated those who lived through it, from those born after it. Covid 19 is a watershed, which has had huge economic consequences and may change social life, as it was known , forever. This makes the reminiscences from a world of mass gatherings, freedom of movement, and crowded family events, even more remote from current reality than it was before the pandemic

It was a privilege and a pleasure to be welcomed into the intimacy of people's homes and to talk with them. The hope is that readers will enjoy these glimpses of village life in the twentieth century.

Colin Campbell, Christine MacLeod
October 2020

Acknowledgements

The following forty four people were interviewed, some more than once: Eric Borland, Mima Borland, Colin Campbell, Evelyn Campbell, John Carlin, David Carlin, Bobby Carruth, Bill Chittick, Nan Chittick, Drew Connell, Graeme Dickie, Helen Dooris, Agnes Douglas, Jennifer Douglas, Lottie Dow, Christine Erwin, Walter Gardner, Irene Gibson, Myra Goldie, Sandy Graham, Anne Grieve, Ethel Hamilton, Jan Howitt, Norrie Howitt, Jan Kier, Helen Miller, Ian Miller, Jack Miller, Alex Murphy, Mabel Murray, Helen McCaig, Cathy McDermott, Eliza MacKenzie, Anne MacLeod, Christine MacLeod, Elspeth Robertson, Arthur Smith, Moira Smith, Georgina Stephen, John Stephen, Ian Trushell, Janet Tytler, Jim Tytler and Jeff Webster.

Good fortune brought retired publisher Derek Rodger into the project. His participation was invaluable: he negotiated a completion date which maintained a reasonable degree of urgency. His editing experience and advice were invaluable.

Thanks to: Andrew Stark of *Stark Images*; George Grant for editing old postcards; Jimmy Carruth, poet, for allowing 'Until the Cows Come Home' to be included and his extract from 'Clochoderick Stone'; Jennifer Douglas for access to family records and the letters of John Meikle M.M.; the Birnie family and Judy Ormond for allowing their fathers' paintings to be shown; and everyone who shared their memories, lent treasured family photographs or answered follow up calls.

Finally, thanks to Evelyn Campbell and Iain MacLeod for their unfailing patience and support.

Old Parish Kirk, Church Street. Built in 1724, close to what was then the centre of the village, the Toonfit

Kilbarchan station, early twentieth century

Cows in Church Street, at the part where the Horse Fairs were held.
Second house is where the Scouts first met in 1909

Chapter 1
Country Life

'The cry would go up that he was burning the hooves.'

WITHIN a century, what were once independent villages have been swallowed by their close proximity to a town, or expanded out of recognition. It is becoming a rare place where within a five-minute walk from the centre of a village, you are in the countryside.

The area around the village of Kilbarchan is not flat land. It is a balance of easy walking, low-lying pastoral hills and challenging steep braes, with rewarding views into the distance. Many from the village, who were not directly involved in farming or other occupations in the country spoke of their links with the countryside around them. It was simply such an important part of their lives.

What we now consider quiet country roads were, for centuries, main trade routes. The existing roads interlinking the farms, the farms with the village. They were the important routes for trade in crops, livestock, milk, and food.

The coming of the tractor, a huge investment, changed farming forever. The slow, plodding horses' hooves had often caused little impact on the soil. Many of the well-worked and productive fields had clay drainage pipes, which lay undisturbed by the beasts. The coming of the tractor broke the pipes and wrecked what had been successful drainage systems. The importance of good land management had an impact on the village, especially from the uphill farms, remembered by David Carlin as a child in the 1930s.

'They used to dam the fields and put in clay pipes. Tractors broke all the drainage pipes in the fields. Cattle and horses do no harm to the fields. In the past they never had pools in the fields and flooding on the roads. Ground was meant for horses. They also don't plough any more.'

Other independent people played their part in ensuring drains were cleared and retaining hedges maintained. David spoke of the roadmen up in the high roads in the country, who greatly assisted those living in the village below.

'There were roadmen for different sections of Kilbarchan, and they called the roads after them. The Hays had a road. They kept the burn open all the time. Now that they have all gone, there was flooding in the village. They maybe slept by the side of the road. They would get about two or three pounds a week wages but could have saved a lot of problems in the village.'

Still seen around the village, the remnants of neglected hedges, which were once cut by hand by well-known local men. 'The Jamiesons cut the hedges, it was hard work.' David knew Peter and Jimock well, they had a mutual interest in pigeons. 'Peter was small, he did the sides. Jimock did the tops.'

Nature study was a common subject in school. John Carlin won a prize for nature when he was at school in the 1930s. Collecting birds' eggs was an acceptable hobby. John and his younger brother, David, were also keen on this. It required a close observance of the habits and habitats of the birds, and of course physical fitness; to know the best way to climb trees. John and David, like boys all over the country would have known the trees well. Now outlawed, a rare bird's egg was a thing to treasure.

The ability to just go for a walk in fresh air, take in the views, the countryside and nature, was for many, a pleasure at any stage of life.

Helen Dooris, who lived in the centre of the village, had a granny who lived at Dampton farm. She and her friend Mabel Murray 'were never off the go, they ran and walked.' They also recalled:

'A group of children would go out – Eddie McMurray, Edwin Muir, George Anderson went with Mabel, the eldest, age 9, pushing her brother in the pram. With a bottle of water, lemonade or juice if you were lucky, jeely pieces, and off for the day. Clochoderick stone for a picnic, home by teatime.'

Their ability to push a pram up the long steep incline, and hang on to it on the same descent says a lot for their strength, not to mention the trust parents had in giving young children such responsibility. It was normal then for parents to trust children to look after each other and allow them freedom. It was a well-known route for previous generations.

Going for a walk was also the thing to do on a Sunday. At a time when attendance at church, and the adherence to the day of rest was still observed, a walk got people out. It gave the young a chance to be by themselves and away from their parents.

> 'With a bottle of water, lemonade or juice if you were lucky, jeely pieces, and off for the day.'

Liza McKenzie:

'Sheila Muir and Jean Keir and I would go for walks up the country, the Dampton Pad, which was good, with its stiles, it was a favourite walk. We would go on the back roads to Howwood, to Clochoderick stone.'

Georgina Stephen:

'When I was about 9 or 10 the wee group would make pieces and walk to Clochoderick stone.'

The group had active imaginations about the surrounding area.

'We went to Faulds Farm to the hill with the hollow, which they imagined might have been a volcano. They could look over and see a lovely big house with trout in the pond. One of the gang, Bob Gardner, would eventually own the property.'

By the 1950s, the village children went to secondary school in the nearby town of Johnstone, as did the children from neighbouring villages. Occasionally, the group would venture to a nearby village. 'We sometimes went to Howwood; we knew others from our class and went to the swing park.'

Some walks were also what would now be called extreme. Ellen McCaig remembered: 'Will Smith walked to Largs for a wee daunner. Seventeen miles. God knows how.'

Visits to the country were often organised. One of the most

memorable was the Sunday School trip. Before the days of train and bus trips, local transport was used. Agnes Douglas recalled:

> 'We went on Sunday School trips. During the war, they went on Currie's lorries up to The Braes. We played races in the fields and tea was a poke with a roll inside, latterly sausage rolls.'

As did Helen Dooris:

> 'Sunday school trips. We took our own mug and stuff was provided to eat and drink. At the farms, we had swings in barns and races in the fields.'

> 'At Easter, we used to go up there [the dam] for tadpoles, with a jeely jor and a net.'

All of these took place before the widespread use of the car. Walking in the country then was undoubtedly much safer than walking the same routes by the end of the century.

The weather, of course played a huge part in activities. John Carlin remembered the long hot summers:

> 'Used to have 2-3 months of good weather. During the school holidays there were 1-2 wet days every 6 weeks. Bare feet. [Melted] tar stuck on feet.'

His brother David remembered the cold winters:

> 'The severest winter was about 12 to 14 below. The van was stuck up the road for weeks. The snow was the same level as the fields. Clearing that was done by manual labour by them that weren't working at that time. They worked in their ordinary clothes. 1947 was a bad year. You had to find your own way, but you always got to your work.'

People found places in the country to make their own entertainment and learn new skills. The local dam, built for the print works, that later became the tannery, was a big draw.

David Carlin and his brother John: 'At Easter, we used to go up there for tadpoles, with a jeely jor and a net.'

The next generation also went to the same place. Jeff Webster would also go up to the curling pond to catch tadpoles and newts. David 'used to go up to the big dam for a swim, up the burn, go bare scuddy into the water. The sun would dry your clothes.'

Jeff also 'learned to swim at the neck of the dam, the depth of which went in stages... then learned to dive off the sluice.'

The dam was also used in winter. David spoke of 'a curling pond, about 20 feet from the side of the dam.' They used to go up to the curling pond as boys. Jeff knew of this too. 'The big dam used to have a lade that worked the machines. People skated on it. The Paisley Pirates used to come up and play there.'

Closer to both their homes was a deserted curling pool: it was a circular dam, which had rushes in it. It was always quite full of water, 'a couple of feet deep'.

David 'used to go to Locherfield in the winter, it had a shallow pond. The Glasgow Mohawks played an ice hockey tournament there before the war. Saw them there when I was about 10. It was a right winter's day – there were cold winters then, severe winters.'

The dam was also used by the Locher Angling Club. Eric Borland was a member. 'Nice trout there,' he remembers. He also fished close by, in the Locher burn. Eric went to 'the pools', as did many, but not just for fishing. Eric explained that these were:

> '... wee dams built by farmers in the burn for cattle to drink, then developed into pools. Used to go up there swimming. There was the channel, at the other side of East Barnaigh, the Higher Linn, near the hump back bridge, and the rocky bottom, that was quite deep.'

Helen Dooris also remembered going there as a child.

> 'We used to go up to The Pools as they called them. Mrs Bradford always built a fire. She would put a match in the can of water to save it from the fumes of the burning wood.'

Everyone had their favourite places to visit. Some had a favourite place, a bit off the 'official' path, i.e. in private land. This was visited by generations of children. 'The Six White Horses'.

Jim and Janet Tytler explain:

> 'The six white horses. You blow down into it and listened! This had been a pond with a fountain, about 10 yards in and 10 yards to the left. It is a sphere of copper, which the water came from. There is still water in it. If you blow, you

'We used to go up to The Pools as they called them. Mrs Bradford always built a fire.'

17

reduce the water pressure and it comes up.'

The sound of horses galloping was meant to be heard. The origin of the story of the number of horses, and what colour they were is unknown. Most visitors just left with wet ears!!

Looking after, buying and selling horses, in all communities, until the twentieth century, was of great importance. The *Renfreshire Gazette* of 1901 referred to the annual Horse Fair held in December at the bottom of Church Street. One can only imagine the deals struck there and advice given. On a cold December day, it is likely that the local bakers and publicans would also look forward to the event.

> 'Horses were not just for use on the farm – the movement of goods to and from the station, and neighbouring towns, the delivery of coal, milk and groceries – all relied on the animal.'

Horses were not just for use on the farm – the movement of goods to and from the station, and neighbouring towns, the delivery of coal, milk and groceries – all relied on the animal. As the use of the horse declined, the sight of one in the village was fascinating, particularly when it was in Geordie Fulton's forge.

Horses would be taken there, up the brae, to be shod. Helen Dooris remembered the smell.

> 'There was no other smell like Geordie Fulton burning horses hooves . . . the best smell in the world! The cry would go up that he was burning the hooves, they would gather round the front and side door of the smithy sniffing up the smell! This was right on the corner opposite Bobbins. At that time the bus came up the brae. Geordie lived above the smiddy; don't know how many times the corner was taken off his roof by the bus.

Jeff Webster had the absolute joy of helping the blacksmith, something to contravene all health and safety laws.

> 'Fulton's Forge was at the top of Steeple Street. Geordie Fulton shoed the Clydesdale horses. Kids would look in the front door. He would pick out a child to help. I held the big horse's hoof between my knees. Fulton would shave the hoof, pull out the old nail, try a standard shoe, heat and bend it to shape and press it onto the hoof. The smell of the shoe on the hoof. The new nails were put in sideways. They were docile beasts. It was great, I loved it. Fulton did all

sorts of things including threshing machines. The fire was red-, going on white-hot. The hoof was as big as me. "Staun here and haud that," Geordie Fulton would say. He wore a leather apron and he fascinated the crowd. His workshop was total darkness inside. The mechanical bellows turned the fire bright cherry red almost instantly.'

Within close proximity to the forge, across the narrow street, was Currie's Pend. Here, on a daily basis, up until the 1950s, other beasts made their way slowly from the field next to the public park. Cows were milked in Currie's Pend, as Ian Trushell remembers:

'Currie's grazed them in the field between the public park and the driveway to the quarry. At around 4pm Annie Miller, of Currie Miller, the hauliers [cairters], would go to get the cows. She would lead them down New Street; turn left at The Cross, and into Currie's Pend. There was a coal yard there, and a byre. She put them into the stalls. She milked them by hand. There were hardly any cars then. Annie then brought the kye back up on the main road. There were maybe about a dozen. This was done every day.'

'Fulton's Forge was at the top of Steeple Street. Geordie Fulton shoed the Clydesdale horses. Kids would look in the front door. He would pick out a child to help.'

What conditions the roads would be like afterwards with the mixture of cattle and horse dung can only be imagined. Nearby residents had no need to go far for organic garden fertiliser!

On occasions, Steeple Square [or The Knowe, as it was called] was the gathering place for a particular group of people who made use of the countryside for their own particular enjoyment. Jeff Webster:

'The Hunt met at Houston House, occasionally at Steeple Square, where the Stirrup Cups went out. They rode past the steeple steps. I could see the hunt from my bedroom window coming up from Pannel Farm. *"Come on the fox."* The Hunt went over the fields. Someone was traumatised when she witnessed the dogs catch the fox. The Hunt did a lot of damage. People had to go round and fix the fences afterwards. This caused trauma. It became a huge issue in the Scottish Parliament.'

The groups most likely to be used enjoying the outdoors were the people from the village. Village and farming life were inseparable. Out and about children, then adults, would be well aware of what was freely available to collect from the roadsides. Pre-war, jam was one of the most common forms of sweetness in the diet. A 'piece 'n jam' sustained children and adults.

Helen Dooris used to go in a crowd up to the Dampton Brae:

> 'My granny used to send us to pick blueberries during the war; she used them to make jelly. My granny used to examine our mouths to see if we had eaten any! This involved hanging over the edge of a quarry, where the biggest and fattest ones were, at Jack Douglas's farm.'

> **'[The Hunt] rode past the steeple steps. I could see the hunt from my bedroom window coming up from Pannel Farm. "Come on the fox".'**

During the war years, reosehips, an abundant source of vitamin C, were still collected, as Moira Smith remembered doing in the 1970s, 'and handing them into Cunningham's shop'.

On the edges of the village, there were the smallholdings. Some of these grew fruit, mainly strawberries on a more organised scale Many children were involved. The use of child labour was accepted – it got children into the fresh air, and occupied them in the early summer school holidays. Many sore backs and sunburn. The ability to eat and pick the fruit at the same time must have sickened some children from the taste of a fresh strawberry for life. A seasonal job, which paid little, but provided work, and a small income, that we might not otherwise have had.

The building of a new road for the benefit of other communities, the Johnstone bypass, in the 1970s, cut through the middle of the village smallholdings. Simultaneously, the mass importation of food easily purchased from the new supermarkets had become the norm, making it uneconomic for the independent smallholders to continue.

By the end of the century to actually walk in the country became rarer. It is more usual to travel by car. The roads were busier with traffic than people. By the 1980s, it was more common to see an occasional runner focussing on a personal best rather than the beauty of nature around them.

As everywhere, the village in the twentieth century has undergone change, much of which cannot be pushed back. One such example is the closure of the station and the removal of the railway tracks. Years later, the making of the cycle track in its place was much to the benefit of those who chose to access it from the village.

The use of the countryside surrounding the village, and the occupations and skills needed have altered or have now disappeared. Babies will still be out in their prams, walks taken, berries picked and wee daunners taken, but on a track designed for bikes. The horses and cattle in the streets are memories. It's a different life; but the potential is still there for new generations to appreciate what is around them.

All ages hay-making on a Kilbarchan farm. Within a hundred years one or two men, with machines, would do the job

Until the cows come home

Until the cows come home
First I will give you names
For names are important
You will take my hand
And we will do nothing else
All day but dance outside
Just the two of us
Barefoot
Across the fields of
Meikle Burnshields
Little Burntshields
Shillingworth
Mid Barnaigh
East Barnaigh
Laigh Auchencloich
High Auchencloich
Laigh Auchensale
The Braes
Not stopping
Until we've covered
The quiet lands of
Law
Lawmarnock
Barnbrock
Moniabrock
Monkland
Dampton
Barnbeth
Clevans
Locher
A sombre waltz in long grass
For the lost herds of the shire

Jimmy Carruth (*Bovine Pastoral* 2004 and *Black Cart* 2017)

Chapter 2
Farming life

'. . . put stobs in the field to mark the peewits' nests.'

FARMING life has perhaps seen one of the biggest changes in the twentieth century. Both world wars had an impact on farming life. The loss of so many men during both wars meant that women were much more involved than usual in the practicalities of work on the farm. Production methods altered and advanced to meet changing local, European and global demands.

The names of the farms around the village shown in the The Poll Tax Record of 1695, have altered little. The landscape has changed little. Similarly, the names of the families in some of the farms continue working the land. The land is much the same.

Bobby Carruth, a descendant of one of the early farming families, the Carruths of Lawmarnock, continues to be involved in farming, and has seen a lot of changes in the latter part of the century. His family farm is High Auchensale.

> 'In grandfather's day, there was no set market for milk. He had a retail round, delivering in Kilbarchan and Bridge of Weir and had the contract for the local hospitals. The surplus went into cans and was taken to a central point'.

> 'The landscape has changed in some ways, not in others. A lot of farming the same way, now a lot smarter, more technical, with seismic shifts in our century'.

Farms around the village were increasingly linked to dairy cattle. Fields around grazed the cows, or were farmed to produce the food for them.

> 'The area is almost exclusively dairy. Crops are grown

largely for sustaining livestock. At the end of the war they were still working with horses. Crops were also needed to sustain the horses. Food was grown for the animals around the village. The amount of grain grown has decreased steeply.'

By the latter half of the century, the local farm, which once provided for the village and surrounding areas, was linked to European law.

'Food security in the post-war period. EU, Common Agricultural Policy, butter mountains, wine lakes, grain storage, all had impact on farmers. Produce as much as you could.'

This undoubtedly had an impact on the local farm, and every part of farming life, in all areas of the country. By the latter half of the century:

'EU milk quotas were beginning to bite. Milk production organisation was changing.'

'It was a game of chance. UK had its own total milk quota, Scotland had its own. If it fell under, everyone fell under. There were stringent penalties. It was very complex, a complete change from the old ways.

'When times were good. . . the farm was producing 3,000 litres a day – 500 gallons a day. There were celebrations when things were good. We all went to the Italian's in Paisley.'

Many families relied on seasonal workers. As Bobby remembers:

'The family tended to have one worker. HND students from Agricultural College, Auchencruive did one-year practical. They lived on the farm, in the house with the family.

'Students stayed in an upstairs room. They had meals with the family. This started with granddad. He would be bringing students the same age as his dad. Some travelled quite a distance. My mother looked after them. They got involved in the Young Farmers. Some were from Islay, Mull,

Kintyre. Kilbarchan was the nearest thing to the big smoke. Other farms would have farm working staff from the village.'

Farmers were well informed. People, through experience, in many cases handed down through the family, would have been well aware of political and economic events that directly affected them. Although living and working in more remote areas, they came together frequently to exchange ideas, livestock, harvests, through necessity of work. They shared those ideas as they moved around the country. They were well tuned in. The working year was built around the farming community.

An example of people who, through principle, gave up their time to make their point, demonstrating and blockading in late 1997.

Bobby's family, along with the majority of farmers in Scotland, were affected by the situation regarding Irish beef imports.

> 'Farmers were becoming political with the Irish beef imports, which affected the local farms. There were blockades at Merkland Docks and at Stranraer. Beef prices were crashing as cheaper Irish beef was coming in. There were a lot of protests.'

For farmers with dairy herds to be milked on a daily basis, taking time off work to travel and protest was not an easy thing to do. The National Farmers Union were important at this stage. Many farmers joined, often through necessity.

There was another place where farmers like Bobby, could come together. A place often where membership ran in the family, Bobby's parents met there.

> 'I Went to Young Farmers instead of Venture Scouts. The local branch was the West Renfrewshire Young Farmers. A robust club, with the odd fluctuation in numbers. Not exclusive to farmers, inclusive of local villages.
>
> 'It's not just about stocksmanship. There were quizzes, speech making, and charity events in addition to the social attraction.
>
> 'The Young Farmers Met at St Machar's church hall, used

local primary schools, village halls, and wherever they could get a room. Weekly, seasonal programmes. Football, hockey and netball in the summer.'

The assumption was that the inheritance of the farm would go to the eldest son even if the first born child was a girl. This changed and families were split because of this, and in some cases, the farm itself was divided. By the end of the century, the children of farmers also had the choice to be a farmer, or pursue other areas of work.

'The children were never pressurised to work on the farm. They always helped out when needed. Everyone helped out.'

Farming is a way of life to many who were born into it, but for some people, the determination to have their own farm and make it work is equally important.

Many of the farms, through varying circumstances, were sold on many times over. One such farm is that of Dampton, situated about two miles from the village Cross.

Andrew Douglas, with some knowledge of farming elsewhere, took on Dampton in the 1950s. The girl Andrew chose to marry, was not a farmer. Agnes Currie was born in the village, from a village family, with no experience of farming life or the reality of moving from the buzz of the village, to the seclusion and hard work of life on the farm. Agnes recalled:

'He came there with his mother. It was at that time, totally run down. When Andrew first came to the farm, it was a mess. The walls had green distemper, it had old ranges, and everything was really old fashioned.'

While life in the village was becoming more comfortable, particularly with the wonders of electricity, comfort took longer to reach the farms. Upgrading costs money. Difficult choices would have to be made on whether to spend on improving family comfort or benefiting the economic development of the farm.

'There was no electricity in the house when Andrew moved in, in 1952. They used paraffin lamps. They went in 1954. Electricity was not that widespread, this was common in farms. They have progressed a lot.'

As was common, farms around the village had been let out for generations, often also resulting in little investment in the farm or land, if it was not owned. Jennifer Douglas, daughter of Andrew and Agnes, did much research into the history of her family farm. It showed how much the farm changed ownership over the centuries and how much it was leased out to others.

> 'It was a series of short-term lets, which didn't encourage people to invest.'

Workers were needed on farms, in many cases they stayed in part of the farm house. 'In Dampton, they lived upstairs'.

Helen Dooris, who grew up in the centre of the village, knew of the farm well.

> 'My mum lived as a tenant at Dampton Farm, my grandpa died there.'

Life on the farm for men was hard. Agnes described how Andrew slowly built up the farm over a number of years:

> 'Andrew started with pigs. They used to be close to the house, and in the byre. Keeping pigs was the cheapest, as he had started with nothing. 2-3 years later, he wanted to have a dairy herd. He had to convert the byres to cattle stalls where the styes had previously been.'

> 'Andrew had the odd casual people at harvest time. His mother did the housekeeping and kept the hens.'

Through time, and sheer hard work, Andrew built up the farm.

> 'The farm had to get bigger and bigger, we finished up with 60 cows.

> 'The machinery came in around the time that Andrew bought the farm. He had horses. He got an Allis-Chalmers tractor, then a wee grey Fergie.'

Life for women was just as hard. In addition to the bearing of children, the rearing of children and general housekeeping, the women were involved in all aspects of farm life.

> 'Lizzie Hamilton and Hugh Thomson. She would do the milking and clean the milk dishes, keep house and hens. It was a tough life.'

> 'The women looked after the smaller animals.'

> 'The house had two ranges. In what is now the kitchen, they boiled the food for the pigs.'

The rearing of the beef calves was Agnes' job.

> 'They were reared until about 6 weeks old, then sold on. They went to market. The bull calves for beef; the female crossbred animals were used for veal.'

Agnes helped to birth calves.

> 'Andrew made a pulley thing, which worked, and didn't do them any harm.'

> 'Pottie the vet from Paisley had to be called, often during the night, but all of the farmers helped each other if they could.'

Agnes kept hens and used to sell the eggs. She had a run of deliveries to friends and some businesses in Paisley. This was on a Saturday, when afterwards she would go and visit gran, then go home.

> 'It was hard work. 7 days a week, not off for Christmas or New Year. We got by.'

For some women, an alternative may have been more favoured.

> 'Women may have been happy to go into service. Women were less inclined to work on farms.'

At busy times in the farming calendar, seasonal workers were hired. Agnes recalled:

> 'If he hired help, people usually would come and ask from the village.'

Agnes' description of a typical day stands as a tribute to the life and endeavours of dairy farmers throughout the land.

The day started at 6 am. She was the first up and brought in the cows. Andrew got all the feeding stuff ready. He originally milked by hand and put it into churns. There was no pipeline or tank. It involved carrying pails to the milk house, cooling the milk and putting it into big churns. The cooling machine used water from the well. Cans had to be steamed every day. New regulations meant that milk had to be tanked though a pipeline. Milk was lifted every day by the tankers.

They had a tank system. They were selling to the Scottish Milk Marketing Board, always to them. There were always checks, random quality checks by a milk officer who took samples to make sure all was well. Andrew was very, very particular. The tanks were washed every morning.

They used to clear out the byres with a shovel, barrow to midden, into the spreaders and onto the land. They got the chance of putting in a byre mucker, a chain that came up and dropped muck into the spreader, meaning that they didn't have to shovel as much. It was then taken out to the fields. This was a great invention; it saved a lot of bother.

In the West of Scotland, the seasons obviously plan out the farming year. With lambing, most of the sheep are left to get on with it, unless they see something unusual. Twins are easy, but sometimes there are 3 or 4. They are kept nearer the house, where a closer eye can be kept on them.

'The farming year ultimately was the health of the beasts.'

Farm hands signed up with farmers for a year, usually on market day over drink and a handshake.

Whatever their origin, farmers needed good neighbours. All farmers were communicators. She had great neighbours, the best you could have. In winter they cleared the road to the farm. When Agnes was shut in for three days, neighbours brought bread and milk. 'That's farming,' said Agnes.

The roads around the farms were once busy with people from the village coming to the farms to work, or leaving the farms with produce. Workers were needed at certain times of the year, many workers were needed. From the daily workers, those who worked with the milk, to the seasonal tattie howkers and fruit pickers.

Alex Murphy, who worked at Smiths farm in the 1940s, as a youth, recalled his story:

> 'I delivered the milk from the farm to Mountpleasant to The Grove, Church Street, Steeple Street, New Street and Wheatlands before going to school.'

There were three farms, which delivered milk to the village. Smith's, whom Alex worked for, Flem Craig and the Co-op. Flem Craig and the Co-op delivered by horse and cart, Smiths delivered by van.

> 'The milk came in 5 gallon luggies. These were delivered to the women in cans measuring half, one and two pints. They were poured into either jugs, which had been left outside the door covered by a wee cloth with beads or straight into the house and poured into a jug. The cans were also cold to carry.'

After the milk was delivered, around 12 noon, Alex went back to the farm and had his lunch. He then worked in the field. They had a tractor and two horses between the two farms. Auchencloich also had two students from the university working there.

He was a boy when the war was on; children were allowed off the school to lift the potatoes for the farmers.

At Smith's farm there was no electricity. They had a generator, which charged the batteries. They had no running water and a dry toilet. The cows were milked by hand.

Robert Smith bought Mid House, between Bridge of Weir and Kilmacolm. Robert, his daughter Nancy and Alex went to Mid House. He stayed with them until he left school.

When Alex was 16, Robert Smith the farmer bought 30 sheep. Any farms around Muirsheil could keep cattle and sheep. It was open land that needed dogs to gather them up. This land had not really been farmed, therefore ditching and ploughing had to be done, with a special spade. It was hard work, soaking wet. No pipes, they just let the water run.

> 'I did every labouring job on the farm, including driving a tractor at the age of 13.'

He loved the farm, but 'there was no money in it.' No money in it was often the reason for the movement away from the farms and Alex left the farm when he was 16, as his 'mother said that I should come home and serve my time.'

The children of farmers were expected to help out, it was a community based on working together. Education was at its widest from learning about the land, nature, economy, life and death, the children of farmers had more of a education in a wider sense than those in villages, towns and cities. School attendance was very different for the children of farmers, for one simple reason, the practicality of getting there.

By the 1980s the idea of farmers children walking to school had changed. Councils provided transport.

Jennifer Douglas, of Dampton Farm:

'The bus driver was called Roy, he was really nice. In my bus load was myself, then up to Robert at Auchensale and picked up Jimmy, Bobby, David and Barbara, then Willie Carruth at Lawmarnock, Marie and Julie Jamieson at Little Burntshields, and there were three Cooks at the cottages at the Bower. John and Douglas at the Overton, and the last one was David Douglas at the Gladstone. Out to Johnstone High and Willie Carruth and Jimmy got off and the rest of us went to Kilbarchan.

'The minibus picked us up at night and I was first off it!'

Things changed even more when Merksworth came into the equation, and the realities of getting to organisations others in the village walked to. Bobby Carruth is a late twentieth century example.

'We lived 2 miles from the village. Getting to cubs, Scouts and football after school relied on someone coming to pick us up.'

Bobby went to school in organised transport. It was more complicated as children went to both high schools, so there were two taxis to be taken.

'Taxi to New Street, then bus to school. Same on return.'

He went to Merksworth, his big brother was at Johnstone High.

Farming life, when times are good, being part of the community, employing people, good harvests, making money. Balancing this and the bad times.

> 'The worst winter was 1963. Andrew had flu, I was the fittest person. I didn't didn't have a clue then about the working of the farm. My brother-in-law came from a farm in Paisley, maybe by tractor and did the milking. Everything was frozen, all the pipes were frozen. There was no heating. We were very lucky; we never had to let any milk away.'

Surviving in farming, or making a success of it, depended on the farmer's understanding of the land, its qualities and how to use it most economically and respectfully. Hard work has been the key. Although farm animals are raised for a specific purpose, to feed or clothe the nation, good farmers empathise with their herds and the birds and wild animals in their parks.

Bobby Carruth recalled his father, Robert:

> 'He caught a fawn once in his mower and had to put it out of its misery. He was distraught that he'd done that.

> 'Dad put stobs [Scots: stakes] in the field to mark the peewits' (lapwings') nests, to avoid mowing them.'

The century saw some of the biggest changes in agriculture, through mechanisation and the reduced need for farm labour. The shift from the close world of farm and village to that of bulk milk buying, international legislation and deals, affected all farming families.

There grew a realisation that much of the ecological diversity of the countryside was being lost. Farmers played a key role in the creation of wetlands, respect for Sites of Special Scientific Interest and in co-operating with organisations such as the Royal Society for Protection of Birds, to protect wildlife in the countryside.

Nurturing the quality and productivity of the land is vital. In an age of concern about food security and food standards, farmers were fundamental to national life. As they are still.

CHAPTER 3
Kilbarchan – a place like no other

'For Habbie's deid.'

EVERYONE and every place in the world is unique. One person, however, distinguishes Kilbarchan from any other town or village on the planet, the now legendary individual who lived in the village centuries ago, Habbie Simpson.

Like most legends, little is known of the real man. Habbie, (a corruption of Robert, like Rab and Rabbie) is said to have lived in the seventeenth century, was a piper, and is buried in the Old Parish church in the village. A headstone with the initials RS and a symbolic shape of a cleaver, indicating the trade of flesher, or butcher, can still be seen.

He was immortalised in Robert Semphill [1550-1620] in his elegy, 'The Life and Death of the Piper of Kilbarchan or The Epitaph of Habbie Simpson'. This was an early poem in general circulation, well known throughout Scotland.

This work, of thirteen stanzas, written in the Scots of its time, is well worth the reading. It highlights village activities at the turn of the sixteenth and seventeenth centuries through a larger-than-life character. Verses record Habbie's public appearances: playing when the cock crows, for the Kirk Town Cause, the sheep shearers, Hogmanay, the Beltane and Saint Barchan's feasts, at fairs, church plays, horse races, playing at weddings, and escorting the bride.

Semphill's lament for Habbie was written in a rhythm that became known as Standard Habbie: lines 1, 2, 3, and 5 are the same length and rhyme, and lines 4 and 6 are shorter and rhyme.

> So kindly to his Neighbour neist, [Scots: next, nearest]
> At Beltan and Saint Barchan's Feast.
> He blew and then held up his Breast,
> as he were weid, [Scots: dead]
> But now we need not him arest [stop]
> For Habbie's deid.

Standard Habbie is also known as Scottish Stanza or Burns Stanza and attained worldwide prominence when Robert Burns used it in, for example, 'To a Mouse'. Semphill's work is one of the greatest poems in Scots literature.

The poem made Habbie famous and stimulated interest in 'St Barchan's toun' and introduced the name of the village to many. At the time of its first publication, readers must have been intrigued by the village and the villagers themselves may have basked in his reflected glory. Habbie was held in such high regard that when the steeple was added to the village meal market and meeting place a niche was built below the village clock to house a statue in his honour and memory. This became the definitive image of the village.

The esteem in which Habbie is held in the village is evident on one particular day in the year when the whole village celebrates in a unique festival. On this day Habbie Simspon comes back to life!

The origins of Lilias Day are lost in the mists of history, and are unknown. The name of the day is believed to have originated around the end of the seventeenth century and is the name of Lilia, daughter of Cunninghame of Craigends. It has been suggested that this was an attempt to 'Christianise' the Beltane Festival, which took place in May. It may also be linked to the farming year, or a communion of people as epitomised by Burns in 'The Holy Fair', where the setting of the poem, the village of Mauchline in Ayrshire is not that far distant. Irrespective of the origin, Lilias Day has become enshrined in the hearts of many, and become an integral part of their lives in the village, no matter what age or stage.

Lilias Day was revived in 1896, but lapsed in 1898. Many localities celebrated by building arches. The villagers followed an old Lilias Day tradition, arch construction over some of the main streets. The arch designs were passed from one generation to another and required cooperation and a variety of skills from people of all ages, building the framework, collecting the heather, foliage and flowers to decorate it, and erecting it. Once complete the arches were admired and criticised by inhabitants of other streets!

In an era when cameras have become an integral part of mobile phones it is difficult to appreciate that the mere presence of a photographer was an event in itself. His arrival , encumbered by his tripod, wooden-bodied camera and a heavy box of glass plates would draw a curious crowd.

Persuading all to turn out in their Sunday best, positioning folk so that they were all seen by the camera, and getting the children to pose took organisational skill and tact. Once everyone, his or her dog and the photographer, were ready, the street group photos were taken. Before the group dispersed everyone would be told when and in which shop the photos could be seen and ordered. Possibly the same camera visited each of the arches, creating a ripple of excitement through the village.

There were other special days in Kilbarchan. The *Renfrewshire Gazette* records that in January 1902 at St. John's Festival, the torchlight procession was abandoned due to bad weather. In December 1905, on Saint Barchan's Day, one caption read: '50 horses at the horse market in Church Street'. The 1907 Pageant of St. Barchan was re-enacted by scholars on St. Barchan's Day, then on the 17th December. Neither St. John's Festival or St. Barchan's Day are within living memory in the village.

Lilias Day was revived between 1929 and 1934, complete with street arches and pageants which were scrupulously planned and timetabled. It was challenging to make them run smoothly, as they were very elaborate historical pageants, lasting two hours, with well over one hundred adults and children involved. [A web page *Lilias Day Pageant: the Story of Kilbarchan* has all the details of the event in 1934.]

Funds were raised for the local and wider community. £1250 was raised in the 1930s to fund a bed in Ward 8 of the Royal Alexandra Hospital in Paisley, badly needed in times before the National Health Service. Like all communities, the willingness of people to help others showed and people dug deep in their pockets for a good cause.

The time and energy involved may alone have made the 1934 Lilias Day the last for many years. Likelier reasons could be that the financial goal had been achieved. The Depression impacted on the ability of families, with little spare cash for charities. Later, people were preoccupied with the growing fear of World War II, preparations for war and the war itself. The long grey period of austerity lasted well into the 1950s; it took a long time for families to recover any semblance of normality.

Physical changes affected the village. With the demolition of many of the old houses and the building of the new, for those who had been in the village for generations, life seemed disrupted. The extension of the village brought new houses and new people by the early 1960s. For many who had just moved from other communities, part of the appeal of the village was an increasing interest in the unique history of the place, its traditions and customs.

Many of the new people had young families. The village school became the hub where everyone mixed. A small group of parents, including some who had experience of parents associations in England, established the Kilbarchan Primary School Parents Association in 1966. It became a forum for educational discussion, social events and fund raising.

Many newcomers, with or without Parents Association links, valued what distinguished the village – its architecture, its surrounding countryside and just things like the pipe band playing through its streets on summer evenings. This new found interest in the community meshed with the pride of Habbies in their own village and its past.

The 1930s Lilias Days had been fund raisers. It was no surprise that the Parents Association soon recognised the fund raising potential of a Lilias Day. It was revived in June 1968. As always this demanded organisation, negotiation and preparation, which created its own cameraderie. One ancient tradition had to be abandoned: times had changed and double deck buses made the erection of street arches impossible. Vast effort had gone into making arches – equal effort in the latter half of the century went into securing cardboard castles or volcanoes on the backs of lorries.

Ian Miller as Saint Barchan, 1968

Lilias Day. Guide float at Burnside Terrace. Precariously perched on stools! 1930s

Community Nursery float. 1990s. Thanks the village for its support

Milliken Drive Arch, 1931. A huge turnout, of all ages, for the big occasion: the photographer's visit

Anne Grieve:

'The first Lilias Day was in 1968 in the school playground. There was a fancy dress parade which started at the old terminus [the War Memorial]. It was opened in the park by Jack House, a famous Glasgow journalist of the time. The Lilias Queen was crowned by Miss Meiklejohn who taught Primary One. It was mobbed and people moved between the park and the school. The historic characters wore some of the pre-war costumes and others were clad in costumes made from old curtains!'

Ian Miller, on the 1968 Lilias Day:

'Remember Anne Grieve and Helen Fulton coming to the Youth Fellowship and encouraging our participation.'

The revival was so successful that it was made an annual event, which customarily took place on the first Saturday of June, although there were a few second Saturdays in June in the 1970s.

As Lilias Day became established months of planning preceded it. Stallholders met on a specific day to have their sites in the park allocated. Early in the year, for many years, was the excitement of the selection of Miss Lilias, and the School Queen, two of the main characters.

Weeks later all the principal characters were assembled to have photographs taken for the programmes, which for many, have become collector's items. Advertising was found to help pay for them. The *Paisley and Renfrewshire Gazette* photographer was in attendance and its sales soared locally when his photographs appeared.

In nursery schools, classrooms, Sunday schools, and youth organisations, children's imaginations had been stimulated and they were eager to dress up and take part. Few Kilbarchan parents can have escaped the urgent pleas of their children to start creating their long promised costumes, or the complaints of a child that their sibling's costume was better than theirs!

Although the day was targeted at children and their relatives, the preparation involved everybody, committee members, parents and volunteers.

John Stephen:

'Georgina always had the ideas and we've decorated the house regularly. I joined the committee for only three years and Georgina was a great help for that. With Evelyn and with Enid – it was a matter of getting people to fill the parts. We visited people in their homes to recruit them for the historic procession. If they said No, we'd persuade them!'

Evelyn Campbell:

'I was involved in costumes. I did a lot of sewing, making monks' costumes, St. Barchan's hat, and finding other people to make costumes – Mrs. Park and Cynthia Birnie. John Stephen and I were organising the parade. On Lilias Day, helping at Tandlehill Road, I was also up at the park with the Guides where we had a pancake stall.'

Jeff Webster:

'Lilias Day was great. The first was in '68 and I'd just started work and it was in the school. I had a big double ladder from my work and I had to put bunting from the Masonic hall right across to the old building and it was high. I'd been at work for about two months, and I wasn't used to going up and down big ladders. I put my ladder right up to the top of the Masonic. . . I got to the top and I was tying it up and there was a stone spire thing and it started to move, I managed to put the bunting over and round the base of it. Then put up the bunting on the school building.'

What made Lilias day unlike other fundraising fetes, was its historical procession. On Friday evenings the arena in the park was fenced off and some stalls were set up. Farmers did the fencing, with Willie Carruth wielding a mel [Scots – maul, heavy hammer] on the fencing stobs as if it was a child's toy.

Helen McCaig: 'The build-up to Lilias Day, the park was just a biz, with what was going on.'

Graeme Dickie:

'Used to go to the park on the Friday night and the wagons

were there and the goldfish were being put out – when it wasn't considered to be cruel to put a goldfish in a plastic bag, you wouldn't get away with that now. . . I won a goldfish and was grief stricken when it died two days later.'

Georgina Stephen:

'Friday nights everyone was out decorating their houses and people used to come up from Johnstone to see what was happening. Preparations for the day demanded advanced planning as well as participation.'

Apart from the historical procession, streets competed to decorate floats. A variety of lorries and latterly large trailers, provided by Malcolm's of Brookfield, were parked at pre-arranged spots throughout the village on Friday evenings. The accumulated materials, paint and imagination of streets and organisations were displayed on them all. The youth organisations, nurseries, teams, clubs and churches threw themselves into the task of finalising their long secret plans. Adults, children and friends were involved. Costumes had been sewn, children recruited and levels of excitement amongst youngsters was high.

Evelyn Campbell:

'One of the best times was when people in their own streets were involved. Clochoderick and Ramsay Crescent. People planned floats for a long time. Loads of people came over from Bridge of Weir to see the parade. Some of the other villages tried to imitate it.'

Anne Grieve:

'The Clochoderick Avenue floats were terrific. We were all at the same stage in our lives. The houses were new, everyone had children. We had 'ins' or sources for paint and paper, and many of the adults had useful skills. People were happy to use their time and every child could join in.

'The floats had various themes over the years, e.g. The Old Lady Who Lived in a Shoe, windmills, volcanoes, Cash and Carry [newly introduced to the market], all made with the use of wood and cardboard. The costumes on the floats were unbelievable, Liquorice Allsorts and Sugar Cubes.'

Cathie MacDermott:

'The lorries came to the Avenue before the parade and everyone was there.'

Jan Keir helped with the Tufty Club – Tufty, a cartoon squirrel, taught road safety:

'We put on a float on Lilias Day and the sun split the sky. The costumes were all fur fabric and these poor children were sweating inside them. We had to have a Tufty policeman and Helen and I went down to the Police Station in Johnstone and we asked if we could have a cadet's uniform. They gave us one and Matthew Blair, a big boy, was standing in serge in the heat.'

Jan Howitt:

'One year we went on the Wine Circle float. It was decorated like a French café.'

In the park people who had been in the procession were involved in stalls. Houses and shops were decorated and prizes awarded. Some families and businesses spent days mulling over themes and accumulating materials, others improvised on the Friday evening. All entered into the spirit of the day, to raise their game, create a novel atmosphere, and, if they were lucky, win a prize.

The procession gathered in Tandlehill Road and Dalhousie Road at 1pm to march off at 1:30. On the way to the start, historic characters, uncomfortable in unfamiliar period costume, strolled or ran along or were driven by friends. Parents clung to eager youngsters and tried to avoid the visitors already streaming into the village to take up their favoured positions along the route. At the meeting point groups gathered, photographs were taken and anxious parents shepherded their children up on to their floats.

Lead organisers throughout the years, like Anne Grieve and her team, ensured that everyone was in order, that the placard carriers were in front of the correct group, and that the horses were maintaining safe distances. All to the sound of bands warming up! At 1:30, led by the Town Crier, the procession swung on to Easwald Bank, with the floats at the rear and proceeded through the ranks of onlookers to the Steeple.

Ian Miller:

'What I most remember is walking through the streets as St. Barchan and the cat calls from your pals as you went by the Trust. It was great. The houses all decorated. It was a magic thing. The incredible Rosie in her bathing costume! In 1974 Joan [his wife] was in the Paisley Maternity and I went in with the gear on. The Pope arrived!'

Graeme Dickie:

'My earliest and fondest recollection of Lilias Day was Rosie, who used to lead the parade with balloons. . . we all took part in the wedding group, probably early, mid seventies. Doing the burger stalls in the Scouts. Then as a parent with the kids at nursery school.'

Jeff Webster:

'I started off as an ancient Briton in a potato sack, not a pretty sight, and then I graduated to the Victorian wedding, I was the bridegroom, I looked like Albert Steptoe. Then I was escort to one of the Ladies in Waiting and every year before that they'd been in a coach, but that year no coach! I was never one of Mulby's monks when he was St. Barchan, I was never one of them.'

The defining moment of the day was the coming to life of Habbie Simpson, who, when he had been summoned from his niche in the Steeple by St. Barchan knocking on the door with his crozier, emerged playing his pipes. Accompanied by his wife Janet he piped the procession to the park.

In the park, for the first few years, the sun shone and few of the stalls had covers. Once, in the early seventies, the skies opened just after the procession had reached the park and stalls had to be abandoned. Stalls had overhead protection after that.

The arena hosted inter-primary school soccer, tugs of war, piano smashing, cycle polo, dog demonstrations and similar activities, which changed over the years. On a few occasions the afternoon was rounded off by parachutists, the Golden Lions, who usually landed accurately, but were once spread over the countryside.

As a fund raiser for local organisations it became an essential venue. Thousands of visitors from neighbouring villages, out to enjoy the day and entertain their families, thronged the park, where every stall hoped to maximise its funds for the coming year. Hospices, clubs, youth organisations, all benefitted. In the early years the beer tent prospered and the two pubs were heaving all day and into the evening. Local shops enjoyed enhanced passing trade.

Stall holders were ingenious in their methods, although largely relying on games of chance! The Young Farmer's stall laid on an event that would not have been out of place in Habbie's or Robert Burns' time.

Jeff Webster:

'There was a tossing of the hay bale [over a bar]. There was a stand and you had to take a pitchfork and you flung it. They're all doing it. Blair Craig from the Monklands, he was three or four years older than me, I'd known him from the BB. "Do you want to win this? You want to do it backwards. Wait until it's almost finished." I won it. I don't think I got anything but the prestige! I was skinny with no muscles.'

Jan Howitt, The Wine Club:

'We had a stall, second hand books, games, but we didn't sell wine! We did have a raffle with a bottle of whisky as first prize, but somebody stole it. The next year we filled the bottle up with cold tea! I kept the winning bottle in a safe place. Somebody won it and whoever handed it over had forgotten about the tea. It was somebody in Kilbarchan that knew us came back and said, "I had just opened it to share it. . ." The real bottle was at the back of the stall. We always gave money to Erskine and other charities. The stalls were great fun.'

When the afternoon ended, many weary revellers went home to take down decorations, peel off costumes, clean off make up, bathe children, feed and look after relatives and friends, tidy up, have a drink, count their winnings or losses, and in many cases a random combination of the above in no particular order, until the climax of the day, Habbie's return to the Steeple.

Georgina Stephen:

> 'The torch-lit parade used to leave from here. Jimmy Clark, the plumber, who lived next door at that time, was the chairman, so it left from the chairman's house, everyone gathered there. We had these poles with hessian soaked in oil [as torches] and later it was candles. Children weren't allowed them. We all left from here. Hundreds of people.'

Lilias Day ended with Habbie leading the crowd to the Steeple, where he was rewarded with a dram, before returning to his niche for another year. As he disappeared the large Saltire, which had hidden his statue earlier in the day, was raised and he resumed his silent watch over the village.

Lilias Day continued annually beyond the end of the twentieth century. Hundreds of children and adults were touched by it, enjoying their family's involvement, meeting friends and neighbours, pulling together as a community. Commitment to participation in Lilias Day, organiser or spectator, could change over the years; possibly through age, time constraints, new interests and freedom of choice. New people filled the gaps, happy to take responsibility and commitment for a few years, keeping a revived tradition alive. Some were constantly enthusiastic and maintained their interest throughout their lives. All, by their combined efforts, have encouraged their children, friends and visitors by perpetuating the legends of Habbie Simpson and Saint Barchan and the unique history of the village of Kilbarchan.

CHAPTER 4
Interloupers

'Anyway, you're no fae here.'

Paisley has its Buddies, Linlithgow its Black Bitches, Dumfries its Doonhamers, Falkirk its Bairns and Kilbarchan has its Habbies! Habbie was, is, and evermore will be, the nickname of someone born in Kilbarchan.

This statement can be the subject of debate. In the past, it was clear cut, a person was either Habbie or an incomer. Talking about interloupers [interlopers] was, at one time, a sensitive issue and for some, a subject not talked about at all. Times changed and what once mattered a great deal, became much less significant.

Some of the older residents just grew up with it, taking it for granted. It was probably like most close-knit communities throughout the world. People did touch on the subject, however. Here is a series of quotations that give a flavour of what being a Habbie, or not, was like. Understandably, for their personal protection, names have been omitted!

'Very, very Habbies are we.'

'He was a Habbie, others were interloupers, that's just how it was.'

'Everyone knows your business, what they don't know, they make up.'

'You had to be careful who you were speaking to as many people were related to each other.'

'I was never aware of being an incomer. I had no problem with integration until Kilbarchan people told you you were an incomer. Nobody ever scorned you.'

A Habbie, rounding off a long contribution to a local debate, delivered the killer blow:

'Anyway, you're no fae here'.

The incomer replied: 'You had no choice, you were born here, I chose to live here, I'm leaving Kilbarchan in a box.'

'The bus drivers used to talk about Habbie Land, "they're aw daft." I said that "we had something over you. . . we know it".'

'When I married, I got called Mrs, which incensed me, as they had known me by my Christian name. A husband from outwith the village however was always known as the female's 'man' or husband.

Some new incomers were known as a 'Blow in'. . . just blown in from outside.

Some had really positive experiences. On her arrival in the village:

'I couldn't have been made any more welcome.'

'Everyone knew who I was.' [New wife of a Habbie]

'The Kilbarchan married women were still known by their maiden name. You still got your Kilbarchan name.'

'Some had very broad Kilbarchan accents. Tomedum, Megedums brither.'

'It was a leftover from the past. People were related to people.'

'People didn't talk about things, maybe too sensitive a subject. People kept things to themselves.'

'People didn't accept incomers at all.'

'My father was born in 1905. He remembered as a reality Johnstone/wee Dublin. They did not like folk coming into the village.'

'They really were nasty to incomers. My mum was Ayrshire and when she came here she had a very unhappy time. People didn't accept incomers at all. Probably she just worked away at it and that was it. She would never have been a Habbie.' [early 1930s]

'My friend came from Houston. I knew nothing about this until very recently. It was terrible, they had things thrown at them, they had windows broken, we never knew about that. I never heard about it. They stayed in the Grove. That was in 1940.'

> **'My husband lived in the village for 58 years, he was not a Habbie.'**

The Grove was part of the first council housing development in the Wheatlands. Housing allocation was always a contentious issue.

'My husband lived in the village for 58 years, he was not a Habbie.'

'I don't know why she had to go to Elderslie for a man when there were plenty in Kilbarchan!'

'I was often called the lassie Campbell, which was my mother's maiden name.'

'There is an intergenerational link, strong; it is there, all these links exist.'

'Some incomers could pick up on this. It was just an understanding, because they had been there for so long. It wasn't always said. They'd know you, and your parents. It was another world. When you came from Paisley to here, it was more noticeable.'

'Kilbarchan had quite a reputation for inbreeding and suicide.'

'I thought it was a reference to a bygone age, couldn't see any evidence of it.'

> 'Stories were heard that certain people could not cross the Cart brig, the boundary between village and town.'

'When we were going together we would meet down at the terminus [War Memorial] and it was chains they had, remember the boy XXXXX from Johnstone. There were others too, all involved. Outside the Co. That was when I was 18-19.' [1950s] That's when there were razor gangs in Glasgow, with the guys with the belts with all the things stuck on them.

Stories were heard that certain people could not cross the Cart brig, the boundary between village and town. The village was not the setting for the 1950s film Brigadoon. Prejudice could be the modern term.

'When you went to the Cart Bridge, you were lucky if you got over it.'

Older generations were aware of this, younger had heard of this, but there is little proof. No one mentioned it, but just as in so many other villages, it always was unlikely to be spoken of in public.

Like many a film script now, incomers to a busy shop or pub in the village, could almost be guaranteed a look, followed by a silence, before conversation resumed. Children playing in the street would have been aware of who the incomers were. It was a close-knit community, like others everywhere. Perhaps more akin to a remote Highland community in outlook, rather than one so close to the city of Glasgow.

One of the main reasons for a surge in people coming into the parish was the need for workers in the mills. Linwood Mill was one of the early water-powered flax mills in Scotland. By the mid twentieth century this was known as the Paper Mill, owned by R&W Watson.

At the turn of the century, the village of Clippens, which later became part of Linwood, housed the many workers in the Shale and Oil Company. Linwood was part of Kilbarchan Parish until 1868.

Although not directly living in the village, the influx of people into the parish was huge.

Johnstone also had a paper mill at the boundary of Milliken Park, on the other side of the Cart brig. In the early days, hundreds of people were required to work there. By the twentieth century the original families established themselves and their descendants populate the area. Many of them were of the Catholic faith.

> 'The area at the edge of the village, nearest the mill in Johnstone is known as Wee Dublin.'

Entering Kilbarchan from the east on the A737 the two and three storey houses to be seen straight ahead at the first roundabout made up Wee Dublin.

> 'There were fights at the Cart Bridge, if anyone tried to get in, there were people there that stopped them. . . just coming in. . . not for work, or rented property.'

There is no Roman Catholic Church or school in the village. There were very few Catholic families. The children of the families travelled to the local town. Catholic and 'Protestant' [non-denominational] children were kept separate in the secondary schools of Johnstone High and St. Margaret's.

> 'Coming home on the bus from the old school [on the site of Johnstone Health Centre], as we went by St. Margaret's Chapel, we're all singing 'The Sash', battering on the side of the bus. Crazy stuff.'

> 'My change came really with the story of the Catholics being met at the Cart and all their belongings being thrown into the Cart. What really alarmed me – I knew the story but I remember at 13 or 14 a retelling of the story, sitting in a house with adults and they're laughing. I thought "what's humorous about that?" and the following day I went in and said, "I'm supporting the Celtic". That was my way of protest.'

A story was repeated, heard around 1955:

> 'He was sitting chatting to a woman in her house, when she

'The area at the edge of the village, nearest the mill in Johnstone is known as Wee Dublin.'

> 'He was sitting chatting to a woman in her house, when she stood up and went to the window and said, "would you look at that, her walking down the street in the middle of the road, and her a Catholic as well!"'

stood up and went to the window and said, "would you look at that, her walking down the street in the middle of the road, and her a Catholic as well!"'

'A nice country village like this would not be something that would touch you, but it's there in bits.'

'A boy in Glentyan Avenue invariably ran in the house chased by a Bridge of Weir boy. His mother stood behind the door with an iron, ready for him!'

'I don't remember any trouble or nonsense.'

'There's a rhyme about Bridge of Weir and Kilbarchan fights. My friend in Leeds knows the words:

From the houses of the Grove
To the Wheatlands big and wide
We fight all our battles
From here to the River Clyde
If the Johnstone or the Brig boys
Ever try to make a noise
They will find the streets are guarded by
The good old Habbie Boys!'

This is sung to the US Marine Corps hymn *The Halls of Montezuma*.

'There were running fights with people from Bridge of Weir.'

'There was gang trouble, noisy swearing and blinding.'

'There was a bad gang that came up from Johnstone to create havoc, The Border. They always had the numbers. Kilbarchan and Bridge of Weir were friends, but they also fell out, and they started fighting.'

'Dress trends then were Barathea blazers with badge. Border was three swords and a wee crown. Kilbarchan gang members probably didnae have a blazer between them. Crombie coats came in with the film *The Clockwork*

Orange, as did carrying umbrellas and wearing braces.'

'Graffiti: Habbies and Border gangs on bus shelters.'

'On the morning of the Royal Visit, 'Habbies' was painted on the railway bridge. It was swiftly removed before the Queen arrived.' [1974]

'The bother in the village. . . what stopped it, what broke the cycle, was when the children went to Merksworth, much further away than Johnstone. Kilbarchan was close and accessible for the Johnstone children.'

'In wintertime, when it was dark, she would walk up Well Road and think nothing of it, it felt safe. I still do that.'

> 'On the morning of the Royal Visit, 'Habbies' was painted on the railway bridge. It was swiftly removed before the Queen arrived.' [1974]

By the end of the century, local tensions had diminished. Various factors contributed to this: as the birth rate plummeted from the 1960s onwards, there were fewer adolescents. Although bigotry still existed, the influence of organised religion on people and families had diminished. There were more organised activities and better facilities, many specifically designed for teenagers. Perhaps the most significant change was the availability of new, affordable technology. Games played outdoors could be replicated on a computer. There were new games where people competed against the computer and had no need to interact with others. Communication could be made on a mobile phone or text, without having to meet with friends. Being part of a group no longer required a gathering of people.

Settling in Scotland in the nineteenth and at the beginning of the twentieth century were communities from abroad. After the Irish, perhaps the most influential in terms of presence in towns and villages throughout the west of Scotland in particular were the Italians. New names appeared in the high street. Usually linked to the ice cream and fish and chip shops, they quickly became favourite places to be. Cardosi, Jaconelli, Porelli, Parducci were all well-known names in Paisley. In Kilbarchan, the Brunetti family settled and were remembered with great fondness, both as a family and for the items they sold.

Giuseppe Brunetti arrived in the village, bought a building and set up shop in Low Barholm. The Cyclists' Rest became one of the most popular places in the village. Three generations carried on the tradition, until the closure of the shop in the early 1970s. Initially he would go round the village with his ice cream barra, then the shop.

Alex Murphy:

> 'Louis Brunetti had three daughters and three sons. Tommy was in the Air Force, Mali was in the Navy and the Cisco Kid was in the Pioneer Corps. He was the youngest brother. My three brothers ran with the sons.'

Following Mussolini's entry to the war on Hitler's side in June 1940:

> 'Bitterness against Italians came to the village when threats were made to break the windows of Louis's shop. My mother stopped this by letting people know that his sons all fought for the British Army at that time. Mr. Brunetti was meant to be interned on the Isle of Man, but instead he was sent to work at Rolls Royce.' [Aero engine plant at Hillington Industrial Estate]

Georgina and John Stephen:

> 'I was in and out of The Cyclists' Rest. Louis and Gini. Gini had not much English. "You wanna hot peas?" The shop had a big marble counter; sweetie jars on their sides, mirrors at the back wall.

> 'Carl played the mouth organ and was a great skater. The whole family were very interesting. His brother had a collection of antique clocks, another brother had old motorbikes. Gini had a plot across the burn. There were no trees there then, so you crossed the burn and went up the banking. She grew the most fantastic veg.

> 'The Cyclists' Rest was also handy for cigarettes, around 1970, until it closed with contents intact. Would have made a great museum.'

The biggest group of incomers, those whose presence altered

'The Brunetti family settled and were remembered with great fondness, both as a family and for the items they sold.'

the village most, both geographically and socially, were those with the 'new hooses'.

The Wheatlands, Milliken Park and Fulton Crescent were areas of social housing mainly for people from the village, and for many years, having a connection to the village was one of the criteria of the Council's allocation list.

Housing was built for Royal Navy personnel based at HMS *Sanderling*, which was on the site of Glasgow Airport until 1963. In the late 1960s and early '70s Chilean sailors were there, awaiting the completion of submarines by Scott's of Greenock. The area around developed into detached and semi-detached homes and flats. All of these were private homes, as was the new estate built along and upwards from Station Road.

People came from Paisley, Glasgow, and even further afield, to what became known locally as 'roon the Station Road'. Much of the locality's appeal was the station, which was within easy walking distance. The train delivered travellers to Saint Enoch's Station in central Glasgow within about twenty minutes.

Close proximity to the new Glasgow Airport, the Hillman Imp car factory at Linwood and a growing electronics industry all brought jobs to the area and house buyers to the village. New houses on the edge of rural Renfrewshire in a traditional village with a long history, had huge appeal.

These houses were built for families, so naturally families grew, making the area full of children all within a similar age range. And the new houses had all mod cons.

There could be jealousy, envy and admiration from all age groups from some of those living in the older houses in the village. There, at that time, some children in the village were still bathed in the kitchen sinks, and lived with a shared outside toilet, while their classmates had all mod cons. The children in the Station Road area could play in the street, it was fairly quiet. With the increasing numbers of cars, buses and trucks the children on the main roads and bus routes from the top to the bottom of the village could no longer play, or cross roads in safety, as they had done for generations before.

There could be envy amongst women, as the new houses had

> 'The biggest group of incomers, those whose presence altered the village most, both geographically and socially, were those with the 'new hooses'.'

kitchens and dining areas, whilst some homes still had 'kitchenettes', or converted bed recesses with a stove and sink and if lucky, a fridge. There may have been much admiration amongst men where the houses had driveways to park the prized possession, the car. Some also had a garage to shelter it safely. For some of the families in the village, living in the same building for generations, often with different generations under the same roof, having 'your own back and front door' was an unattainable dream.

Bill and Nan Chittick, originally from Paisley, were the first in their house. They arrived 1964. Their eldest son Neil was 10. They had two other children, John and Allison. All of the children were born in Brazil.

Originally from Glasgow, Jan and Norrie Howitt, with their young family, also bought one of the new houses. A big attraction was the bus service, which she could use to visit her parents in Shieldhall Road.

They had the choice of any of the houses when they were being built. The competition for houses in Glasgow was great: they looked at a house in Low Barholm, but, as in Glasgow, they would have had to compete in price. They bought their home for £3,310 and never regretted the decision.

> 'Sometimes when it was clear, I could see the Moss Heights, which made me kind of homesick, being away from my friends, family and community. I have been very happy here.'

> 'In settling in and getting established most neighbours were similar. They came from the 26-34 age range, with a few golden oldies, who were about 40! There was a big mix of people. A few worked at the airport in traffic control and customs.'

> 'Not many from Kilbarchan had homes in this area. Some weren't pleased, one was exceptionally unpleased and for many years "wouldn't look at the road we were on", as the new houses spoiled his view.'

> 'Everyone was having babies. Nappy valley, Spam valley. There were newly marrieds and English people.'

> 'We knew everyone in the area because we were always walking. We were all there on a wing and a prayer; the big thing was paying the mortgage.'

> 'The children played outside all the time, now there are so many cars. It was a much safer place then. We grew a hedge to keep the ball out.'

> 'The children also went to the Bog Park; they played football and built houses and dens. They were a gang that played. The Bog Park was a very popular place to play; they were allowed to go there. They were always back for their tea.'

> 'The amount of traffic is the biggest change, there's nothing new about difficult people.'

Other people's reaction to going to Kilbarchan from Glasgow included some who'd never heard of the place, to a deep intake of breath and the thought that there were 'funny folk there'. That didn't bother them.

Norrie Howitt:

> 'My wife got to know others through the children. All the children played with each other. There were dozens of them around. I used to have to go and dig them out the mud when they were building the other houses around! They all got on quite well.

> 'It is quite isolated at the top of the hill, even more isolated, especially after they closed the railway. There is nowhere to go, there is no coming and going.'

Evelyn Campbell, from Ralston:

> 'They were also the cheapest new houses we could see anywhere. We saw the ground before the building started. There were no show homes. We chose the second one.

> 'There were two sizes of homes. We had a smaller, two bedroomed house; the one next door had three bedrooms. A

lot of the houses have extensions on them now.

'There were lots of other children around, all of a similar age. Some families came when their children were up a wee bit.

'We had a black and white TV, other children used to come round to play. They watched *Playschool*, as was the thing. What we had, which not all of the houses in the village had, was a bathroom. It was very small. We were welcomed into the village.'

In the 1970s grants became available to repair and upgrade the older houses. Rules on bathrooms having windows were relaxed and use was made of the old bed recesses. The fashion for open-plan living/dining areas encouraged many to knock down walls, combined rooms, expanded the houses, all with ample room for the essential new colour TV. In came the coloured bathroom suites [Avocado being the most luxurious], and space made for the big kitchen complete with washing machine, tumble drier, fridge/freezer and microwave.

Evelyn:

'Nappy Land was Station Road; most washing lines had nappies out going along the road. There were no disposable nappies then. We had a washing machine, a twin tub, so that they could be boiled. The washing was done at night and put out in the morning. There was quite a competition to see who got their washing out first.'

She was befriended by Elma Holmes, Betty Gray and Cynthia Birnie and some of their children played together. She:

'. . . never found anyone unfriendly.'

The heated discussion on Habbies and interloupers is perhaps now history, but it was an intergral part of village lore. Perhaps the best way to end this chapter is to relate the story of a Habbie meeting an interlouper in the Clydesdale Bank in the village.

'I'm an incomer.'

To which the reply was. . .

'Thank God for you all.'

As the children of the new families grew up, they began to outnumber Habbies. Being born in the village became a rarity. The century began with almost all babies born at home, giving them the automatic ability to call themselves a Habbie. It ended with very few children being born at home. Almost all babies were born outside the village in Thornhill Matenity Hospital in Johnstone, and later, Paisley Maternity Hospital.

The ancient, rigid, definition of 'Habbie' has gone with improved maternity services! If the name is to persist, it will perhaps be assumed by those who have a deep commitment to and affection for the village, and who choose to be called Habbies.

> 'I'm an incomer.'
> To which the reply was...
> 'Thank God for you all.'

Chapter 5
Three Rs

BASIC EDUCATION used to be focused on the bare essentials of reading, writing and arithmetic, known colloquially as the three Rs. In Kilbarchan lore this expression embraces a totally different set of circumstances This is not going to be a detailed chapter or a scientific analysis: it is a difficult chapter.

In the hundred and fifty years before the twentieth century there had been ethnic cleansing after the Battle of Culloden in 1746, cultural repression in the Disarming Act that followed, banning tartan and bagpipes, and the systematic suppression of Gaelic. Add the Clearances in both the Highlands and Lowlands, where people were forcibly evicted by modernising landlords, shifted to marginal land, or even forcibly exiled to rapidly expanding towns and cities or abroad and there are the causes for generations of insecurity.

Suffering much the same lack of respect and human sympathy from those who controlled their lives, Ireland was devastated by widespread potato blight, which caused famine, between 1845 and 1849. A million died and two million left the island. Starving and desperate for work, many came to Scotland, where they swelled the farming and industrial labour forces and shared the same hardships as everyone else.

The Industrial Revolution exaggerated this. People moved into grossly overcrowded towns in search of jobs. They were paid minimal wages for working long hours in dangerous conditions. They had no job security, few rights, no access to free medical attention, no secure home and no future. If all their efforts failed, the poorhouse was the last resort.

Social mobility was possible but rare. Society was strictly

stratified by wealth, birth, education and accent. Aspiring individuals were expected to acquire their social superior's styles and accents. Indigenous accents, along with their grammar, words and phrases, were almost lost. Many families had lived with generations of disparagement and few or no prospects.

To which, across all society, can be added professional or business failure, broken marriages, bad health, family tragedies, poverty, lost loves, unemployment, depression and loneliness. Nobody is identified in this chapter. The three Rs, in Kilbarchan, are linked to suicide.

> 'The minister told me about it. We were hardly in the village when he told us there are three Rs in Kilbarchan – the rope, the razor and the river. He stated that, at one time, Kilbarchan had the highest suicide rate in the country.'

One villager had never heard the phrase but added:

> 'And heids in ovens.'

North Sea gas is not poisonous, coal gas was lethal. Revolvers were mentioned too.

> 'Suicide was known as the Kilbarchan disease. When I was a wee boy, somebody had killed himself and my mum called it the Kilbarchan disease.'

> 'I grew up just accepting it. . . it was just there.'

> 'I've always joked by saying Kilbarchan was the original site for the film *Deliverance*. The inter-breeding – and so a little mental instability, so that the exit out of the village was ropes, rivers and razors. Whether it was a myth or maybe the allegation was that "they're all daft".'

> 'I've often wondered about that. I do remember two or three.'

> 'Maybe it was intermarriage, you know.'

'I can never think of that word Bowfield, without thinking of this man who went and drowned himself in the Bowfield Dam.'

'Kilbarchan was famous for the three Rs – the rope the river and the razor – the suicides. I was aware of that as I grew up. Whether it's true or not, I don't know, but the story we were told was of someone walking down the Branscroft in the dark and there was this body hanging from a tree.'

'A lot of the men when they were out of work did away with themselves. That was kind of well known, on the railways.'

One graphic story:

'My grandpa was manager there for years, before he slit his throat. I remember it clearly, vividly. I was nine or ten, we were still downstairs, my mother had been called to Paisley, because her brother had been killed on the railway. And she came back in that night and my Aunt came out of her house and said, "Grandpa's cut his throat and is away to hospital." So he had gone to the bathroom, locked the door and put down a white towel – it had to be white, y'know, and slit his throat. My father kicked the bathroom door down and found him. They got the ambulance, they took him into the RAH [Royal Alexandra Infirmary, Paisley]. He survived for a day or two.

'I was upstairs with my granny and the rest of them when the bell went in the house. There was no phone, and it was the police, they'd had a phone call – he had died. It's one of these. . . because this village is known as the village of the three Rs, the rope the razor and the river.

'It's part of the family, why hide a thing like that? No reason given why he did it.'

They never found out.

'He'd been round the week before to all his friends and said, Goodbye and nobody knew it. He was retired, aged between 60 and 70.'

Where did he tell his friends he was going, or did they even ask?

The opportunity to have someone to talk to became widely available. Society and its culture have changed radically over the century. By 2000 the Samaritans had been set up to help those in need and their families.

Listen Closely

Parkview, towards the Branscroft and Brookfield. Coal delivery by the Co-op

Old homes in New Street, before demolition, looking towards the Cross

Low Barholm and the Trust Inn, site of the original tram terminus [Stark Images]

CHAPTER 6
Homes

'The single end bed was never cold.'

IN ITS use of slate, stone and later, roughcast, Kilbarchan's traditionally built environment is typically Scottish. It shows the effects of time, the rise and fall of the economy and changing styles. A huge draw for many is the history of the village, the very name of which is historic. Many believe it is the location of a very early church or cell [Gaelic – *cille*] of St. Barchan, like Kilmalcolm, Kilmarnock and Kildonan. These were early Christian missionaries, of the Celtic Church, the most famous being the 6th century Saint Columba. These missionaries settled in places that were often established places of pre-Christian worship, or simply local gathering places. Many were close to running water. It makes sense therefore, that the early church in the village is near the burn.

For those who have lived in Scotland most of their lives, this history is all around, and is taken for granted. Ancient remains pre-dating Christianity lie in the area surrounding the village. Whitemoss Roman fort is at Bishopton and the beginning of the Antonine Wall, the great Roman defence system is just across the River Clyde. Much earlier settlements at Dumbarton Rock, capital of the kingdom of Strathclyde are within easy reach of the village.

For people visiting the village, especially those with a relatively new national ancestry, a village like Kilbarchan, with a built history which pre-dates the founding of their nation, is a lot to take in. Many visitors, especially those from countries like America, Canada, New

Zealand and Australia arrive to seek evidence of their village ancestors. They want to see where they lived, the streets they walked, their family church, their workplaces and their graves. Anyone who has met these visitors can see how proud they are to have the connection.

> 'Getting up in the morning with patterns of frost on the windowpanes.'

To live in a house, any house, in a historic village is something special. Many thousands visit recreated examples in museums or places like Beamish in County Durham, Greenfield Village Michigan, Upper Canada Village, Ontario, the Ulster Folk Museum and the Weaver's Cottage in the centre of the village! These give an experience of what ordinary life was like in the past. In this chapter are people who lived in homes in the village in a century in which some of the biggest changes in the development of houses took place.

Something striking about entering many of the older houses at the beginning of the twenty first century is how comfortable they are. Indoor plumbing, toilets, baths, showers, electricity, central heating are all standard, even individual privacy. In the same homes at the beginning of the century, it was a very different story.

It was common, by the end of the twentieth century for a house to have only one family with perhaps two children. A hundred years ago the same space could, and did, house four families. The building could also be their place of work. There would have been no bathroom, no hot water and an outside toilet, shared with all the neighbours in the building. Families lived together, with grandparents and other elderly relatives often sharing rooms with younger members. Cramped, poorly lit by gas mantles. Coal fires were normal and created polluting clouds which hung over communities everywhere. In almost every home widespread pipe and cigarette smoking created its own unhealthy atmosphere. A sink by the window, a basic coal-fired range to cook on.

Some of these conditions existed in the village as late as the 1960s.

> 'The living rooms were in the front, the bedroom at the back. Each had a wee scullery. As you went upstairs, door on left and right, and one facing you.'

> 'Getting up in the morning with patterns of frost on the windowpanes.'

The memorable smell of the outside toilet was paraffin, to keep the pipes from freezing. The houses were cramped with set-in beds, all the children sleeping in the same bed. A drawer could be used as a cot for a newborn. Shift workers in a mill made use of the empty bed during the day.

'The single end bed was never cold, hot bedding.'

Hard to imagine, although not that long ago.

The coming [and going] of the railway altered the village. Apart from the demolition of a few houses, the village was little affected by the new track leading from Glasgow to the coast. But the new station may have encouraged house builders at St. Barchan's Road and Dalhousie Road. Milliken Park's large detached houses had followed the opening of Milliken Park Station in the nineteenth century.

Throughout the twentieth century, much change occurred, for example, council homes at the Wheatlands and Fulton Crescent and private housing at Clochoderick Drive and Station Road. Differences between the styles of houses, the land or no land, garden or no garden, bought and rented, old and new, caused comments, probably typical of villages throughout this land and abroad.

'The ones from the bottom end, Easwald Bank area were that wee bit better off.'

'The bottom of the village was thought to be a better class. Many lived in bought houses.'

'Thaim roon the Station Road.'

'She thought that those who lived round the Station Road had pan bread. I lived there and liked plain, like Mothers Pride, with the white crust at the end. It was not all pan loaf round here!'

Previous generations would not have grown up in bright, open, minimalist homes. Having things meant having disposable income to spend. New items were looked after, polished and cherished and in many families, expected to be handed on to the next generation.

> 'It was not all pan loaf round here!'

After the war a group of over seventy pre-fabricated houses were built on both sides of Meadside Avenue, at the Wheatlands Farm end. These were built as there was a shortage of houses and work, making work and providing houses.

> 'We played here when the German prisoners of war were laying the drains. In this bit here, where they built the prefabs. They walked from Johnstone Castle.'

> **'You have no choice as to who ends up living in the close.'**

> 'All of my brothers came home from the war. Houses were allocated, but not all to servicemen, which caused a lot of bad feeling. Some went to police.'

New to the village were three storey flats, built in the 1960s by Renfrewshire Council and the Scottish Special Housing Association in Fulton Crescent, once the grounds of Spring Grove House.

> 'We had a council house. The Scottish Special houses went in overnight. They were poured in. Poured concrete walls.'

> 'A November morning, misty, cold, horrible. Out of the mist came this built house. They were nice houses, still up.'

Walter Gardner spent his life in the village.

> 'I was born in 1926 in Gateside Place. I don't remember living there! The family moved to Milliken Drive, where I stayed until I was married. My grandmother lived in Low Barholm, Adam Lightbody's family were downstairs.

> 'When we married at first, we lived in Park View and stayed there until we moved to Station Road. Around 1968-9 we moved to Rock Drive. I bought a plot and chose the design of the house.'

Later he downsized to Burnside Gardens, his sixth village home.

In the old village, life was busy with the noise and bustle of people, of all ages and stages. Their work, or unemployment, hobbies, friends, visitors, trades people and personalities, forged the character of the place.

> 'Everybody knew each other, what they got up to, and what

they didn't know, they made up!'

'You have no choice as to who ends up living in the close.'

Often in the old houses, families lived together, or close by. Everybody knew each other and there was a sense of trust, security. Daily routines, taking turns.

> 'My family moved to stay above The Cyclists' Rest in Low Barholm until I was 5. They then moved to Steeple Street. All of my family stayed in the building. My uncle Willie stayed in the next building. My great aunt Mary and her husband had a shop.'

As in all communities, neighbours were known to help each other out. Like all communities with strong church connections, helping neighbours was a duty. Before Care in the Community, with local councils taking responsibility, the kindness of neighbours was the only thing that some people could rely on. Some neighbours were good, others not so good and some were mildly eccentric.

In the old house between Weavers Cottage and the Parish Church, an old woman wrote letters and put them up at her window. She wrote letters about characters in the village.

David Carlin:

> 'In New Street, a man bought a young horse and kept it through at the back door. Later he couldn't get it through the close as the horse had grown. A lot of comedians stayed in New Street.

> 'An old lady lived next to the Weaver's Cottage who put newspapers on her windows, which he and friends would stop and read. She would come out and shake her fist. Children were fascinated.'

It is the kindness of people, and their spirit, which can be most affectionately remembered. Miss Mary Gibson lived in High Barholm, in the house where she was born, along with her sister, Maggie, brother, Walter and Habbie, her cat. Mary looked after her sister, Meg in the 1970s, when both unmarried women were in their 70s. Evelyn Campbell knew Mary well:

> 'People have always gazed into a fire, it was alive.'
>
> 'You are always drawn to a fire.'

'Meg's mother died when Mary was in high school, so she couldn't stay on with education, she had to come home. She made a big sacrifice, but made the most of it in terms of helping other people in the community. She had her wee flower shop on the step of her house at High Barholm. She loved her garden.

'Meg lay at the back of the hole-in-the-wa' bed in the living room. She didn't speak a lot, but she was included. Mary never complained, the saddest time was when she left her house to go into hospital.

'She ran the Church Flower Festival. She did flowers for others, including weddings. In her house there was a fire in the living room, with a wee kitchen, enough for one person to turn around in. She sat on a wee stool by the fire. She had a lounge that she didn't use; it had a lovely fireplace with tiles, maybe of Walter Scott. Beautiful chairs and table, this was where she kept her flowers.

'Upstairs were the metal beds that she had slept in when she was younger. The building was creaking. She moved to a better organised wee place. She very reluctantly moved. She loved her TV.

'She had her 90th birthday party in the Steeple, she loved that, all the old folk from the church were there. She had a garden party in the house in High Barholm before she left.'

Perhaps the most memorable of all the things that remained unchanged in the older houses was the fireplace. It is not to us now. Heat sources changed from a single fireplace to electricity and gas. Coal fires were replaced as the main source of heat. Fireplaces were converted, many were ripped out or boarded up, replaced by central heating radiators. The traditional focal point and heart of the home was removed. Screens, both television and later computer, became the main items in the room.

'You are always drawn to a fire.'

'People have always gazed into a fire, it was alive.'

'Through good times and bad, sometimes when nothing can be said. Look into it thinking your own thoughts.'

'We were bathed in front of the fire, maybe once a week, on a Sunday night, before school in the morning.'

'The fire would have been banked up with dross to be kept lit overnight.'

'Clothes were sat on the fireplace to warm them up and children dressed in front of the fire on cold mornings.'

'Fire had the ability to destroy, to let things go, it was a cleansing thing.'

'The toasting fork was used at the open fire. Everybody had a companion set on their hearth with a poker, brush and shovel behind it, which at one time went with the picture of the woman with the green face above the fireplace!'

> 'Many of the older photographs distinctly show the close steps scrubbed and chalked, by women, usually on their hands and knees.'

Coal needed someone at home to keep it going. And having smoke coming out of the chimney was a sign that someone was in and up. When coal fires were the only source of heat, noting the chimney smoke, or lack of it, of a vulnerable person, enabled neighbours to tactfully monitor them, without interfering. Neighbours would be aware if the fire was not on by a certain time of day, which would be of concern.

> 'Big newspapers like *The Herald* helped to start the fire by drawing the draught up the chimney; the *Daily Record* was smaller, so not so efficient. At New Year, a tall dark handsome male carrying a lump of coal to put on the fire was the best first foot!'

Coal was burned in the village until the 1960s. A lot was needed, each house having their own coal cellar, although many of the newly designed Council homes of the 1930s also incorporated an inside coal bunker.

> 'The bags of coal came from Barr's. The coal man would come through the close. He was paid in cash; the women all

> complained about the mess. I remember, age 9 [1960s], it was my job to go and get the coal. A wee lassie carrying two buckets of coal upstairs. I also would clean out the fire and put the ashes out. To make the fire, the cold ash pan was emptied into the tin bucket. It was swept out neatly. Scrunched up newspapers were put in the basket, with sticks on top. Rolling up newspapers made paper sticks. This was then topped with small pieces of coal. I never used firelighters, so must have been skilled!'

The village eventually became a Smokeless Zone. This greatly contributed to the demise of the coal fire. Although the comfort of the coal fire was lost, it did result in less work and cleaner air! With the loss of the coal fire to dispose of much accrued domestic rubbish, the Council waste collection service was invaluable to the village.

> 'The bin men came through the close. I could see inside the bin lorries from my upstairs window, they had big sliding doors, which were usually open. There wasn't so much stuff; hardly any plastic.'

People were house proud, and women, of course, did the work. This extended to the close. Many of the older photographs distinctly show the close steps scrubbed and chalked, by women, usually on their hands and knees. The close was cleaned weekly. This was hard work, with the amount of footfall in all weathers and the visits of the tradesmen.

Anyone, adult or child who to put their dirty feet on the close steps just before they were dry, was likely to bear the wrath of the woman who cleaned it! Neighbours who didn't take their turn of the close were not popular, to say the least. However, by the end of the century, the cleaning of the close was no longer the issue of great importance that it once was, with many of the older buildings having fewer people in them, and no coal fires!

From early times the course of the Kilbarchan burn influenced the development of the village. Water powered the small scale mills for grinding corn, their lades and weir. It was rechannelled into bleach fields for linen manufacture. When these old industries disappeared, less care was taken of the waterway and its flow was interrupted by sediment, branches and crumbling banks. The deterioration created a problem which troubled parts of the village for many years.

Georgina Stephen grew up and spent her life in the same house in Low Barholm. She and her husband John recalled their story of living close to the burn.

'My first memory of flooding when I was about 3 in 1949/50. My downstairs bedroom had a lino floor. I stepped out of bed into cold water. The garden was built up slightly to stop the flooding, but that didn't work. Dad and John built a wall around the garden. Boards were at the back door, hammered in, with wedges. They would stand all night with a shovel to stop any water that came beyond that. The wall was 2 ft. on one side and 3 in the neighbour's.

'I remembered times when the water flowed in the back close door and out the front onto the street. Mrs. MacMillan, the roofer's granny, stood in her house next door putting water into the bath, the water level was the same [as it was in the room]. On one occasion, the window cleaner jumped the wall, not realising it was deeper on the other side and it was pitch black at the time. At least he could swim! It always happened when it was dark.

'John and Hector continued to build a wall around the whole garden, Hector estimating that they had moved the equivalent of 214 tonnes of rubble. That worked for a few years. Once the whole village flooded when Glentyan's sluice gates were opened, the whole works came down, in my time. The people opposite were not affected by the burn, but by the water coming from the fields above.'

John remembered standing on top of a manhole cover, which was about eighteen inches off the ground due to the pressure of water coming down. The wee burn is a trickle now at times.

'If something jammed under the bridge at the tunnel to the old railway, that could cause problems, we frequently had to clear it of tree trunks, branches and weeds that had floated down and got caught.'

Water, and the fun of it, was a big draw to play in. Although

> 'My first memory of flooding when I was about 3 in 1949/50. My downstairs bedroom had a lino floor. I stepped out of bed into cold water.'

generations of parents would have well warned their children of the hazards and dangers of playing in water, many could not resist.

Mabel Murray:

'The backdoors were long, right down to Kate Aitken's Burn; they used to play there. Kate Aitken lived in the house next to the burn, the big grey building.'

Helen McCaig's son was like so many children in the village.

'Barry had wet boots. . . are your boots wet, no. . . you've been in the burn?. . . no. When he took his boots of, his feet were all crinkly!

'In the Barholm, you could fall in the burn at one end, and get out at the other! One Sunday morning, one of the four youngsters that lived in The Trust fell in the burn. Francis Kerr's wife's dad got the wee boy out. He got an award for that.'

The development of groups of houses ended in the 1970s with Rock Drive. Many parts of the village became a Conservation Area in 1970, meaning that planning permission was severely restricted. Occasionally independent plots were released, with some individual homes added, but generally new building ceased. By the end of the century expansion of the village, thanks to groups like Kilbarchan Community Council kept an awareness of what was, and was not, acceptable for the village, helping to keep its character.

All of the contributors to this book have lived in the village. Some have upsized, some downsized, and some never moved from the house in which they were born. Homes shelter individuals and families. There are both good and unhappy memories associated with them. Their situation, size and structure, in part, shape the individual. They are part of life's journey.

CHAPTER 7
New Houses from Old

'It was as if electricity had just been invented.'

Weaving fine cloth on a handloom had been was the main source of income for most of the village. It involved entire families, in almost every house. Buildings were designed with weaving shops (workshops) downstairs and families living above. Many had their weaving shop in their garden. The Barholm and Gateside Place still show typical examples. Every available space would have been utilised to accommodate the large looms and the equipment that

Four weaving veterans:

(back) William Meikle, John Houston;

(front) Francis Stewart, William Anderson

went with them. Weavers could, and did, employ their families, and whole families worked together. They could set their own working hours. They could be their own boss. It was a distinct and specialised way of life.

Much has been written about Kilbarchan's weaving past, but by the early twentieth century, handloom weaving was very much on the decline. By mid-century, the handloom, as a main source of income, had virtually disappeared.

On his travels around the country in the 1920s, an amateur film maker, Claude Friese-Green, came to the village and captured the sights on camera [Weavers in Kilbarchan, 1926 You Tube]. He used a medium that was ahead of its time, colour film. He produced one of the first ever examples of the use of colour moving film, which has been preserved. Giving the village a quaint look, not yet with audio, and unable to film indoors, the film shows the pride of the weavers showing off their work, smiling and laughing, and children of the village toddling around.

The photograph on the previous page, which featured in the 1951 Festival of Britain Kilbarchan Week brochure, shows the last four Kilbarchan handloom weavers, sitting on the steps at the Steeple. All were well known locally, but Willie Meikle [rear left], became the most famous of them all. He took part in the Empire Exhibition in 1938 and became known as the King's kilt maker. He was also, probably the first to be filmed for posterity [National Library of Scotland, Scottish Screen Archive, Weaving of the Kilt (1938) 4 minute video]. He was reputedly quite a character. Visitors flocked to see Willie in his weaving shop in Gateside Place and New Street. He was very proud of his grandfather's loom, going to the 1949 Toronto Trade Fair in Canada, he and the loom travelling by ship.

In Kilbarchan, weaving was a predominately male profession, with countless women and children supporting them in the background as pirn [Scots: spool] winders, and all of the other essential, detailed processes unseen, unrecorded, and often overlooked.

Census records show, handloom weaving was the work of the head of the family. Here, from 1841, the women are recorded. The unmarried woman, the mother of, the daughter of, and the widow of a weaver, was very often the 'Head of the Household'. These were workers in their own right, their skilled work was equal to those of the men.

Miss Agnes Christie was a weaver, as were her three sisters. As was her widowed mother. Shortly before her death, Agnes was befriended by a woman, very much an incomer to the village, by the name of Mrs. Halifax Crawford. She had an interest in history and the decline of the old ways of life. She was aware of the quaintness of Agnes's house and had an eye for rare objects. She was particularly interested in the architecture of the building. The roof had a cruck structure and she recognised how rare this was in Lowland Scotland.

Following the death of Agnes, the campaign to save Miss Christie's house at The Cross began in earnest. A committee headed by Mrs. Halifax Crawford was set up to encourage the National Trust for Scotland to open it as a museum.

Much work needed to be carried out to repair the cottage and village joinery firm, Connell and McIntyre, was assigned the task. Miss Christie's house, Number 1, The Cross, changed from a family home, lived in for generations, to a museum in the care of the National Trust for Scotland. The Weaver's Cottage, as it became known, opened to visitors in 1954. Since then, it has attracted thousands of visitors to the village and is a village landmark.

Willie Meikle's loom was brought from his weaving shop and set up in the cottage, to recreate the tartans of the past. Tom Adam and others from the village worked the loom and demonstrated its use to visitors. Jimmy Clark, 'the last of the Calton Weavers', a Glasgow weaver of fine cloth, continued the tradition. Several people worked the loom since then. Christine MacLeod began in 1983, taught traditional tartan weaving techniques on the original handloom in the cottage by Jimmy Clark.

The staff were helped by local people, a core group of whom volunteered their time for many years, to show visitors, of all ages and nationalities, around the cottage. They shared their expertise, skills and enthusiasm. They helped preserve the cottage and told the stories. They listened to, and helped visitors to understand how lives were once lived.

Promoted as a Visitor Attraction, many came to the Cottage as they discovered that the village was the home of their ancestors.

Many were fascinated by, and proud of, their association with its weaving past.

By the 1960s many of the old homes and workshops of the weavers in the rest of the village were in a poor state of repair. The looms were virtually all gone. The once thriving workshops were disused; with many left empty. Dampness, dry rot and woodworm set into many of the old homes. For people living in many of the old weaving houses, there must have been a great sense of a bright future when they were offered one of the new council houses, with all mod cons provided, their 'own back and front door'.

Weaver's Cottage had become, by the 1960s, just about the only building that was an example of a trade that had been at the core of the village of Kilbarchan.

But there was also the new generation of those who had an interest in the past, who were aware of the potential of these houses with a unique character in a unique village.

In 1959, Jim and Janet Tytler bought a building in the village, which belonged to a weaver in Gateside Place. It was the typical weaver's home, with the loomshop downstairs and the living accommodation upstairs. They, with their growing young family, slowly and painstakingly made it their home.

Janet's grandfather had lived in Mosside Farm, before moving to Johnstone.

Janet:

'We knew of Kilbarchan, we liked it, it was rural.

'It was all happening in the late 1950s, early 60s. Lots of houses were renovated in this area at the time. We were living in a room and kitchen in Elderslie and Jim was a DIY man. And the house needed a lot of work done to it, it was derelict.'

Janet recounted what they expected to have to do to make the house habitable.

'There was no connection. It had an outside staircase, no working running water and no bathroom. Downstairs was bad to walk on. There was a trap door underneath the floor. The bloke before worked on the railways and there were

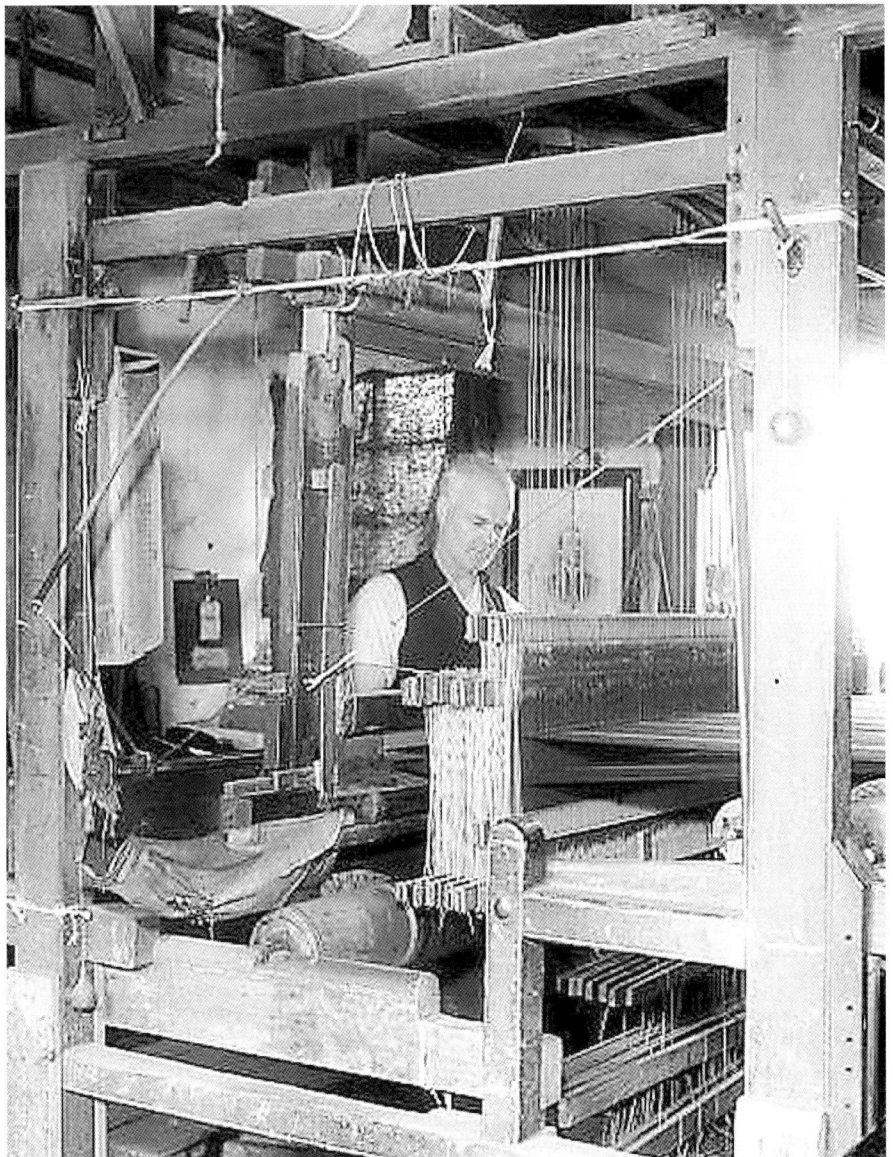

Willie Meikle's loom was brought from his weaving shop and set up in the cottage, to recreate the tartans of the past

things like bags of cement gone solid.

'There were holes, large holes, where the treadles of the looms were, which were covered over with wood, which had since rotted. Three at the front, three at the back, making a six loom shop. The holes had to be filled in.

'It was a lot of work taking down old washhouses, using the rubble for infill, which went into the hole. Quarry scalpings from the local quarry were put on top, with a final coating of sand. A damp proof course was laid and finally concrete, which was the easiest to lay.'

An unexpected problem occurred when renovating, not exactly building related.

'They had been weaving in it for so long, oose [Scots: fluff] had gathered and stuck to everything. The oose was infested with fleas, discovered when one child had a rash, which turned out to be fleabites.

'We knew Jack Gibson the doctor through our mutual interest in ornithology and when we told Dr. Gibson about the fleas, he made a special request. He asked to get the fleas, as they were so rare elsewhere, he wanted to study them. Jim seemed to be immune to the fleas, but he was taking them back to our flat in Elderslie with him.

'His brother was a sanitary inspector, so was able to get rid of them. They put six slates on the floor and six capsules of gas, and retreated quickly as it began to smoke. . . for six months! That got rid of any woodworm as well!'

Jim and Janet Tytler were doing up an empty space. One week they'd buy plasterboard, the next cement and so on. 'We were living in squalor, while others were living in posh council houses with bathrooms and everything! We saved every penny we could.'

They had first to make a habitable home of the rooms upstairs, two room and kitchens.

'Fifteen doors were taken off upstairs, providing strapping for plasterboard, as they were good $1^{1}/_{2}$ inch pine.'

There was no kitchen as such; there was one cast iron sink in one of the rooms. The first winter the outside toilet was under the outside stairs. Fortunately it was a good summer and they mainly lived outside, when they were pulling down the walls.

'John Connell across the road helped with the water supply. They were just able to use plastic pipes. Clark the plumber put in the bathroom.'

The kitchen of the old house was typical of the old houses in the village.

> 'There was a built-in bed recess, made of brick, the cooker was in there. It was as if electricity had just been invented. One room had a socket in the wall. If selling a house at that time, a big seller was having two electric sockets. When Jim took it off the wall, there were no wires attached!
>
> 'The garden had big holes in it where plants had been. It was derelict as well! There was a "rock garden" about 6 feet high, which was a midden, a collapsed washhouse. And the main sewer ran from the front of the house under the close. The main drain was at the washhouse. There were sandstone coal cellars, which were used to make the stairs.
>
> 'The fireplace was original, but it was blocked by birds' nests. Jim cleared it from top and bottom, but had to take the wall down upstairs to get to the bit in the middle.'

Working on a budget, as well as sheer hard graft, practical ingenuity was also needed. And at the same time they had to comply with new Council Regulations. They put in the new stairs; they had to deal with British Standards and planning permission. After 16 stairs you must have a landing, they had 17, so they had to be chipped.

> 'The walls were mortared, whitewashed and rough. They were changed for insulation and to provide a smooth wall. A damp proof course came up three feet. We chipped off all the mortar, using it for infill.
>
> 'The feature wall in the living room was a big job. We had to remove the old plaster. The room wasn't complete until ten years later, in 1969, when we had a wee party to celebrate.'

Janet 'did apply some pressure to get on with it' – they had lived in one habitable room for ten years. There were several young families around them in the cul-de-sac. Their neighbours, the Lauders, had the bottom of the house opposite, with tenants upstairs.

'Some people who had no expanding families just left the loom shops downstairs and lived upstairs; they had no need to convert.'

Fewer people now remember the arduous reality of converting an old, now historic, property. New generations, living with their families in similar converted buildings, enjoy much greater comfort and luxury than those before could ever have imagined.

Families, working together, the sound of the shuttle, the discussions on the intricacies of the cloth and the realities of feeding the family solely from the loom, by the end of the century, were a thing of the distant past.

Once transformed to modern standards, many of the old homes and workplaces of the weavers and their families were converted into beautiful spacious houses with large private gardens. Having a home with a history became highly desirable.

CHAPTER 8
Keeping a Roof Over Your Head

'. . . hit the deck. Lived to tell the tale.'

Tradespeople are many and varied and vital to the building and maintenance of homes and businesses.

Here are three typical tradesmen who all, in their own way, and with their own unique character, contributed to keeping a roof over villagers' heads. Two come from long established trades which ran in the family, the other was an independent worker.

Eric Borland began to serve his time as a slater in 1970. It was a 4-year apprenticeship, which included slating, plastering, roughcast and tiling. He worked in his father's business in the village.

One of his father's contracts was for doing the smallholdings in the village. The Scottish Agricultural Board built these for soldiers after the war. They were on Milliken Road, Nether Johnstone and the 'Coo Road' [Barrhill Crescent]. 'I got a shot at doing everything in them. I worked on them in Dalmuir, Muriend and Chryston. We were well travelled, even as far as Eaglesham!'

Gables in Ewing Street from Rosehill. An autograph book sketch [Bill Birnie]

'My father also worked on turrets. I had to acquire this skill to become a journeyman. The building trade was good to work in. I worked a lot with different tradesmen.

> 'It occasionally involved a bit of travel. I worked on an automatic telephone exchange in Carradale, when they were doing away with the operator service.
>
> 'And of course I worked on the farms nearer to home. The keeping of animals indoors created its own problems. Cows sweat a lot indoors in winter. This would rot the nails, nail sickness. The slates were recycled, dressed and re-slated with copper nails.'

Like a lot of young men in the village, Eric tried out different work. He took up the opportunity to move away from home. Hearing of work from his pals in the village, he moved to Plymouth with Charles and Michael Adams from Fulton Crescent. He had stayed with them in Plymouth.

> 'After working in Fine Tubes for two years, I went back to the trade in the village.'

Industrial accidents were common. Accidents working on a roof were a daily occupational hazard.

> 'Always bounced back. Bounce was nearly the word. Always been lucky. Went right from the top of a roof and hit the deck. Lived to tell the tale.'

Eric was a familiar sight, like other tradesmen in the village, carrying a ladder on his shoulder.

> 'When you got it balanced right, it's nae bother.'

Drew Connell was another village tradesman, of Connell and MacIntyre, joiners. The workshop was just down the road from Eric's father's. Drew explains:

> 'I must have been in every house in the village doing work, and in every farm.'

He also worked in the neighbouring village, Bridge of Weir.

> 'Willie Fullerton's sister lived in Kirkintilloch, worked there, worked away down to Faslane.'

One of the more unusual jobs when he was a young joiner was on the dismantling of a ship. The *Empire Medway* was moored at Faslane on the Clyde.

> 'The owner wanted to do his stables up. He bought a lounge on the ship, which was all wood panelling. My hands were blistered taking the screws out.'

He also had to remove the decking and scrape all the caulking off. He told the owner the history of the house and she wrote it down. Three years later he saw this in print in the schedule when they tried to sell it.

When Drew was on a roof of a house on Merchant's Close to repair fascia and slates, his father left him to work for a while. He was told not to do any more until his father came back, but Drew thought he would just take the fascia off.

> 'I slid right down the roof. Fortunately my foot stuck in the cast iron gutters. I never told my father that!'

A similar thing occurred when fixing skylights at Melfort House. A ladder was taken away when Drew was working on the roof. The rain came on and Drew slid down the roof, which was only a single storey. As he came down, he took five lengths of gutter with him.

> 'My father was more concerned about having to put back five lengths of gutter; he didn't ask me how I was!'

Drew eventually took over his father's business at the age of 38. He always 'enjoyed responsibility'.

Probably like most men of their time, wives supported their husbands. 'Catherine says I'm always right!' Like many men of their time, those in the trades had their own unique dry sense of humour.

The third tradesman is Dan Trushell, an independent worker, who built up his own business. Dan attended junior secondary school in Kilbarchan. His son Ian told his story:

> 'He left there and got a job as an apprentice engineer in Johnstone. He was going to be a turner. He worked on the surface table. However, three years into the apprenticeship,

the Depression came, and he was made redundant. He managed to get a job as an apprentice slater and plasterer. Served his time until the beginning of the war.

Dan wasn't called up; like many men:

'. . . he was a class C in his medical. Through his experience, he was a key worker. He was taken off the trade and put back into engineering. He worked in the Rolls Royce factory in Hillington making Merlin engines. Then came the Clydebank Blitz.

'All former construction workers were called to the Broo. [Scots: Labour Exchange] He went back in as a slater and plasterer. Dan was a featherweight, so he was often called upon to work on dangerous roofs, as he was lighter in weight.'

Dan Trushell went to Clydebank to help salvage slates from wrecked buildings. 'One day he was there when a mate picked up something in a roof valley – and gasped and blanched: it was a child's decomposing hand.' [John MacLeod's *Rivers of Fire* page 157]

After the war he stayed in the construction industry as a journeyman slater and plasterer. When he did some work in Rankine Street in Johnstone, Ian remembers going down with his father's piece at lunchtime.

Dan eventually set up his own business in the village.

'He borrowed £500 from grandpa and bought an old building in Ewing Street. The property had been a plasterer's before, and he was desperate to sell. This became his yard, with the full length of the feu running from Ewing Street to the burn.

'My mother called this "his wee play hoose".

'He started with a handcart with ladders, buckets and everything you needed to do the job. He then progressed from cart to a bicycle, which held a bag of cement and a good few slates. He had some customers in Bridge of Weir. The neighbouring village was up and down steep braes and it must have been quite an effort on a bike, but like most people then Dan would likely think nothing of it.'

Eventually he had an Austin Shooting Brake, which was clapped out. Notionally a five seater, it was well used by the family. On holidays the parents, two sisters, Ian, granny and grandpa all fitted in, with Ian and Jane sitting behind the back seat, looking backwards. Ullapool, Gruinard Bay, and Scourie were all destinations for the family with the big ridge tent, and all the gear. A Hillman Husky was another vehicle, and lastly, a Bedford.

> 'Dan also did a bit of painting for the professional painters in the village, like Jimmy Jackson and Tom Gould. They got him to paint bargeboards, gutters etc. He wasn't real competition as these were hard to reach areas for the painters.'

> 'Mrs. Halifax-Crawford once asked Ian, in her own inimitable way, "Who are your people?" When Ian replied that he was Dan Trushell's son, she described him as "A fine tradesman". Praise indeed.

> 'He rebuilt the steps of the Steeple, working all day with cement, laying treads and risers, using a nibbler to make indentations, to prevent people slipping. He went home for his tea, then back to the Steeple until about 9pm, to make sure that no wee boy would write his initials on it!'

> 'He was never out of his working clothes, dungarees. And he was inefficient, he took forever. Dan always seemed to have had about 10 jobs on the go at the one time. He would just do enough work to calm his customers down. He never got paid until the job was done, much to the displeasure of his wife!

> 'Mum and dad seldom, if ever, went out together. Dad was a good singer, singing at concerts. His mother went to the Rural and country dancing. Father would stay in when she was out, that was the way it worked.'

Only once did he have a baby sitter, which were his uncle and aunt. 'It was an incredibly secure home, family were together, and

Looking down Church Street towards the Bank Brae
[Frank A. Walker]

always a parent in the house.' Once when my mother was out, a neighbour commented that she was "away wi' a sodjer", and I believed him!'

Dan's son, Ian, could have been a typical child of a tradesman before the days of hands-on fatherhood. Dan was a man of his time.

'Dan was a great dad. He was aye workin. He had to work to put food on the table, and he did that.'

Chapter 9
Schools

'Naw, yer . . . gauin' tae rip it up!'

'In the school system that emerged after 1900. . . pupils could, at the age of eleven or twelve, instantly be classified as 'academic' or 'non-academic'.
 A Century of the Scottish People 1830-1950 T.C. Smout

THE 1872 Education Act made education in Scotland compulsory for 5 to 13 year old children. To meet this requirement in Kilbarchan a school for 300 pupils was built between April and October 1876 and officially opened in October 1877. It was built on ground previously occupied by Meadside House.

Opposite, on the corner of Gateside Place, stood the former Female School, which, with a room in Kilbarchan Steeple, had previously provided schooling, in addition to less formal schools in individual homes. By 1900 the new school roll was 511 and the Female School became the Infant School.

Conditioned now to free state education, it is strange to find that fees were charged at weekly rates: Reading 2d (old pence), Reading with Grammar, Writing and Arithmetic 3d, and if Geography and History were added to these 4d. If other subjects, such as English literature or sewing were chosen the fee was 6d a week. Parents with little spare money had to make difficult choices. This would have a direct impact on the family and limited the life opportunities available to children.

The leaving age was raised to 14 in 1901. Kilbarchan School

offered continuation classes, beyond the age of 14. In a ground breaking political decision, the 1918 Education Act funded free secondary education which meant all families could have their children educated.

In 1923 only those offering five year courses were designated as secondary. The others became the Advanced Division, retitled junior secondaries in the 1930s. Kilbarchan was a junior secondary.

The Kilbarchan School Centenary Brochure 1887-1997 includes the perspective of Agnes Storry, Windermere, Brookfield, who arrived from Glasgow with her parents and older brother, Alexander:

> 'I was enrolled in Kilbarchan School about 1909. My first classroom was at the back with high arched windows. There was a coal fire in every classroom. From Standard II we heard the clanking of hammers and chisels and smelled the tar when they replaced the old stone floor with parquet bedded in tar. We were going to have a school hall!'

> **'I was enrolled in Kilbarchan School about 1909. My first classroom was at the back with high arched windows. There was a coal fire in every classroom.'**

A staff toilet was provided, which did away with the staff crossing the road to use the facilities in the old Female School.

> 'Our headmaster was Mr. Thomas McCrorie, known as Whistling Tom. He made a tornado-like passage through the school, letting the doors swing behind him, whistling *sotto voce* all the time. He was a redoubtable headmaster.'
> [Agnes Storry, taught in Kilbarchan Primary from January 1925 until July 1962. Thomas McCrorie was appointed headmaster in 1877 and retired in 1927 at the age of 81. He was active in the parish church and the parish council and became County Coucillor for Kilbarchan.]
> *Kilbarchan School Centenary Brochure, 1877-1977*

Forty to sixty percent of recruits to the British Army in the Boer War had been rejected as unfit. Near universal unfitness was of national concern. In 1906 free school meals were provided for poor children and in 1907 school medical inspections began. Awareness of the need for improved fitness assumed great importance and was widely supported.

In 1911 a former Sergeant-Major and Boer War veteran, Tam Dunning, doubled as janitor and P.E. teacher: physical education was known as 'drill' partly because it was often taught by ex-military personnel but primarily due to a fashion for Swedish Drill, which still, but rarely, persists.

Getting to school, until the 1960s, contrasted with school transport later in the twentieth century. Pupils had no option but to walk from the village and its surroundings. There was no dinner hall and only an hour for lunch.

John and David Carlin lived at Mountpleasant, the two storey cottage at the top right of Shuttle Street. John enrolled in 1929 and David in 1931. They had an uninterrupted view of the school and village from their home, as Wheatlands Drive and the Grove were not built until 1938.

> 'We used to go down through the field there to the school, there was nothing there. The headmaster got us one day climbing over the big wall into the school and made us go down the road after that. The headmaster was Walker, he played football for Queens Park or Kilmarnock. He was a very lenient bloke. He wasn't boisterous at all.'

Agnes Douglas, 9 Easwald Bank:

> 'Rain, hail or snow, you went up from Easwald Bank and back.'

Walter Gardner lived at Milliken Drive:

> 'My mother always had soup for lunch. I hated soup. In the bad weather the school sometimes closed, but I had to walk there to find out.'

Although everyone had to endure bad weather the Carlins were particularly sorry for the children from Overton Farm who had a 1.8 miles (2.89 kms) journey to school:

> 'wee boys walkin' doon wi rain and snaw runnin' oot o' them.'

The morning was the easiest stage of their journey, the return journey was mainly uphill.

Christine Erwin spoke about her mother Margaret (Meg) Holms attending Kilbarchan school in 1918:

> 'She went to the wee school at the top of Gateside and once

'wee boys walkin' doon [to school] wi rain and snaw runnin' oot o' them.'

she was older she would go across the road to the big school. She never went to Johnstone . . . never. She completed her education in Kilbarchan. Her older sister Helen went to a private school in Glasgow on the train with her Dad.'

Until the 1960s many thought that children should be seen and not heard, which inhibited or damaged developing personalities. Classes were large, discipline was severe, corporal punishment was frequent and often excessive, conformity was the norm. Some teachers spoke their minds and could be discouraging, scathing and unkind in their criticism. Many were strangers to nurturing and were not constrained in their judgements.

The Carlins enjoyed school, John went in 1929, David in 1931. Pupils sat in pairs on a hard seat, at a desk with an ink well. Misbehaviour was punished by being put in a dark room for half an hour or made to stand in the corridor. David:

> 'There was a girl in John's class who drank the ink, I saw her doing it. We had a singing class and I was told I had a voice like a jackdaw.'

Some teachers recognised talent and encouraged pupils to fulfil their potential, but society and economics were powerful barriers. David Carlin:

> 'We went to Johnstone High. In Kilbarchan I won all the prizes for drawing and I was good at it in Johnstone. The boy that was runner-up to me at Johnstone: he went to be a designer at the carpet fields (Stoddart's, Glenpatrick Road, closed in 2004) up at Elderslie. The art teacher said to me the last day that I was at school she wanted me to go to the Art School in Glasgow. I said: Ach, No. My parents weren't that well off.'

In Glentyan Estate, Elspeth Robertson, then Hunter, had a contrasting experience in 1934:

> 'I started off being educated with PNEU, Parents' National Education Union, when you were four or five, taught at home for only two years, then shared a governess with two children, down at Milliken Park. I went there on my bicycle to Melfort. When the boys went off to Cargillfield and then

Sedbergh, a lovely lady from Greenock came over and taught me at home until the war was well under way in 1941. I was then sent to a boarding school, evacuated to Ballikinrain Castle, near Balfron, it was an Edinburgh School, St Hilda's. Then I was sent to St Leonard's.'

Myra Goldie, 38 High Barholm, dressed in a pale blue knitted jumper and white pleated skirt started school in 1935:

'I went to the old female school. There was a great big tree at the corner and it was used as a toilet a lot. Because there were two wee poky places (toilets) you were supposed to go to. Boys and girls used the tree. Boys on one side girls on the other. . . if they bothered!

'We were given slates with a straight pencil and I, being a corrie fister [Scots: left handed], I had to sit on my left hand.

'You got mugs of Horlicks every day in the wee school, in mugs with wee figures on them, you knew your own mug, they provided them. The Horlicks was warm, made in the kitchen of the wee tottie [Scots: small] school. We got it in the morning. When that stopped you got wee bottles of milk, a third of a pint, with cardboard tops that you could stick a straw in. When it was cold the milk was frozen; you had to sit and hold it in your hand to be able to drink it.'

> 'We were given slates with a straight pencil and I, being a corrie fister [Scots: left handed], I had to sit on my left hand.

Myra went to school up Well Road and through the park and the narrow lane leading to Gateside Place. On Monday mornings everyone fired up their boilers to boil their washing. There was a wash house over the high wall of the lane and on cold Mondays Myra and her friends leant against the wall to enjoy the heat from its boiler.

Memories of school however, were often not what formal lessons had been learned.

In 1939 a new single storey annex was built in the playground for the younger primary classes.

Eliza Mackenzie started school in 1939:

'We went to the old female school for about a month. They were building the new school. . . it wasn't quite finished . . .

and then we went on to the big school. They did have meals but my Mum said, "You have time enough to come home." We had good fun in the school.'

Mabel Murray and Helen Dooris [1939-40] both went to the old Female School. Mabel thought she would only be in the Female School for about six months. Helen remembered that it was the dining hall. Mabel:

> My memory of that was getting injections. The nurse said we'll give you this and that'll give you a *V for Victory*. I already had two and they gave me this one *V for Victory*.

> 'Anything that you had to have done, like the nurse or when you were weighed or they took your height, was in the dining hall. The smell of the dining hall still lingers, it was mince and potatoes.'

Alex Murphy was approaching leaving age during the war:

> 'My mum and dad worked. They worked shifts. My mum worked at Bishopton (Royal Ordnance Factory) and at the firelighter factory in the old laundry in Merchants' Close. My brothers were all away at the war. I did milking at the farm and dug the front, side and back gardens at 6 The Grove.'

Alex was preoccupied and his school attendance was erratic: he was summoned for truancy.

> 'The judge said that I had missed a hundred half days from school. He was not a happy man. I got fined ten shillings. I paid it myself. I was working!'

Drew Connell attended the new annex in 1941. On his first day:

> 'My mother had to come up with wellies at lunchtime because the snow was so deep. That must have been in 1941 or thereabouts. The teachers were there for so long. Miss Stewart who stayed opposite the quarry and Miss Storry who stayed in Brookfield. They seemed to have been there for ever. I was taught by them.

… his school attendance was erratic: he was summoned for truancy. 'I got fined ten shillings. I paid it myself. I was working!'

'The headmaster at that time was old Danny Livingston who stayed on the old farm road between Kilbarchan and Johnstone. He was a great guy. Rangers were playing Moscow Dynamo, he brought in a wireless, just a big speaker, into the classroom and let us listen to it.'

Lottie Dow was in the February 1943 intake:

'I think I was four and a half, I think I got in in the February. We lived at the Grove and there was a lane right into the school playground.

'There was class distinction, as well. One teacher was quite good at that. We were brought up at the top of the village. The ones from the bottom of the village, like Easwald Bank, were classed as that wee bit better off, maybe it was us. The bottom of the village was better class, I don't know why – some of the people lived in bought houses.

'You went with your pals. I remember having boils and Miss Storry – she knew my mother as being quite poor, giving me these pills to take home to my mother – iron pills, she said I was lacking in something. Apparently Miss Storry was awful good with my mother with my brother Archie: she was quite fond of Archie, who was a bit of a scamp!'

Ian Miller went to school in 1949:

'My memories of school in some ways are a kind of a blank. I don't think I was a good scholar . . . I do remember being sent to the headmaster once, to tell him that I hadn't been belted that week. He congratulated me but I was so thick I didn't realise its significance. 'Very good, keep that up!' he said.

'I didn't excel at school. I liked to be the class clown. I left school with a 3rd year leaving certificate. These were the days when they gave out the numbers, Smith 97, so and so 95 down and down it went, I hoped I might get about 50 – 20. There was a script left – "Miller," he said and he let it drop to the floor, "16 percent." And then he said, "like the prairies" as I came out to pick up the paper. "How the prairies, sir?" "Wide open spaces".'

I do remember being sent to the headmaster once, to tell him that I hadn't been belted that week. He congratulated me .

Lasting friendships were made at school, but some existing friendships suffered: Helen Miller's best friend was Jane Trushell:

> 'She was the same age as me, we started off in P1 (in 1951), all in the same class, a bumper year after the war.'

Their jotters were taken from them at a morning break and after the interval they were organised into two classes. Previously there had been only one class per year and that was the first time there were two classes. The friendship survived the enforced separation!

Ian Trushell went to school in 1953:

> 'Primary school was a great integrator, some of them lived in bought houses. Nobody at the top end had a bought house and that was the only contact we had.

> 'The classes were enormous, 36-40 in the class, half girls, half boys. There was one class in each year and you started in the infant school and worked your way along that corridor to the old school, then you went across to the big school. You ended up with the qualifying teacher – she set you up for your qualifying exam [similar to the 11+, assessing a pupil's academic prospects]. The preparation for that entailed maybe an early bath and early to bed. One boy turned up on the day of the qualifying exam in long trousers and was duly mocked. We were in short trousers until secondary school – second year was long trousers. The first year was shorts. It's tough!

> 'The reason I did not go to Paisley Grammar School was that you had to wear a cap in first and second year and you had to play rugby, which was not "the beautiful game".'

> 'There was a drama in my qualifying year because you had to select which secondary school you wanted to go to. Most elected to go to Johnstone High. I chose John Neilson. There were two girls who elected for the Grammar and they didn't get in because there were competitors from all the primary schools. They were to be sent to Johnstone High School and the parents kicked up hell and said that they should go to the John Neilson as the second choice, as the hierarchy was

the Grammar, the Neilson and Johnstone. No, no, they (the authority) said, you applied to the Grammar and failed, so Johnstone High it is for you. They obtained places in Greenock Academy.'

The pupils parodied:

'Oor wee school's a great wee school. . .

'Chaddie is a holy man,
He goes to church on Sundays,
He prays to God
To give him strength,
To belt the weans on Monday.'

Moira Smith 1964:

'There were two Primary 1s and it seemed to be like that all the way through. There didn't seem to be much movement between classes. School was good fun. I played netball and I remember the music room and singing, the teacher was quite strict, but I just loved it .We were into plays and acting.

'The sports days were in the Public Park – they were great.

'In Primary 7 I sat the IQ test, not that we knew what it was for. We all had to sit the test and then it came out: "Where do you go after that?" Paisley Grammar, Glasgow Road, two buses at least, unless you got one going to Glasgow? Jean [Moira's twin] decided to go to Paisley Grammar and I decided to go to John Neilson, at Ferguslie, which had moved there in 1968. My sister Kay went to the dome (the original John Neilson). One or two people applied for Paisley Grammar. A load applied to John Neilson and I don't know if some didn't get in, but a whole crowd of us went.

'Before we went there we got a list – my parents got two lists – tennis bags, tennis racquets, hockey sticks, tennis whites. Looking back I wonder how my parents managed. Second hand tennis racquet, second hand sticks, second hand hockey bag, it was naive but we just did it. Coats had to be a specific type. I had a beret: my father said when I put it on that it was like a pea on a dumplin' so it never went back on.

'There was an unspoken expectation that you would achieve. No questions asked. Mum was the dux at the local primary school and never had the opportunity to move on. Dad was clever as well but never got the chance to go to university – he went to Paisley College.

'Ian became a quantity surveyor, whereas Alan went to Strathclyde and came out at Jordanhill. I went to Strathclyde, Jean to Glasgow and Shona to St. Andrews. Mum and Dad never said, "We can't afford to do this." Saying that we all worked through university.'

Jeff Webster related the following, unthinkable nowadays:

'In Primary 4 we got this wonderful teacher,. In the morning a teacher taught us maths and all the horrible things. In the afternoon another gave us reading and art and the good stuff. She was the first woman that I ever realised smelled differently. This woman smelled lovely. And she would get you onto her knee and you would read a chapter and then someone else. . . she had all these boys and girls on her knee, we absolutely loved her to bits. However she ran off with someone. And the illusion was shattered.'

This is equally unthinkable:

'In school you have seasons for marbles, so you play marbles for three or four weeks, then it came autumn you get chestnuts and you play conkers for three or four weeks and then rounders for three or four weeks. We had a season for all these and then we had a season for hunting the two brothers. The bell would go for the interval and we'd all look out "Where are they?" at the corner of the playground – all chased after them, the poor souls were running round the playground – it was really awful – there were two of them and twenty five of us, giving them the full Bhoona. We never

caught them, they must have been terrified. I don't know
what we'd have done if we'd caught them.'

Warning to Millenials. What follows are unattributed quotations, which reflect a time and regime now long past. Physical punishment was part of life in most Scottish homes and schools.

Teachers were well remembered, although not always affectionately. When one of the female staff strapped a boy's arms they were lacerated by the belt. It was the only time that his father ever intervened in anything that they did.

> 'He went down at night to the house to see her . . . it never happened again. It was real cruel. She was a Sunday School teacher too! She did a lot of walking with her sister and if she saw you misbehaving she would give you hell on a Monday morning – nothing to do with her.'

> 'There was a teacher in there who was in the First World War and he was all blue blotched on his face – I think he was gassed in the war. Now and again he went mental and, see the strap, it was all curled up and he would hit you in the face with it.'

> 'At school I was belted often, for nothing. If you came home and said it, you were told that you must have deserved it; I mean that's it! You'd be taken to court now. If you were late during the war, you were strapped for that. It wasn't your fault, it was the Germans!'

> 'If you weren't paying attention he'd [the headmaster] throw chalk at you.'

Two boys tried to go to the Houston Races:

> 'They dogged off (truanted) from school and I think some of them had chalk all over their faces to make them look ill. A girl in the class who lived near one of the boy's mothers was sent to tell her that the boys were refusing the belt. She was in the wash house and when she arrived in the class, told the teacher: "Just take the belt right across every wan o' their legs." She lived too near the school. She was being

sent for too often. Her son was mortified.'

'In Primary 5 or 6 we didn't have a teacher and they were filling in with teachers from the secondary school, and that was horrendous. Pulling people up by the hair, throwing dusters at them, prodding them with a pointer, that wasn't for me at all. I ran away from school – home. When my mother heard what the problem was she said: "We're not having any more of that."

'We went back again to speak to the headmaster who said: "It's been very difficult, but there is a new teacher coming after Easter."

'I got belted for forgetting a reader in Johnstone High and also because someone did something in the class and no one would own up to it. Everyone got belted. One of them was a vicious teacher who took great delight in belting the girls in my class.'

'Some of them (the pupils) were troublesome, some just wanted to be doing anything else other than school work and anything that distracted them – and by the time the whole class had been lined up and belted that was half the class gone – it didn't leave a lot of time for learning.'

'One teacher was a great big guy and he used to fall asleep. One day he picked somebody up and said, excuse the language, "I'll fucking fillet you." Now he'd be on the front page of the paper.'

'Another thing, there was a bit of a melée in class and somebody threw a rubber that stotted off [Scots: bounced] my head and hit someone else. "Out!" said the teacher. I remonstrated with the teacher and explained the ricochet but he was not interested. "Right, OK, one of the belt and that's it." I refused. Class are saying, "Don't take it!" "We'll go outside and talk about it."

'Here we go! "I'll belt you – end of story, or we'll go to the headmaster." "No, sir." So he's belting me all over the place, legs and everything, so I go back and they're all going, "Get yur faither in an' he's tae stiffen him." My father never stiffened anyone in his life. So I told him and showed him the weals and he asked me what I wanted him to do. I asked him to go and see the teacher and my father said he would but asked: "Have there been times when you should have been belted and you weren't belted?" "Oh, aye, quite a few." "He shouldn't have done that but maybe it'll even it up. But if you want me to go in. . ." I thought, "Don't bother."

'One teacher – if you were in line to have the belt, his approach was to build up the tension: he would bring the pupil out to the front and place a piece of chalk on the desk in front of him and before he got the belt he would hit the chalk, which would go to dust and add a bit more fear.'

In 1982 the European Court of Human Rights declared against corporal punishment. The legislation was passed in Scotland in 1987, but it had fallen out of use well before that date.

Graeme Dickie, to Primary in 1975:

'There used to be a playgroup that ran at the Steeple Hall, the equivalent of the modern mother and toddlers' groups. My Mum didn't work. She was involved in bringing up me and my sister. And then it was primary school in 1975.

'I briefly remember the centenary celebration in 1977. There was some sort of certificate or badge. I played badminton in the primary school with Alan Penman. We got to the Scottish Badminton championships at the Cockburn Centre, near Braehead, first round, totally hammered, knocked out, but we got into the second round of the boys' doubles because we had a bye for the first round! That's as far as we got!'

It's safe now to confess to smashing a window whilst playing football.

'I remember staying in at lunchtime to help the teacher to

take down the friezes, and being a gallus [Scots: mischievous] wee boy I decided to sit on the Portakabin windowsill, above a large drop, and the teacher walked in and gave me what for. I can imagine the paperwork she'd have had if I had fallen!

'Other memories? Playing conkers, a seasonal round, at the bit close to the road. We would all play marbles. There was the big hill that ran parallel with the Masonic Lodge, where the big slide was in the winter. If you had your brogues on people would check: "Naw. Yer Segs (metal sole protectors) are goin' tae rip it up." You're not allowed! Playtime would pass and the Jannie (janitor) would come out and salt it.

'There was the Jannie's dungeon and we used to go in to play on the coal heap, run up it and just slide down it, like coming down a hillside.'

'Mr. Hand – he was great throughout the school and on the piano. We had a bright yellow minibus. The swimming pool we first went to was at Quarrier's Homes. They used to have a small pool.'

'Once, the school bell rang and I had it in my head that it was home time. I remember David Blair stopping me at the gate and saying "Are you sure? It's not time to go." He did his best to stop me. I walked home.'

'There was a ban on leaving the school grounds, never mind walking all the way home! We used to sneak out at the back of the blaes [Scots: red shale football pitch] to the footpath that brings you out at the sweetie shop across the road. You'd spend your dinner money on Battlezone or Pacman. There was the baker's just down from the antique shop: we used to nip in and get a pie or a sausage roll, but of course you shouldn't be there. The woman that ran the baker's, one time, she clocked one of the teachers coming, so the two of us are hiding in the back of the shop. She obviously valued our custom!'

'The one and only time I've been involved in a scrap was in

primary school. I've no idea what the argument was, but these playground things happen: "Fight in the park after school!" When I got home my mum sat me down at the kitchen table to wait for my dad to come in – I was absolutely terrified about what was going to be said. My mum said, "Tell your dad what happened." His words were: "Did you win?" A great burden had been lifted from me!

'As I moved into secondary school that was the year it that the belt was banned.'

Since Kilbarchan had ceased to be a junior secondary in September 1956 all Kilbarchan pupils who were not going to schools in Paisley, attended Johnstone High School. What follows split families, divided village opinion, infuriated most of Kilbarchan and temporarily ended the long established local link with Johnstone High School.

In 1975 local government in Scotland was reformed and a two tier system emerged with education and other services controlled by Strathclyde Regional Council. The outgoing Renfrewshire Council had senior high schools with associated junior highs, which fed into them at the end of S2 or S4. The principled decision was taken that all secondary schools would be six year community comprehensives.

Johnstone High was overcrowded with 2000 pupils and there was a potentially under-occupied new school in Paisley, Merksworth High. It was decreed in early 1976 that Kilbarchan pupils should be bussed to Merksworth in the north of Paisley, which included areas of multiple deprivation. To stop the removal of Kilbarchan from Johnstone High, its community high school, was the principle for which Kilbarchan fought.

Ian Grieve led the Parents' Association's campaign. The first public meeting, attended by three regional representatives took place on 8th January 1976. They were faced by a crowded and angry but orderly audience.

Mr. McKechin, Vice-Chair of the Region's Education Committee, declared:

'Johnstone High School is overcrowded and has to lose one of its feeder schools and that one was logically Kilbarchan –

> Johnstone was a community: Kilbarchan did not belong to this community and so its pupils have to join the community in Paisley.' [*Johnstone Advertiser* 5.2.76]

On Feb 4th 1976 the region's Education Committee voted 26-7 in favour of the Merksworth solution.

Colin Campbell was chair of Kilbarchan Civic Society and depute head at Merksworth High:

> 'I was caught between my colleagues, who were eager to have Kilbarchan's children and Kilbarchan parents whose fury knew no bounds. People were upset, impassioned and imaginative: one friend asked: "Will you have a job if Merksworth burns down?" Another suggested: "If things do really get bad I know the best sniper positions round the village! Captain Nichols showed us them when I was in the Home Guard." '

Anne Grieve:

> 'Clemmie Cowan and I went to the City Chambers in Glasgow to one of the big meetings. We met Janey Buchan [the local regional councillor], going up the stairs. "Now don't you worry," she said, "everything will be all right." Then the vote came and she put her hand up. We couldn't believe it. She had to toe the party line.'

It was a heated and fast moving environment for six months. On 10th February 1976 Kilbarchan Parents' Association obtained an interim interdict from a Paisley Sheriff preventing a final decision on Kilbarchan's future at the Education Committee on 11th February, which was to ratify the decision. The case was heard and the decision, on Monday 16th was that the interdict should stand. In the meantime arrangements for the rest of the area went ahead.

The final decision was up to the Secretary of State for Scotland. As June passed Kilbarchan P.7 parents were increasingly anxious about their childrens' destination in August. The summer term ended on Wednesday 30th June. On the morning of Saturday 26th June the verdict arrived in the village: Kilbarchan parents had lost their battle and accepted the decision.

In 1977 Jim Moffat, Chair of Kilbarchan Parents' Association, wrote:

> 'Some parents have been successful in securing places at other secondary schools through applying to the Schools Council. With children from the same village attending different secondary schools, the whole principle of comprehensive education is open to doubt as far as this area is concerned. With the continuing uncertainty surrounding the future of education, in particular the possibility of a surplus of secondary schools due to the falling birth rate, the problem is likely to be raised again and it is hoped the matter will be resolved this time with the maximum consultation and good will.' [Kilbarchan Primary School Centenary Brochure 1977]

In 1984 KIlbarchan children resumed at Johnstone High School. Later half of Johnstone High was demolished and that site and Merksworth High School's became housing developments.

Graeme Dickie, went to Merksworth in 1982. Graeme was in the last group to go to Merksworth High School from Kilbarchan.

> 'In first year there must have been five double-decker buses. The volume of pupils they were transporting from here into Paisley... At that time Gryffe [High School, Houston] was coming on the scene as well and when you think about it, the whole planning of the education system – it was bananas. All this resource to build a new school at Gryffe, there's Johnstone High School, they should all be able to cope with the capacity and the continuity within your community.
>
> 'It was quite challenging with the social mix of the kids you're going to meet: you've got all that apprehension, as you would going to any high school. The catchment area included Ferguslie, Abercorn, Gallowhill and Mossvale – the social mix worked very well. The balance was great, and that's how I met my wife!'

Bullying can go unchecked if it is not reported and silence is expected by the bully. It was not fashionable to clype (Scots: tell tales).

'One of the boys I came across on the bus was from the village, just one of these stupid confrontations. I was sitting on his seat on the bus and he said "Are you moving?" and I said: "No." And he punched me. Just one of these daft things, but it did knock your confidence as a child. I didn't retaliate and he did get his seat!'

Before Graeme left the school, the roll (originally planned for 1240) was down to a few hundred pupils.

'We were in fourth or fifth year and full of too much nonsense and some of us decided amongst ourselves to take on the role of managing the smokers' corner. We went a couple of floors up, filled a bin with water out of a fire hose and poured it out of a window onto the smokers. We were all full of high jinks and ran down the stairs – we didn't realise that the physics teacher had his head out the window below! Most of us had never been in trouble for over five years and we all were sent to the headmaster. He eventually came out and with a bit of laughter in his voice said, "Just leave us to deal with the smokers, please." It was a great experience overall.'

To round off a century of change is Eilidh MacLean, who went to school in 1995.

Her experience contrasts with what has gone before. Corporal punishment did not exist, parents had acquired a greater right to participate in their childrens' schools through school councils, and the negativism that had characterised some teachers had been supplanted by a more nurturing philosophy. In the winter:

'We were inside and we had A3 paper that was folded and stapled and you had a clip and you could do colouring in. Didn't go outside when it was raining, but if it was cold and windy we were still out. We would huddle around the doors, the brick doorframes. Some of them were in the corners and we'd all pile around them and huddle together for warmth.

'When it was snowing, it was inside. There were a couple of times if we were outside before nine o'clock we would have snow ball fights but we'd get into so much trouble for if

anybody got wet for the rest of the day. . . we were
sheltered. We *were* sheltered!

'We were mostly driven up to school; we were allowed to
walk home. Sheena and I went up together, we were about
the same age, in the same class and lived in the same
street. Either my Mum or her friend and colleague would
take us and drop us off. If it was a wet day or a not very
nice day we'd be picked up; if it was dry we'd be allowed to
walk home as long as my other sister was walking home
with us. When my sister left we were allowed to walk home
ourselves!'

The previous three short paragraphs contrast vividly with the conditions which prevailed through to the 1960s, when cars were rare, nearly everyone walked and, except in exceptional circumstances, the authorities paid no attention to the weather. Parents had become more protective, demanding and empowered.

Walking home Eilidh's route was:

'Past the old school, although I remember them building there
– there was rubble and stuff on the road. Either through the
park or where the old girls' school was and walk on the wall or
go into the jungle and find a path through, then go down New
Street and stop at Max's (general store), probably.

'Always excited when they [the wall bars] came out, other
than that . . . we played rounders in the gym hall which
must have been quite dangerous. We were very protected.

'There were Nativity plays but I don't remember doing a
Nativity play at school. Every class had a specific decade
they were to sing songs from. We had the Twenties one year
with Mrs. Allison, and we learned to dance to the
Charleston; we had fringed dresses, that was really cool. I
remember doing The Yellow Submarine and we made a big
cardboard yellow submarine and some of us were playing
instruments as well. We also did songs from The Wizard of
Oz. I wasn't a principal. The decade I was talking about
was for the Millenium concert.'

In a hundred years major change had taken place, particularly in expectations, which had increased amongst both parents and teachers. Until the 1950s barely five percent of secondary pupils went to higher education. With the introduction of comprehensive education, O grades for Fourth Year in 1962, the raising of the school leaving age to 16 in 1974, and O grade replacement by Standard Grades in 1984 the percentage of pupils able to access tertiary or higher education soared to almost fifty percent.

In the village and elsewhere in Scotland doors to professions and skills which had previously been out of reach because of restrictive systems and financial hardship, were opened.

Opposite

Back Row: Jim Arnott, Alex Harper, Brian Hector, Douglas Stewart, Eric Caldwell, Tom Miller, Jim McDonald, John Preiss, Jim Wilmott, Alan Leaman, Ian Murray.

3rd Row: Mima Borland, Janette Borland, Christine Honeyball, Margaret Metcalf, Agnes Munro, Lorna Munro, Sheena McIntyre, Evelyn Ford, Fay Layton.

2nd Row: Elizabeth Withers, Alan Menzies, Barbara Davidson, David Smith, Jean Hawkins, John Graham, Elizabeth Winters, ——, Gail Neilson, Daniel Downie.

Front Row: Frances Cleghorn, ——, Margaret Gardener, Sandy Clark, Mary Adam, Kenneth Holmes, Alex McGowan, Helen Reid, Johnny Neil, Mary Lion, Robert Rennie, Margaret Collins.

an oral history of Kilbarchan 1900 – 2000

Kilbarchan Primary School
[Tom Shanks]

Miss Leggat's Primary Two 1953. A group bridging the century's generations

Listen Closely

The war memorial in the West Church.
There are sixty nine names on the First War section.
Some thought it so bad that it was the war to end wars.
Whatever was originally on the lower portion of the memorial made way for the twenty seven lost in the Second World War [Stark Images]

CHAPTER 10
World War I

'I am the only one left in your photo.'

WHEN war began in August 1914 it was met throughout Europe with resignation by some and enthusiasm by others. Kilbarchan had few army and navy reservists so there was little public fuss when they left. The Kaiser declared that his troops would be home 'before the leaves fall' in 1914: in Britain men rushed to join in case it would all be over by Christmas. All ages responded to the message on Kitchener's famous poster 'Your country needs you'.

Local pride inspired rolls of honour of volunteers, which were displayed in churches and published in newspapers. Kilbarchan's roll of honour totals at least 420 men and 4 women nurses. To these can be added names accidentally omitted and the uncounted women who replaced men in factories, farms and transport and served in the armed services.

The home defence Territorial Force mobilised in August. Kilbarchan's Territorials reported to E Company, 6th Argyll and Sutherland Highlanders' drill hall in Dimity Street, Johnstone, marched to Paisley, mustered in Perth as part of the Highland Division and moved to Bedford, where they trained until they embarked for France in May 1915.

Fear of invasion and sabotage was real and spy mania gripped some people. The Kilbarchan Citizens' Training Corps was set up in late 1914, a voluntary body, like many that had sprung up throughout the nation. They were regarded with suspicion by the authorities, but in 1916 they were formally established as the Volunteer Training Corps and incorporated into home defence.

On the initiative of Chief Scout Baden-Powell a Boy Scout Corps, to train 15-17 years old Scouts for the army was established. The Kilbarchan Boy Scout Corps began in April 1915. The Bridge of Weir Leather Company gave the Scouts the use of its baths!

The Kilbarchan column of the *Renfrewshire Gazette* recorded items of local interest week by week. A work party began when the war started. Using their well practised skills of knitting and making clothes, mostly by hand and a few treadle sewing machines, the women sent hospital night shirts, shirts and socks to Paisley. Their output rapidly increased to meet the unprecedented flow of wounded. This Comforts Group evolved and by 1918 was seeking more help and allocating work and receiving it in the Congregational Church Hall every Saturday. The school and Kilbarchan Co-operative also made garments.

By November 1914 the village had collected £21 towards the Scottish Lassie ambulance. In 1915 the parish minister reported that £525 had been raised and had paid for a Red Cross ambulance. The Red Cross was a destination for a variety of fundraising fetes and concerts throughout the war.

Whatever general fears there were about the war, nothing compared to the anxiety of people whose husbands, brothers, sons and sweethearts were at the Front. Each time they saw a telegram boy in the street they would have feared the worst. They must have had great sympathy and understanding for the family to whom he was delivering the news that nobody wanted to read.

Archibald and Margaret Houston of Gateside Place were the first in the village to encounter the telegram delivery that would change their lives. Kilbarchan's first overseas war death was their son, Private Robert G Houston, who was killed with the 1st Seaforth Highlanders on 9th May at the Battle of Aubers Ridge where his battalion was 'so badly hit by enemy fire that no men got beyond their own parapet and the front line.' He has no known grave. He had been a dye worker at Anchor Mills, but was better known as a footballer, having played for Abercorn, Johnstone and as goalkeeper for Partick Thistle.

Robert Trushell, as related by his grandson Ian

'Grandpa Trushell had been called away early as a Terrier and he was on the Somme in 1915. Soldiers knew the sound of a shell that was going to miss them or get them. They were lined up for their rations and a shell came across and they knew that they were going to get it, so they scattered and tried to take cover.

'Grandpa was behind a stone wall, the shell landed and shrapnel came straight through his jaw, broke it, and came out of his throat – he was drowning in his own blood. The battalion medical officer performed a battlefield tracheotomy, and that saved him. It was a Blighty wound [a wound that would get a soldier back home].

'I don't know when he actually came home, but dad was born in 1915, he would be at least three, maybe four. Grandpa came to the station at Kilbarchan and dad was taken by his mum to meet him, but he didn't know him, because he'd never seen him. The only thing that dad wanted from him was the metal protector they put behind the buttons to protect the cloth from the Brasso – a button stick.

'He was the leader of the Comrades' Orchestra in Paisley. They played at concerts in the cinemas. They had evening wear in these days. They used to have white stiff fronts, which they changed at the intervals. He was a talented guy, he played well.'

Conscription

The diminished flow of volunteers in 1915 and the need for a Continental size of army led to the start of conscription on 1st January 1916. Men who felt that they could not reasonably be required to serve because of work or family commitments, or who had a conscientious objection to war, had to face tribunals to state their case, e.g. a farmer was exempted, as food production was important, a shop manager was not. Conscientious objectors who would not serve or undertake to serve in any way that would aid the war effort were jailed: others were prepared to serve in non-combatant roles.

The Hunter family in Glentyan House made their grounds available for several events between 1915 and 1918. These included a garden party for the wives and families of serving soldiers, an afternoon treat for wounded soldiers from Gallowhill Auxiliary Red Cross Hospital and a Daffodil Tea to raise Red Cross Funds. Springrove House ran a number of fundraising fetes.

In 1916 the Princess Louise Scottish Hospital for Limbless Sailors and Soldiers opened at Erskine. The proximity of the new hospital inspired both a concert for limbless servicemen and a performance by St. Barchan's Amateur Dramatics for Erskine's funds.

Life went on at home, but not as usual. By mid-1917 another thirty five householders had received the news of a serviceman's death. The collective grief was incalculable and the expectation of even more deaths was high. The visible evidence of the battle fronts were clothed in bright blue uniforms, with white shirts and red ties – the wounded were as close as Castle Terrace, Bridge of Weir [Ranfurly Auxiliary Red Cross Hospital] and Johnstone and District Auxiliary Red Cross Hospital. There were servicemen convalescing in Rosehill, Well Road. For every death in the Great War there were roughly three wounded, of whom two were returned fit for duty.

Entertaining the wounded

In March 1917 they came from Johnstone Cottage Hospital and Craw Road to be given tea, songs, dances and a gramophone recital by the staff of Glentyan Laundry. In April men from Barshaw Hospital were treated to Bovril, cigarettes and sweets at a Cartbank Laundry event in the school. The following month Glentyan Laundry entertained men from Dykebar Hospital and repeated the event in June for men from Gallowhill Auxiliary Red Cross Hospital.

By 1917 drinking times had been curbed, public lighting had diminished, because of the threat of bombing by Zeppelins, Air Raid Precautions had been established and the ringing of church bells had stopped. This was required by DORA, the Defence of the Realm Act. The need to produce food was paramount as unrestricted submarine warfare by the Germans was depriving the Allies of essential foods. Allotments were made available and awards judged for the best allotment. For the first time there was food rationing. All of these measures impacted on everyone in the village.

Two Kilbarchan men left evidence of their Western Front experiences, John Lee and John Meikle.

John Lee was interviewed in the 1970s in his Kilbarchan home, freed of censorship. His account highlights the squalor, confusion and waste of the Third Battle of Ypres, better known as Passchendaele, which lasted from 31st July until 10th November 1917. British Empire casualties, killed, wounded and missing totalled about 250,000.

John Meikle's letters have been treasured by his relatives. While he was training his letters were open about his activities, but letters from France were restricted by censorship and by the need to reassure his parents that he was safe. The contrast between the two contributions is stark and partly explains the difficulty people at home had understanding what their relatives were enduring.

Both men had five to six months training: drill, physical education, weapons training, bayonet fighting, shooting, discipline, tactics, grenade throwing, trench digging and long and challenging route marches. Both embarked for France from Folkestone,

Like millions of others they endured slow French trains, old buses, bad accommodation, mixed weather, coping with fear, boredom, the routines of trench warfare, holding the front line, raiding over No Man's Land in the dark, random killing and maiming of their friends, relating to replacements, training for the next assault, resting, which usually included fatiguing manual labour, and very infrequent leave.

John Lee, France and Flanders 1917-1918

In February 1917 John Lee was called up and reported to the 56th Training Battalion, formerly 12th [Reserve] Battalion of the Cameronians, in Kinross. John Lee's overseas draft replaced casualties in the continuing Third Battle of Ypres. When he moved towards Poperinghe, west of Ypres, in buses, other buses were withdrawing troops:

'A voice called out from a passing bus going back, full of Argylls, "Hello, Jock, this is Willie Keith here." But I could not pick him out as all their faces were dirty with mud. . . he came from Bridge of Weir, and I met him months later at Arras.'

Posted to the 10th Cameronians, his draft moved immediately through Ypres, at night, to the front.

'We later found out that ten of our number were killed or wounded on the road up.'

When they arrived at their destination:

'We seemed to be at the base of a hill. No one knew where to lie down, and there was no front line, only mud and shell holes. No one was there to be relieved. There were no trenches, no duckboards, simply uneven mud with shell holes. What a sight for sore eyes, dead mules, men and equipment seemed to litter the place. And what a smell!'

John Lee was a bomber [hand grenades] in the battalion's next action:

'We tried to get up the hill. . . so many were being killed that the word was passed along to retire. The German machine-guns simply mowed down most of those to our rear. This went on until our division was withdrawn. During this time all had various narrow escapes. . . at times the Germans used shrapnel. . . I had my helmet holed by a piece, which luckily didn't get into my empty head! Another piece tore a piece off my chin. . . I was very lucky.'

Once the Company Sergeant Major made his way towards them, bearing a rum jar, from which he had refreshed himself. The Germans opened fire, and the CSM dropped the jar and ran. It was rescued from the mud by Lance Corporal Chadwick, who was in charge of the section of six men.

'We were all frightened and frozen, but after we had a drink of rum that would have filled an ordinary bottle of whisky, we were all in a good mood and started singing *Mademoiselle from Armentieres*. The Germans started shelling. . . and by the time we'd gone blotto, the battle was over! The Lance Corporal lost his stripe!'

After Third Ypres [Passchendaele] his division, the 15th [Scottish] Division moved south to the Arras sector.

> 'On going up for the first time we reached the front line trenches of Monchy-le-Preux. We were overlooking the German trenches. We now had a worse enemy than the Germans – lice. It was impossible to get rid of them. Baths were the order of the day, plus insect powder, and lighted candles to burn the lice out of the seams in your underpants.

> '[At Christmas 1917] we did not get our Christmas dinner until January. Jock's boxes were sent from Glasgow, and the cooks were slightly under the weather, and nearly every cake was burned. This resulted in the cooks being turned into stretcher bearers, much to their dismay.'

In March 1918:

> 'From our outpost at Monchy officers could watch train load after train load of Germans arriving for our sector, and those on the left and right. By about the 20th [21st] the Germans began to paste our back areas and Arras, which was reduced to ruins. The position was very tense.

> 'On a fatigue party with barbed wire I slipped off the duckboards, rupturing my right side. I was carried to the rear and found myself at the hospital in Abbeville. Cheers! What next?

> 'Next was a Blighty [soldier slang for the UK] ticket. I had a few days at a hospital in Calais then I found myself in Edmonton in London. I had never imagined while in Ypres that I would survive to sleep in a bed once more. . . At the end of the month. . . back to Kilbarchan on sick leave.'

After convalescing he reported to the 5th Reserve Battalion at Invergordon.

> 'I had another stroke of luck. One day the Regimental Sergeant Major asked me if I would like to take a stripe [i.e. promotion to Lance Corporal]. I said 'No', but on being

told that the alternative was to return to France I changed my mind very quickly.'

He was sent on a two months course at Edinburgh Castle, followed by another course at the Scots Musketry College in Madras College, St Andrews.

'There we actually had table covers, cups and saucers and waiters. The kippers were very good!'

He returned to his reserve battalion, by then at Bridge of Allan, where he trained recruits until the armistice, 11th November 1918.

John Lee was lucky to avoid the German offensive on 21st March 1918. He was in Scotland when he was offered the chance of a promotion course, which he accepted. John lived to see another war.

John Meikle, France 1916-1918

Before conscription began on 1st January 1916, John Meikle [27], a plumber, signed on under the Derby scheme, which had been established to encourage men to show their readiness to serve, when required. He volunteered in Paisley on 12th December 1915 and returned home until he was mobilised on 21st March 1916. He reported to 3rd/7th Argyll and Sutherland Highlanders, a training battalion, at Ripon, Yorkshire.

Throughout his letters from Ripon John asked for news of family and friends, sent home washing occasionally, described the details of weekly inspections, and asked for his parents not to send butter, which could be 'lifted' at tea time, eggs, or pears. Home baked scones were wanted and parcels from home were shared.

Subsequent letters asked if his mother was receiving her share of his pay, if there is truth in the rumour of a new thread mill in Kilbarchan, how various family members were getting on. He recorded a bombing [grenade] course, trench digging, inspections and leisure time walking and listening to bands in Ripon.

Ripon, 26th March: 'I have met some fine chums, three from Glasgow and two from Edinburgh and we are all in the same hut. . . Saturday we had tea, ham and bread for breakfast, steak and potatoes and pudding for dinner and at night we were in the town so we had supper there and visited a Picture House. . .

29th March: 'We go to the range every day for a fortnight, it is seven miles from the camp and we get the train up but have to walk home.'

9th and 11th April, to his mother: 'I have been to church this morning and I am just after hearing the evening service in the hut.' [Family church going was well established: this would have pleased his mother.]

26th April, to his father: 'I would be obliged if you would send me a Postal Order for a few shillings. . . a photographer visited the camp and our hut was all taken together and in groups so I will have to take some [photos].' [A fading photograph might be the only future record of a lost soldier: John and his father would understand that.]

10th May: 'There is Measles or some other trouble. . . to keep the men from mixing together we are each confined to our own lines and all the refreshment huts are all closed and we are not allowed into Ripon. . .'

Measles killed. There had been an outbreak in Kilbarchan school too.

5th May: 'I will be forgetting very little I learned about the trade. . . but it is good for me to smarten up a bit and have to fend for myself.'

28th May: 'If you would really like a photo you will have to send a few shillings.'

18th July, to his father: 'I am to be allowed a weekend home this Friday night so please send me 10/- to pay half the railway fare.'

13th August, to everybody: 'We are at Folkestone and going to France tomorrow.'

He joined the 1/7th Argylls, on 15th August and was assigned to 8 Platoon, B Company. He met Robert 'Dandy' Crawford of High Barholm, Kilbarchan, who was in D Company.

> 19th October: 'I had a parcel from Mrs. Hunter, Glentyan [the wife of the owner of Glentyan Estate, west of Kilbarchan] on Monday, it was a very good parcel. The weather here is very wet and it is very uncomfortable but of course we will just have to take what comes and keep on smiling. . .' [Reassuring his parents that his spirits were high!]

On 28th October John was suffering from trench fever, which was widespread. Its cause was unknown. He was in No.3 Canadian General Hospital in Boulogne, which described his condition as *Pyrexia* [slight], sometimes diagnosed as *enteric fever*. Scientists struggled to identify its causes and established that it was transmitted by body lice.

On 12th December he was in the 14th General Hospital at Wimereux suffering from *'Suspected Enteric'*. On the 13th his division, the 51st [Highland] Division captured Beaumont Hamel, incurring over 2000 casualties. Trench fever had saved him from the battlefield lottery.

New Year's Day was a public holiday in Scotland. Many worked on Christmas Day. John wrote an exuberant letter to his parents on Christmas Day 1916, on his new writing pad!

> 'This had been the happiest Christmas Day of my life, my only regret being that I cannot see you all for some time yet . . . we found a stocking on each bed. . .

> 'My stocking contained a trumpet, a writing pad, shaving soap, cigarette holder, two packets of cigs and one orange. . . we had a very good dinner. . . the sisters entertained us with songs. . . on going down to tea we found another present on each of our plates. . . after we had eaten cakes and sweets until we could eat no more, we had Cigars and Cigs. . . we each had a draw in a tub and I got a small mirror and comb in a nice leather case, so what do you think of all these presents on one day?'

The delight of this 27 year old at such simple gifts is painfully touching, or is he simply reassuring this parents that everything is normal? After three months recovery he returned to his battalion on 28th January 1917:

> 'The weather here is dry but very cold and keen frost, and as we have the kilt yet, it is pretty healthy about the knees.'

The Battle of Arras began on 9th April 1917 in disgusting weather conditions: the German line broke, sagged and held, in a bitter and expensive attritional battle. The 1/7th Argylls suffered 521 casualties.

> 29th April: 'I am the only one left in your photo which I sent you from Ripon about a year ago, who is now in the Battalion. So you might take extra good care of the photograph as I would like to have it when I come home.'

The odds of surviving lessened the longer a soldier remained on the Western Front. The photo may have been the only one in which he featured and both he and his parents would be calculating his chances of coming home alive.

The Third Battle of Ypres lasted from 31st July to 10th November 1917. The Highland Division was engaged in it twice. On the second occasion, on 20th September, John was wounded in the left leg, and arrived at the 25th General Hospital on 30th September.

> 1st October: 'Don't worry, mother, I was slightly wounded in the recent advance getting a bullet into the left leg just above the ankle, however I am getting on very well indeed and have not too much pain. If I were back with the Batt. again it is about my turn now [for leave].'

> 6th November, feeling guilty about church going: 'My leg is now nearly all right again and I believe I would have been out of Hosp. but that I have had a large boil on my neck. On Sunday night I was over at the recreation room and had a game of billiards. What do you think of that for a Sunday? I am sorry to confess that I did not go to Church but I will go next Sunday if I am still here.'

> 9th November, enclosing a card: 'I was sent for by the colonel of this hospital and he handed me the enclosed card which

had been sent down here for me. You will take care of the card as they are not given to a great many, in fact I only know of one of our pals in the platoon who has had one, and he was presented with the Military Medal some time afterwards, but of course that does not mean that I will get anything more than the card, but of course, you never know. I don't want <u>any</u> of you to be going out talking about this card, as you all very much always over-rated anything that I ever did all my life, so please remember, no talk outside.'

Was he a taciturn male of his time? Don't fuss, don't embarrass me by advertising it! The decision he announced in the next sentence was life changing. The hospital staff had decided that he had done enough, with a wound and a Military Medal to his credit and that he should have a chance of avoiding the risks of the front line:

'I had an offer of a job at my trade in the hospital for some months, perhaps, but I am longing to see you all so I think I will get back to the Batt. as soon as possible, as my leave must be almost due.'

Was it leave or his chums in the battalion that influenced him most? The next letter suggests it was the latter.

15th November – he had heard that the Highland Division might be sent to Italy: 'I hope it may not be true as I then would be sent to some other Battalion and I would much rather go back amongst the boys I have been with ever since I came out.'

On 20th November the Battle of Cambrai began, with 1/7th Argylls heavily and bloodily involved. He had missed another major battle. He rejoined the battalion on 21st January, and was granted his coveted leave, from 25th January until 8th February 1918. On 26th January he was promoted corporal.

March 11th 1918. His last letter, to his young sister:

Dear Bella,
'. . . there is nothing for me to write about at present. . . we are having very warm weather, fairly good rations and Jerry not bothering us too much. I am sending you <u>all</u> <u>the</u> <u>news</u> from

the part I am in at present. I was pleased to hear you had
letters from Charlie and Willie last week and that both were
enjoying good health. When you next see Willie you may tell
him my address is still the same in case he does not know.
So you have been having a real good week-end instead of
writing to your big brother, you were walking round the
Dampton and visiting the Picture House with Bill. Well,
you are a lovely girl and I would like to be doing the same
thing. However, it may not be very long now before we are
all home enjoying ourselves again.
I will stop now by asking you to remember me to all at
home.
Your loving brother,
John

On 21st March 1918 the Germans launched Operation Michael to destroy the Allies on the Western Front. The British army was battered by artillery fire, assaulted by storm troops and forced to retire. On 23rd March the last major rally of the Highland Division took place on the Beaumetz-Morchies line, primarily manned by remnants of the 1/4th Seaforth Highlanders and the 1/7th Argyll and Sutherland Highlanders.

1st May, 1918
Dear Mr. Meikle,
I have just heard from one of my company that you have
not been informed about your son's death. I am extremely
sorry but the Minister of the regiment usually writes to the
relative, thus the reason I did not write sooner.

On the 23rd March our company was ordered to hold a
wooden track at all costs, about 10 o'clock in the morning a
Major of the 4th Seaforth Hdrs. was seen to fall about 50
yards in front and Johnnie jumped out of the small trench and
crawled out to where he lay and bound up the officer's wound
which was very serious. Having finished he turns and was
coming back and a German sniper, who had crawled forward,
fired and got him through the head, killing him instantly.

About half an hour afterwards, the German Hordes started to
advance and owing to casualties we were forced to withdraw.

I have been his Company Sergt. Major for some time and during the three and a half years I have been out here I have never met a braver soldier or better man. He was first and foremost at everything, sports as well as fighting, and Mr. Meikle none of those who knew him out here know how he is missed in this company. He was loved and respected by all in the regiment, his comrades along with myself send their deepest sympathy in your [loss].
I remain yours in sympathy,
C.S.M. Cunningham D.C.M., C de G. [Croix de Guerre]
B Coy. 7th A&SH
B.E.Forces

John Meikle's desire to have his leave and return to his chums cost him his life.

27th July 1918: The Infantry Records Office in Perth, asked John's father if he would like John's Military Medal to be presented in public or posted. It was posted on 6th August 1918.

23rd July 1919: Desperate for some tangible memento of her son, John's mother wrote to the Infantry Records Office at Perth asking if she could have any of her son's property. None came, as he was never found. He may be under a stone engraved 'Known unto God' or in a field near Beaumetz-les-Cambrai. His medal, his name on Bay 9 of the Arras Memorial and Kilbarchan Church's memorials, is the only evidence of his 30 years – along with lines in the local newspaper and his letters.

When hostilities ceased on 11th November 1918, Kilbarchan Steeple bell rang all day, the school closed and flags and banners were displayed. In the homes of the bereaved and the seriously disabled there was little joy, only shared relief that it was over. And the unanswerable, 'Why did it happen to me?' Seventy names are on the village memorials.

The men that returned had been altered by their experiences, some appeared to readjust quickly to normal life, others concealed their torments, or some may have drowned them with drink. Most slept uneasily. For the homes to which they returned, there had been months if not years of separation, individuals may have matured, children were unfamiliar to their fathers and older brothers. Wives and mothers had become accustomed to being in charge in the family home. Many had to abandon this.

Colin Campbell:

'Dan Trushell told me of a soldier who had just returned home at the end of the war. His wife had been struggling to raise the family and the oldest boy was defying her and she asked her husband for support: 'Leave the boy alone,' he said, 'there's been too much discipline.' What did that do to their resuming relationship, or her authority within the family and to family discipline? Or, in a village, the fabric of the community?'

Christine Erwin:

'My mother used to tell the sad tale of being frightened of her father when he came home from the war because there was this "strange man" who suddenly appeared at the end of the war and came to live in their house. She'd just been brought up with her older sister and mother up to that point.'

Colin Campbell:

'I visited Robert Gardner and his two sisters in their home in Langside Park in the 1960s. He was a Kitchener volunteer in the 10th Cameronians/Scottish Rifles and had been seriously wounded in a leg by machine-gun fire at the Battle of Loos on 25th September 1915. He was hospitalised for four years and when I met him he was still being treated for the wounds.

'On his first visit to Paisley after his discharge from hospital in 1919 he was leaning painfully on his stick at the tram stop on the High Street, near New Street, when a Kilbarchan contemporary saw him and asked why he had not seen him for four years. As Robert explained his predicament the tram arrived and the man leapt on, leaving him slowly failing to board it as it moved off.

'The French used to have special seats set aside on public transport for War Wounded.'

Listen Closely

Glentyan House. From the rooftop of their home, Mr and Mrs, Hunter and their daughter Elspeth, watched the bombing of Clydebank. A bomb dropped near Glentyan Estate's North Lodge. Like other families in the village, the Hunters hosted evacuees from Clydebank and Glasgow after the Blitz

The Home Guard was initially made up of volunteers, but later in the war men were told to join. The photograph represents a mix of ages, brought together for home defence. At least fifteen men wear First World War service medals

CHAPTER 11
World War II

'Shoot it doon, Willie.'

WHEN the Peace of Versailles was signed in June 1919, the commander of the victorious Allied armies in 1918, Marshal Foch, prophetically declared, 'This is not a peace, it is an armistice for twenty years.'

As the people of Kilbarchan gathered to unveil their war memorials, they would have had conflicting emotions of grief and resentment at their heavy losses. The memorials at the Parish Church, the United Free Church, the Scout Hall and the main focus, the village memorial, record for posterity the effects of war on their community, their homes, and their families.

For many women, there was the loss of their wartime jobs and a return to a subordinate role. There was disillusionment with the absence of 'homes fit for heroes' and job insecurity. The social divide had been reinforced by fear caused by the overthrow of old orders and the new Soviet Union's international promotion of Communism.

The damage to communities, large and small, by the loss of young men in the war was heightened by emigration: the desperate and the ambitious sailed away, leaving some communities bereft of many young men and women; their youth, skills, fun, enthusiasm, laughter and love.

The 1926 General Strike paralysed the nation and increased fear of revolution. Strike leaders were black-listed and resentment simmered for years. The 1929 Depression unleashed unemployment on the capitalist world. As an austerity measure, in 1931, unemployment benefit was means tested, which was deeply resented by the long term unemployed. In John Brown's shipyard in Clydebank, Hull 534, the future *Queen Elizabeth*, rusted on the stocks from December 1931 until April 1934, symbolisng the precarious nature of the British economy and the perennial lack of continuity in shipbuilding. Many of the men who had often gathered after work by The Cross, or at their close doors, to talk and pass time, found themselves with nothing else to do, as their jobs had gone.

In Germany the Depression created fertile ground for Hitler. He won power in 1933 and created jobs with conscription, enlarged forces, military industries and the construction of strategic highways.

It was clear that the nightmare of 1914-1918 might be repeated. The French and British governments ignored Hitler's infringements of the Treaty of Versailles, connived at the weakening of Czechoslovakia in 1938, then made it known that Poland's territorial integrity must be respected. British preparations for war restored employment to many.

In March 1939 limited conscription began, followed by full conscription for all 18-41 years old men on 3rd September 1939. In 1942 the upper limit was raised to 51 and all females aged 20 to 30 were included. There were exemptions for people in manufacturing jobs and services which sustained the war effort. Conscription ended in 1960.

At 11:15 on Sunday 3rd September 1939, Prime Minister Neville Chamberlain broadcast:

> 'This morning the British ambassador in Berlin handed the German government a final note stating that unless we hear from them by 11 o'clock this morning that they were prepared at once to withdraw their troops from Poland, a state of war would exist between us. I have to tell you now that no such undertaking has been received, and consequently this country is at war with Germany. You can imagine what a bitter blow it is to me that all my long struggle to win peace has failed.'

Newspapers were still the main source of information on national and international affairs throughout Europe. Radio had begun to overtake them by being more up to date with events. As Europe stumbled into war the BBC's nine o'clock news became a daily ritual for anxious citizens.

Irene Gibson: Easwald Bank:

'I remember coming from the church with both my parents: we got to Easwald Bank and a lady called Nan Love opened her window and shouted out, "That's it, war's been declared, Willie." My parents stopped and said, "Is that right?" and she said, "Yes, it was on the radio this morning." I remember a great discussion of what would happen and what could happen.'

Elspeth Robertson, Glentyan House:

'We moved in before the war actually began. I remember standing in the entrance bit which had black and white squares and hearing on the radio the announcement and then a small friend said, "A bomb could fall on Woolworths! And Woolworths would be gone!" '

On 3rd September Kilbarchan's Territorials reported to the drill hall of the 6th Argyll and Sutherland Highlanders on Paisley High Street. They trained there daily but everyone lived at home, with subsistence allowances, until the battalion moved to England on 15th October.

Sirens, shelters, wardens and blackouts were fundamentals of wartime life. The destruction of Guernica in April 1937 in the Spanish Civil War by the Nazi Condor Legion had demonstrated how effective bombers could be against civilian targets. It was believed that bombers would always penetrate anti-aircraft defences. Initially navigation depended only on maps, stars and eyesight, which justified blacking out all lights. Radio and radar soon played an important part. Poison gas attacks were expected.

Throughout the village, people prepared blackout curtains, brown sticky paper was criss-crossed over windows to minimise shards of blasted glass, car headlights were reduced to a dim slit of light, street lights were off, and trees and lamp posts had white stripes painted on them to make them visible in the dark.

Air Raid Precautions [ARP, later Civil Defence] wardens patrolled their allotted areas to maintain the blackout. When the sirens sounded they directed people to shelters and helped rescuers after a raid. There were specialised ARP/CD rescue teams who were trained to dig out casualties.

Fire watchers were posted on major buildings, equipped with sand, water and stirrup pumps, for dealing with incendiary bombs and minor fires. The police, fire and ambulance services had volunteer reserves.

Kilbarchan was only a few miles and minutes flying time away from Clydeside's shipyards, the Rolls Royce aero engine factory at Hillington and the Royal Ordnance Factory at Bishopton, all potential targets. As Kilbarchan had no military installations or manufacturing centres little priority was given to public shelters.

Lottie Dow, The Grove:

> 'Where the bus stop is on Wheatlands Drive, there was an air raid shelter. It was shaped like two upside down baths, that's the only way I can describe them. . . brick, we used to climb up and play there.'

Irene Gibson, Easwald Bank:

> 'Very few people had proper air raid shelters. The people at the top of St. Barchan's Road, they had one, an Anderson shelter in the garden.'

Helen Dooris, Steeple Street:

> 'There was a shelter up in Steeple Square and the minute the siren went all the bed clothes were lifted and we went en masse, with my granny. It was at the church gate. . . the dampness and a dank smell and the smell of cats was horrendous. There was a wooden door and down some steps.'

Eliza Mackenzie, Low Barhom:

> 'At Kilbarchan School they had a wee sort of shelter and we practised. It was at the end of the new school – you went down. You had to have your gasmask at all times.'

Walter Gibson, Milliken Drive:

> 'We used to go downstairs to the neighbour, Alec Shaw, underneath the table, ten of us!'

Myra Goldie, High Barholm:

'When the bombers came over we went into our Aunt Jean's lobby, and sat on chairs in there all night. My father and Uncle Willie were ARP: the police office was two doors down and the police officer would come up and chap the window "Right, Matta!" and he went out checking.'

Eliza MacKenzie:

'They were very strict with the blackout. They came to the door and said "There's a chink." Mathew Muir was a warden. My dad had to take turns in Renfrew, he said it was quite eerie sitting in this big office.' [Fire watching at Babcocks]

Mabel Murray, Church Street:

In Church Street the first night the sirens went our next door neighbour came in, and they said, "Would you like to come in with us?" They were an elderly couple. We did go in. Then the next night, as I was putting out the milk bottles, the sirens went again and my mum said, "And we're just staying in here tonight." But they went down Church Street and went under the Roarin' Brig.'

Irene Gibson:

'Mathew Currie used to hammer on the wall when there was an air raid siren and he and my father went out together. I used to hear that from Mattie, she was a first aider. I don't know where the First Aid Post was but her neighbour used to get her out and they walked together to the First Aid Post. We had sandbags, I think they were delivered to us. You were supposed to put them on an incendiary bomb.'

Agnes Douglas, siren memories:

'Irene's dad was a fireman and he used to chap through, for my dad was a warden and the firemen always went away first, he would knock through and my dad would know that he would have to go next. John [her brother] was being cheeky to my dad one night and my dad was giving John a row and John said, "Be quiet. Dad, there's the sirens." And my dad had to run. We used to go below the table.'

No bombs exploded in Kilbarchan but there was a near miss.

One bomb, unreported by any of the witnesses, quietly fell near McMurritch's farm (now Milliken Mill Farm), between the river and the railway: it did not explode.

An unexplored bomb, its fuse removed, being recovered from McMurritch's farm (now Milliken Mill Farm) by Royal Engineers. It fell in a field between the river and the railway line. Nobody who was recorded spoke about it.
[Photo: James Henderson]

After the disintegration of Allied forces in France from 10th May 1940 onwards, the government set up the Local Defence Volunteers, later the Home Guard. Men rushed to enlist. There were few weapons, and after the evacuation at Dunkirk, all available weapons were given to the full-time army.

Kilbarchan's Home Guard was No.3 Platoon, Number 5 [later E] Company of the 2nd [Renfrewshire] Battalion of the Home Guard, which covered Johnstone and the villages. Initially Kilbarchan platoon assembled at the Steeple Halls, later at Spring Grove House.

The later BBC comedy drama *Dad's Army* captured some of the improvisation and public scepticism of the early days, when the virtually unarmed volunteers were facing invasion. Eager amateurs had to rely on veterans for the basics.

David Carlin:

'We used to laugh at the Home Guard, some of them had wooden guns, we used to say what if the paratroopers came? The new recruits, they were marching with pieces of wood.'

The unit was well organised for an era with few phones. Named people would be contacted and they would call out others from their allocated list. John Lee, had been on a non-commissioned officer's course in 1918, which gave him the experience:

'. . . to train our local Home Guard in 1940 to a degree which enabled them to be the first company to fire at Foxbar range. After some time I was sent into Paisley and made the official sergeant of intelligence for the battalion.'

Eric Borland:

'My father was a corporal. He told me they had a dummy gun that sat down on the Branscroft – to fool the Germans. It was made up of canvas. . . They're sitting there with this gun that couldn't shoot and they're bombing Clydebank. He could see it all happening.

'The Home Guard Headquarters was at the Steeple Halls. My father was on guard duty and this plane was circling above, and the gun he had couldn't shoot, a kid-on gun. It was a Heinkel bomber, whether it was coming back from a raid or what? They had a dummy airfield [one of many 'Starfish' decoy sites, with lights and fires to simulate bombed airfields and buildings] up at the Peesweep [Lapwing Lodge] – maybe it was looking for that. Jessie Mitchell, she was a kind of far-out relation of mine, she came running out and shouted "Shoot it doon, Willie." He went, "Bang, bang"!'

Colin Campbell:

'I was told many years ago that the only man to discharge his rifle inside the Steeple Hall was a William McCaw. The bullet went through an internal wall, but harmed no one.'

Walter Gardner-sole survivor of Kilbarchan Home Guard:

'We used to meet up in the Spring Grove. When the Sten gun came out and when I first tried to fire, it went up in the air, with the recoil. It was a cheap weapon. Went twice a week. . . it was all right.'

There were tactical exercises to which they were taken by truck:

'We had to take this wood on the road to Largs: there was a farmhouse and a wood at the back of that and we had to get there unrecognised.'

They failed.

The photograph of members of the Kilbarchan Home Guard shows the reality. There are men of all ages, some possibly over-age, whose military inexperience was leavened by the fifteen men wearing World War I service ribbons: one wears pilot's wings. The people in the picture only represent the number available that day. Many others would be at work.

From high up in the outskirts of the village the Clyde valley and the Kilpatrick Hills are clearly visible. In 1941 an attack took place on the shipbuilding town in the valley. It began at 9pm on Thursday 13th March 1941 and lasted until 5.30am on Friday 14th. It is remembered as the Clydebank Blitz.

The Luftwaffe pathfinder Kampfgruppe 100 was guided by radio waves to Clydebank and deluged it with incendiaries. These illuminated the target for the next two waves which dropped high explosives, to destroy buildings and obstruct the fire and rescue services. More damage was done to civilians than to military targets. About 9pm on the 14th bombs fell again and continued until the small hours of the 15th.

The Clydebank conflagration was so great that its flames and glow were seen throughout the village.

David Carlin was in the field behind Mountpleasant:

'I think we were catching rabbits. Our John was there, and Peter Ritchie, the three of us. We sat up at the wall up there and watched the lights, the flashes, and the noises. It was like a firework display, right enough. I saw a lot of Ack-Ack [anti-aircraft] fire. It was light all along. It was amusement at first but then it was serious. My mother and father were worried we hadn't been in. We got hell.'

Eliza:

'My aunt had come up from Renfrew for a few days. She brought a dog, she was safer up here. There were noises of the bombs but I was told it was just a big noise. You could feel the vibrations and I remember my mother saying, "It's just a big bang" to shut me up.'

Agnes:

'. . . the night Clydebank got it. It was like fireworks. The brightness – the sky was all lit up.'

Lottie Dow, The Grove:

'I remember getting shoved in a pram and a bomb fell in that field [in front of Monklands] and all the windows were falling out. My mother and father and maybe all the others all went up the brae, to that field where the Law Farm is, and they were in that field the night Clydebank was bombed. They could see it was lit up. When the sirens went. . . the other place they sometimes went was over the quarry, over the Milliken. You had to evacuate the house.'

Myra:

'I can still hear the bombers, you knew the difference, they went over once – I still remember the Clydebank Blitz, there was a difference [in the sound]. I know now they were lighter, they had dropped their bombs – there was one in Johnstone and one or two in Paisley when they were jettisoning their bombs.'

Elspeth Robertson:

'My parents were both air raid wardens, their station was up on the roof of Glentyan. There was a flat roof outside and from there they could see the whole area. We had some staff and evacuees, we were all down in very bottom floor of the house and every time the sirens went off I was frightened and they said, "Come up and have a look, it's not all bombs."

'I would go up on the roof and watch what was happening. It was fascinating watching the searchlights and hearing all the bangs and noises. There was one amazing night when there was an air raid and my parents were up there with their tin hats with a white 'W' for warden. This plane came roaring over, pretty low and they put their hands up to cover the white W on their helmets! It dropped a bomb just over the North Lodge and that was in the field in front of Monklands. My father couldn't walk very far. . . but there wasn't even a window smashed in the North Lodge and he came back tossing a bit of metal! I've got a bit of the bomb!'

Irene Gibson:

'I do remember being wakened up at the height of the Clydebank Blitz because my grandmother was in Clydebank, and obviously the fire brigade were out. And the next day, it was a Saturday [15th March], my father came back, he might have been there a couple of nights – he was absolutely black. They [Kilbarchan NFS] had been there. He said, "It was absolutely terrible. I tried to find out what happened." My uncle worked in the shipyards. My mother's sister was there and my granny was staying with them. He said, "I don't know what to do, I think you should go over." So my mother went over and took me! She obviously didn't have any idea of what it was like. We went by public transport, across Renfrew Ferry and we took a tram car up to Dalmuir. We walked after that because the sewing machine factory, Singer's, was still alight and there were still firemen there.

'I was more worried about my mother's reaction. I always

thought it didn't matter what the situation, she kept calm – she was obviously getting a bit worried, but then we found out that they had gone to Skye in the morning, on the early train. They stayed there for the rest of the war.

'As soon as we knew that they were all right we came away. But I remember seeing in their house two budgies, a blue one and a green one, the cage was there and the budgies were still perched.'

Her uncle stayed there, to go to his work.

Irene Gibson:

'There were evacuees from Glasgow. The two old Miss Gibsons, Lizzie and Jeannie, in Easwald Bank, had a 12 year old boy and they were maiden ladies, and what would they do with him? He had friends, and I played with them in the garden.'

Elspeth Robertson, Glentyan:

'We had two families from Glasgow. Some of them had never seen a tree – mother and children, they lasted 24 or 36 hours, they were terrified by the trees. They had to walk from the terminus up that avenue, which was three quarters of a mile and they were absolutely terrified.

'Then we got three boys, Patrick, Alfie and Graham and they were staunch Roman Catholics so they had to go to Johnstone every Sunday to church. Wee Graham was only five and my mother was looking after them, feeding them all the time. They were lovely boys. I often wondered what happened to them. Rough and tumble but salt of the earth.

'When the crisis was over or their parents wanted them back, we had two adult families and they became special friends. They had their own accommodation and cooked for themselves.'

Helen:

'We had my mother's two cousins from Shettleston, they were

refugees. How they packed in I don't know. They stayed with my granny most of the time – they would come and sleep at our place and one night my cousin got up and he was looking out the window: "All's quiet on the Western Front" and just at that the bomb fell on Johnstone, around Quarrelton Road way. He was back into the bed before you knew it.'

Kilbarchan School was closed on the Monday and Tuesday after the raids. The teachers were involved in finding accommodation for evacuees in the village. Two weeks later the school hosted forty five pupils from Holy Cross Roman Catholic Primary in Clydebank: later in the year they transferred to St.Margaret's in Johnstone. [Kilbarchan School Centenary Brochure 1977]

Everyone had clear memories of the 13th-14th March 1941. The deepest blow fell upon Mr. and Mrs. William Borland of Easwald Bank, whose son John [44] and daughter-in-law Georgina [43] were killed in their home at Whitecrook Street, Clydebank, on Friday 14th March. [*The Clydebank Blitz,* I.M.M.MacPhail Clydebank District Libraries 1974]

Four thousand of Clydebank's twelve thousand homes were completely destroyed. Only seven properties were undamaged. The official death toll was 528. Most of the population was homeless. On the same two nights Glasgow suffered 647 deaths, Dumbarton 60 and bombs fell randomly in the surrounding counties, doing no harm or killing and maiming serendipitously. [*River of Fire*, John Macleod Birlinn 2011]

The devastating effect on a relatively small concentrated community made Clydebank Scotland's worst Blitz victim: it was Scotland's Coventry.

Mabel Murray:

'The Hunters lived in Glentyan Estate and their son (Richard, Elspeth's brother) was an officer and one day, standing and watching at the close, part of his regiment came down Church Street in their full army gear and branches sticking out all over. They were well camouflaged. This was them going up as a unit, I don't know where they were going. His troop was at the Hunters' at the weekend.

Elspeth Robertson:

'They'd done a route march from Achnacarry, the Commando Training Centre, and they billeted themselves at Glentyan two nights or more. I was away at that time. My mother said what they left was marvellous, hunks of meat. They thoroughly enjoyed it, apparently the pipers came round the dining room table. There were a lot of them. He [Richard] wasn't in charge. He was a very junior officer.

Elspeth's family was to receive the news that every family feared most. As in World War, I news of casualties was delivered by telegram. James McIntyre was the son of the Kilbarchan postmaster and in October 1944 he had the unhappy task of delivering the Hunters news of Richard's death. The minister had been briefed and would visit after the telegram had been delivered.

Elspeth Robertson:

'There'd already been one delivered, which never should have been. Mother was sitting in the car, at the bottom of the main avenue, waiting for my father coming along from his train, and a telegram was delivered to her in the car saying that he was missing. If you like, it was a breaking in, for they knew something was wrong.'

After his visit to Glentyan:

'He went off to North Africa, where he was wounded. They wanted to send him home and he said, "I'm not going." He stayed with them and was only able to do certain things– he'd been badly wounded. He didn't get back into the battalion until they had gone into Italy. It was only just after he rejoined the battalion that he was killed.

'I was very close to my brother.'

The Ministry of Food was established at the outbreak of war. It advised on food economy, waste and maximizing available resources. It published simple recipes and encouraged self-help. Complementary to this was the Dig for Victory campaign, to reduce the need for imported food. Marginal land was cultivated, allotments were encouraged and gardens made more productive rather than decorative. Food imports had halved by 1941 as a result of this campaign.

For a fair distribution of food, rationing began in January 1940 and clothing and food ration books were an essential in almost every daily shop. Rationing was not phased out until June 1954.

All the old houses in Kilbarchan have long gardens, which were always well cultivated to provide vegetables and fruit and there was a flourishing Horticultural Society.

Myra Goldie:

'During the war the hens were numbered, they came every week and took the eggs and x number of people in the building got one each and the rest went away in a van.'

Eliza Mackenzie:

'Up at the smallholding they had to give them back to the government, and we got one or two. You had your coupons and it was cut off if you wanted half a pound – you never got half a pound. Two ounces. They were very strict about that. I quite liked Spam [when it arrived]. My mum never really bought a loaf, we had scones. My Mother must have wanted to strangle me, I was such a fussy eater.'

Their garden was well cultivated:

'People said it was like a miniature show garden, it's such a big garden. Grandad got a lot of horticultural prizes for flowers and fruit.'

Agnes Douglas:

'MaryTaylor had a sweet shop at the corner of Tandlehill Road. Somebody would say, "She's got sweeties in, dolly mixtures or something" and you'd take your coupons and get your dolly mixtures. Tuppence or threepence.

'When I was at college I worked at the papershop, Alexander's. The coupons were Ds and Es – Ds were two ounces and Es were four ounces. I counted the coupons at the end of the day.'

Christine Erwin spoke of her mother, from the village and her wartime romance with a soldier:

> 'Mum went to work at Bishopton. Her younger sister worked at Bishopton as well. Her Polish husband arrived in her life through a contact at the Ordnance Factory. There was another lady at the Ordnance Factory who met a Polish chap and Jarko had a friend, Witold Mazurkiewicz. She went on a blind date and she and her friend met up with the two guys at the top of the Hillhead Underground on Byres Road. At that point Witold was at Maryhill. He'd been round and round Scotland. He came through Europe, out to France, a boat I think to Liverpool, then he was posted to Scotland, Fochabers, East Coast, Central Belt. Then he was sent back, he'd done Monte Cassino then Falaise. At one point he'd been in tanks. They got engaged towards the end of the war. Would he go back, would she go with him? They got married on Christmas Day 1947.'

They settled in Kilbarchan.

Victory in Europe triggered an outpouring of relief and elation throughout the nation, tempered by grief for those who would not return. For many there was still anxiety – the unfinished war against the Japanese in the Far East.

Witold Mazurkiewicz, Polish Army

Agnes Douglas:

> 'There was a party and they were dancing but John and I weren't allowed out. Just my mum and dad. They were all dancing in the street, at Easwald Bank, up at the foot of Milliken Drive. I can remember the lights going on. My mum took me up as far as the old terminus to see the lights.'

Myra Goldie:

> 'Everybody was up in the public park. It was great. I had got a bike from somewhere – it was my own bike. Everybody was happy.'

Ian Trushell:

> 'My elder sister Ellen, who was born in 1940, she had only experienced the blackout, and after VE Day they took her to the top of Milliken Drive and they looked across the valley and saw all the lights. . . that she'd never seen. . . she said, "Is that fairyland?" '

David Carlin was called up. He went to Pinefield barracks in Elgin for his basic training: the staff were Lovat Scouts.

> 'I went in about 1943 or '44. We were in Elgin. We were used to tackety boots, there were some who had shoes. One of them, he must have been a mummy's boy, he worked in an office in Glasgow, you want to see the feet he had from marching, he wasn't used to big boots, they put him into one of the foot regiments. That's the way it was. You did a test, Morse code and different things, to sort out your regiment.'

David was selected for the Royal Corps of Signals, whose depot was at Catterick. On a night out:

> 'Once there were four of us going to Darlington. And we were skint and we got a taxi back, it was about twelve miles from Darlington. We took him right into the centre – we opened the door, none of us had any money, and shouted, "Churchill will pay!" He's running after us. Once we got into the camp he didn't know where he was.

> 'After Catterick I went to Norfolk. I went down to Havant, near Portsmouth – the flying bombs came over at that time. I was in a private house that had been taken over at Southsea. The houses along the front of the town were rubble – every house was a shambles. We were bombed regular. One night I was on the toilet upstairs and I landed at the bottom of the stairs!'

His unit returned to Norfolk, destined for the Far East.

> 'I came home on embarkation leave. There was a pigeon race on the Saturday and I was due back in Norfolk on the Saturday and I stayed over till the Monday. Right away I

was marched in before the colonel. . . the one that marches you in and knocks the bunnet aff your heid, you feel that low. The colonel raves on and raves on. I told him my mother was badly. And he says, "You're a lucky boy, your unit's being moved in three days time." I was lucky. That's one of the worst crimes in the army, especially when you are on embarkation leave.'

The troopship sailed from Liverpool to Bombay.

'We arrived in Bombay, then travelled by train all the way across to Calcutta. Went from Calcutta to Comilla, on the border of India and Burma. The river drowns thousands every year. That's where I seen the biggest snake in my life. We were in tents and I woke up in the morning, it was nearly into the tent, about two feet away and about seven feet long. The worst snake of the lot is only about six inches long, the poison in it was deadly. We used to be warned about it in the army. Used to get them under corrugated sheets. When you went to the toilets, you looked down first!'

'The snakes don't go for you, it's you that disturbs them. I was in a barber's shop, the floor was bamboo, and one of them came up through the floor and he caught it at the back of the neck – they must be trained when they're young – the back of the head, they're useless, they can't do anything to you. That's the only thing I was frightened a wee bit about, snakes.'

David did not offer to describe engagements with the Japanese and this was respected.

'You do things on the spur of the moment. See, if you panic or that, you know, you'll do things you would never do before. You wouldn't dream of doing them. There's some things it's no right tae talk about. It's better keeping them to yourself.'

In late February or in March 1945 his detachment was posted from the West African Division to Ramree island for six weeks. His time there was idyllic.

'There were some buildings there and I found a bag of paper, drawing sheets, and that's what I did, swimming in the morning and all afternoon, that's when I drew. I did umpteen different designs of pigeon lofts for when I got back home. I had them in a bag and somebody knocked [stole] it!'

When the war in the Far East ended:

'There was a big estate, say 10 miles in diameter and the houses were built there for Burmah Oil, and I was in one of these houses. Football again. I was in charge of the ration store for the unit. The Regimental Sergeant Major and the Regimental Quartermaster Sergeant – I got in with these two. One of them played for Bristol City . . .

'They had unit teams, the sergeants' mess, officers and 1st battalion team and 2nd battalion team and a regimental team. You had to be good to get in. Most of the others were professionals.'

David met his brother in Rangoon:

'I got new clothes for him in the store. I got him a bed. Our John's a different nature from me. He was in the Royal Artillery. They had tournaments, sweepstakes and if the enemy got a direct hit the winner got fifty bob. He was always scrambling at the last. He never thought much about the army.'

Alex Murphy:

'What's not been seen is the amount of people lost in Kilbarchan during the war.'

Walter Gardner:

'In Milliken Drive, there was four never came back. Ramsay Stanners, he lived across the road, he was a bricklayer and finished up a Sergeant Pilot in the Air Force. I always remember he was home on leave. He must have flown into Abbotsinch [RNAS airfield on the current site of Glasgow International Airport] and when he went away, he must have told his mother, he dipped his wings as he went out. Alec Sallows and Roddy MacKinnon and Tom Bolton – he wasn't a Habbie. He married a girl up in Milliken Drive, Agnes Craig and he was killed as well. Eric Soutar, he just lived on the main road. He died – he was a prisoner of war in Japan.'

Twenty seven men from Kilbarchan died in World War II.

People and families were changed by the war by the loss of so many fathers, sons, mothers, daughters, friends, neighbours, and their homes. This war was not only fought on a foreign field, but through aerial bombing, came physically very close to home for the first time. When the war ended, people had to live with its consequences.

Alex Murphy's brother William served in Burma as a Royal Marine Commando:

'He was wounded in the left hip and the left elbow and the shrapnel could not be taken away. Willie didn't neglect his family, but he did have a drink. One of the times I was taking him to his house from the Trust he was very low and I made him a cup of tea and just talked away and what he said was they were in the jungle and a mate next to him got

Willie Murphy (front row, left) with his Royal Marine comrades

shot and he had thought, Thank God it wasn't me. And he regretted that ever since. That had affected him. The thought of his mate dying and he was glad it wasn't him. That shook him to the core. He had to live with that.

'When he got wounded he was shipped to China, I think, but they wouldn't let him home, I don't know why. He had to sign a document that absolved them of all blame, so he didn't get a pension. Because he had discharged himself they washed their hands of him. He came home and what he had to do in the winter was make a mitt of stookie [Scots: plaster cast] for his hand so he could pick up a brick, because he couldn't hold the brick with his fingers. He laid bricks with a stookie. He worked, he had to work to tire himself out and then he fell asleep. He died aged 48, leaving five of a family.'

David Carlin:

'I was serving my time. I found it strange going back into work. First month or two I could have gone back. You had to buy a weekly ticket for your job. Your money didn't go that far. See, when you're in the army, you go to bed at night, no worries about taxes and rent, your bed's there. The only thing is the military side.

'When I came home, the pigeons attracted me, Ronald was grown up. I missed the comradeship a lot. No worries. You got three months, and you didn't lose your service. You signed on for 25 or 12 years. Never had a drink before I went into the army. I thought, I'm going to sign back in.'

His mother did not think this a good idea:

'She took me into Hepworth's in Paisley and she rigged me out from top to bottom. I looked a million dollars. Demob suit? I never wore it in my life, the trouser legs were half way up my legs. Naw, took the raincoat, it lasted a couple of years. When I was demobbed the boy says, "What about your medals?" I said, "Gie them to Churchill." Neither of us took them. You see them down there with their medals. I wouldn't do that. I've no time for that. The only thing I took was a regimental dress cap. It was blue, but somebody knocked it.

'I had to be dressed when I went out in Kilbarchan. I was always dressed. Here folk would say, "Have you still got that old bunnet with the big hole in the back of it?" I went about here more or less in rags but the minute I went out that gate – smart. The army learned me that.'

Chapter 12

The Kilbarchan Churches

'It was a happy place, a good place.'

IT IS DIFFICULT today, when many mainstream churches are closing, to appreciate the part churches played in society in 1900. A significant residue of the judgementalism of Robert Burns' time over a century before was alive and well. For the first half of the twentieth century ministers and priests enjoyed a status, albeit declining, that today's clergy could hardly imagine. The churches still had huge influence on lives, locally, nationally and personally.

History explains much about the formation of attitudes. How churches work is not an exciting topic, nor a subject of widespread discussion, but the next 450 words are critical.

Before World War I there were four churches in Kilbarchan.

The old grey Parish Church of Kilbarchan, built in 1724, was overshadowed by building works, begun in 1899, which created an impressive one thousand seat red sandstone building. It opened on 13th January 1901 – a church for a new century. The two buildings are on Church Street.

> David Carlin:
> 'See the parish church there, it's got a beautiful entry to it, when someone gets married there and gets their photograph, it looks lovely, at the steps.'

The parish church's constitution gave the Kirk Session, its governing body, which was chaired by the minister, custody over both spiritual and temporal matters. This put the minister in a dominant position in all church affairs.

The Treaty of Union in 1707 had safeguarded the rights of the Church of Scotland, but the right of each Kirk Session, since 1688-1689, to select a minister, was supplanted by Act of Parliament in 1711. This restored the local laird or landowner's right to appoint his own man. Such patronage was alien to the Presbyterian tradition: the 1711 Act was abolished in 1874.

Believing in the Kirk Session's right to choose a minister, some left the parish church in 1786, and built a church at the Knowe, now Steeple Square, which joined similarly minded churches as the Relief Church. Several organisational amalgamations later the East Church was back in the Church of Scotland in 1929. Its constitution separated spiritual affairs, supervised by the Kirk Session, from temporal affairs, carried out by an elected Board of Managers, presided over by a preses [chairman]. The minister, on administrative and financial matters, was subordinate to those who held the purse strings. This system persisted until 1988.

The two ministers covered for each other during the summer holidays and some organisations straddled the two churches. There was always some co-operation.

> 'Christian Aid had joint soup lunches and we went round the doors. Book stalls, a Johnstone and District thing, that was a good way of getting the different churches together.'

In the minds and speech of many the West Church remained *the* parish church, despite there being two parishes, East and West, in the village since 1929.

These mindsets partly explain the failure of the two to unite, even when diminishing rolls made it an obvious outcome. The greater capacity of the West Church and its grander design allowed its members to assume that it would contain a united church. The East Church realised that too and felt threatened.

Longstanding family associations and memories of baptisms, marriages, social events and remembered personalities bound congregations to their respective buildings. Loyalty to influential peers in each church and loyalty of individual ministers to their members' view, combined with the very human instinct to resist change. The subject was deep rooted, complex, and very emotive. The church, for most, was part of everyday life, in one form or another. It was the central point, in so many ways, of a traditional village in Scotland, from cradle to grave.

> 'I was taken to church when I was three months old and laid along the pew. The church was just part of you, that's what you did. As soon as you were a certain age you took a Sunday School class and then you went into the choir. For years I was in the choir. And the Bible Class. All the boys and all the girls. The Sunday School was huge then.'

> 'My brother took me to Sunday School when I was three. That's my association with Kilbarchan East. I went in the Sunday School. I became a Sunday School teacher. When you were a Sunday School teacher you had more to do with the teas and that sort of thing. I remember going to the David Livingstone Centre at Blantyre. It was a great trip. It was good. And the Sunday School teachers always had their meetings.'

Sundays until the 1960s

As the century began the Scottish Sabbath was marked by avoiding any activity that could be remotely construed as work. In extreme cases this could mean having Sunday's meals prepared on Saturday, dressing in the Sunday best, going to church several times, and possibly going for a walk. No games, no running about, no healthy recreation – stultifying, boring and wearisome for anyone other than the most pious. No shops or public houses were open, the swings in the parks were chained. Sunday cast a pall of dullness over children. Places remote from the major conurbations were conspicuously oppressive.

> 'Started in Kilbarchan West then Kilbarchan East. In my grandmother's day, she was a great knitter, but she'd never knit on a Sunday [1900s]. A Sunday [1940s and 1950s] was quite strict in those days. You were just supposed to sit

and be pleasant. You didn't go out and play or anything like that. That was the way of it.'

'On a Sunday we'd walk up the country, the Dampton Pad and that kind of thing. We used to walk to Howwood sometimes, by the back roads. That was a Sunday.
There was a Bible Class, both churches went to it in the West Church. Dr Alexander took the class. It met in the early evening.'

'Sunday School? Oh, yes, first prize every year for attendance. Junior choir, I've got all the photographs to show you! That's when there were services in the evening as well. Morning, noon and night. I dreaded Sunday. It must have been worse further up North where they did nothing on a Sunday. There was no fun on a Sunday. We all went to Sunday School.'

Sunday School

Sunday Schools ran throughout the century. Staff volunteered, leaders were sometimes persuaded. Moira Smith recalled making her way from Gateside through the New Street gate to the church:

> 'Along the path, get a sticker [for the Young Worshipper's League] from Mrs. Stevenson. Irvine's was the best place to shop, open for the Sunday papers and after church. If I got away without putting my money in the collection, I'd go there.' [1960s]

Bill Chittick, Sunday School Superintendent, 1980s:

> 'There was a session meeting and the minister was looking for someone to take over the Sunday School. After a lot of discussion I agreed.

> 'It grew immensely because the minister used to go up to the school and talk to the kids and used to come and give me a list of the names of kids he'd spoken to. The numbers started going up because the minister was a good recruiting officer.

'The seniors were in the large hall, the juniors in the small hall and the tots were in the ladies' toilets! At one of the prize givings I had put out 'reserved' notices on the pews and they were going to take up more than half of the church! We had more than six classes in the big Sunday School and the small Sunday School must have been as big as well.'

Trips

Sunday School trips were a universal institution in Scotland. Before higher living standards in the 1960s, job insecurity and poverty were endemic. Many families did not have resources to go on holiday, or even a day trip. The trip was an escape from a crowded home, a visit to an unfamiliar venue, and something to anticipate. Before and during World War II trips were local. After the war, until the railway shut, trains carried trips, then it was buses. Over a generation the decline in interest in Sunday School and trips was marked.

Agnes Douglas, during and after the war:

'Went on the Sunday School trips during the war. Up to the Braes, we went on Currie's lorries. Remember being up on the fields at the back of the Braes. We always had races, you got your tea, in a poke [paper bag], there was always a roll and latterly we got sausage rolls and things like that when the Sunday School trips went down to Troon, to South Beach. We'd always go to a church hall down there.'

Mabel Murray, during the war:

'We went up to the Braes. You were in the lorry and you took your own mug. There would be stuff provided to eat. They would put up a couple of swings in the barn, then there would be races in the fields.'

Myra Goldie:

'During the war we got wagons with horses or Currie's lorries and went up to Whinnerston – for years we did that. The same bit of ground, the teachers must have made all the picnics – you ran wild. For some unknown reason it was always good weather.

'After the war we started going on trains with streamers, hanging out of the windows. Prestwick, Saltcoats, Prestwick was one of the favourite places. You were controlled, you didn't get wandering. You had your pie in a church hall and you had races. Nobody went away anywhere. You were frightened to go away. Jean and Adam Lightbody were very much in control. You didn't even go for an ice cream, nobody had any money. Bus home and off at the War Memorial, exhausted. It was a day out at the seashore. A lot of singing on the bus, 'The back of the bus cannae sing!'

Helen:

'You went to the station and got on the train and that was a big deal and you always went to the seaside and had all the races and everything. Everybody joined in and then it got that it was a bus and they took you to a field somewhere.'

Moira Smith:

'Earliest recollection was catching a train to the coast: long carriages, streamers. Must have been '64. Going up the tunnel [the station had a central island platform between the tracks, approached at both ends by tunnels] and coming back at night. The Sunday School was absolutely mobbed.'

Irene Gibson:

'The first time my son David went to a Sunday School trip, my mother and father took him, he said it was the best day out he'd ever had, he'd got a pie. "It was absolutely great. Can we get one?" He'd had a great time, singing in the bus.'

Bill Chittick:

'For the Sunday School trip we had two double decker buses. One year I phoned the bus people at Inchinnan and said I might need three buses, and they said, "Oh, Mr

Chittick, don't order three buses, two buses will be enough, some of the children can sit on their mothers' lap".

'When we were initially involved with Adam and Jean Lightbody the teachers used to meet up in the hall and Jean had made a mixture of Grant's meat loaf, big cans of it, all the way from Aberdeen, mixed with tomato sauce, and we made up the sandwiches, every year. We used to put our hands in a bowl and mix it all up.

'When we had the trips we used to order 14 dozen Scotch pies, that gives you an idea of the number involved. Knox and Finnie's Scotch pies plus a cake and diluting orange. Eventually we ordered the pies from the trip location. You and I carried a bread board of pies through Helensburgh from the shop to the trip. We always went by bus, never lost one child. Their mums and dads were there.'

General Assembly 1993

The ancestors of both congregations would be birlin' [Scots: spinning] in their graves at what followed.

Ian Miller:

'I always thought that the chances of the East and West Churches in Kilbarchan coming together were as remote as the Berlin Wall coming down.'

The Berlin Wall started to come down on 9th November 1989!

There were vacancies in the East Church in 1971, 1980 and 1991. On each occasion a committee from the Presbytery of Paisley came to discuss the prospect of union. The proposals were resisted. Latterly, in congregational meetings, folk who had come quietly to church for years found themselves witnesses to heated debate. In the time of the last vacancy Kilbarchan East was so persistent and impassioned that the matter reached the General Assembly of the Church of Scotland.

Representatives from the East Church put their case for

maintaining its independence to the General Assembly on Monday 17th May 1993. Following a debate and a vote, both churches continued as separate bodies, working hard, but facing an increasingly secular society. Until the century's end . . . and beyond.

Baptist Church

A Congregational Church stood on the site of Kilbarchan Guide Centre. It was established by the Hunter family of Glentyan Estate. In 1915 the Congregational Minister left: it became a Baptist Church in the same year.

Helen Dooris:

'There was the big platform where the bath was and I was very frightened of water. All I could think about was, "If I'm still here when I'm eighteen, they're going to dip me in there." That used to terrify me.

'My granny took me to every tea meeting because we got really nice food there and all you had to do was listen to Mr. MacNiven playing the piano in the hall. There was a big hall downstairs: whoever looked after the hall stayed in the small flat underneath the church.'

David Carlin:

'That's where we went to at first, the Baptist Church. The minister there used to have hens, black Minorcas about the size of a turkey and they laid a big egg, nearly twice the size of a hen egg. He was really friendly with my father. We used to go to Sunday School there and the Hunters of Glentyan used to go too. I think he kept it up, moneywise.'

Irene Gibson:

'I always thought he had built it. I remember old man Hunter coming to church. When I was in Sunday School in the Congregational Church they used to go to Arran in a reserved carriage on the train, and get on the boat. It was my father who organised that: he said it was because a lot of children who came had never been on a Clyde steamer before. He thought that this was a great adventure and it obviously was.'

The Memorial Hall

Helen Dooris:

'My granny took me to every soiree – the Memorial Hall, we went everywhere.'

Myra Goldie:

'We saw lantern slides, Jesus on the cross, dripping blood etc. Went as often as it was on. You got something to eat – bun.'

Lottie Dow:

'Used to go to the Sunday School. I went to the Memorial Hall, it was always better fun. They had a soiree every so often, children would read out of the Bible. I was too shy to perform.'

Ian Miller:

'I loved my time there. My father played the organ and it was just different They had these meetings on a Saturday night with a guy giving Hellfire and a cup of tea, so it was worth going to.

'There is no doubt that with all the music and the hymns they sung, it was much brighter than the dreich Church of Scotland. It was a happy place, it was a good place. In the days of my childhood in the evening there'd be eighty there. In the morning maybe fifty or sixty.

'The morning service was unique. There was no structure. Someone would get up and say Hymn 42 and we'd all get up and sing it. Then we sat down, silence and somebody would get up and say a prayer, and sit down, silence, a reading, silence. There was always communion, the breaking of bread, but as a child. . . the silence. . .'

Disliking long silences was not exclusive to children. Women were not allowed to speak and had to have their heads covered. One elderly lady made her first and only statement:

'Oh God, save us from this abominable silence.'

As a teenager Ian began to attend the village Youth Fellowship in the West Church, after he had attended the Memorial Hall's evening gospel meeting. This challenged his faith and his debating skills. The Gospel Hall made it clear that he could not be in both organisations – 'You're either with us or with them.' Ian left.

> 'I became more involved in the YF, became the President. We arranged three big charity concerts in the Kelburne Cinema [Paisley] with music groups and Arthur Fawcett, minister of Johnstone High. The Concords were the first electronic gospel group: they were sell-outs. Organised from Kilbarchan and involving all the youth fellowships in the area. There were Sunday nights at the YF when as many as a hundred young people would come.'

Ian had happy memories of both churches: he was an elder and Sunday School Superintendent in the West Church. He had clear memories of the intoxicating aroma of port as communion wine was decanted in the vestry.

> 'The beautiful white covered pews, the absolute silence of the communion service, broken only by the steady footsteps of the elders as they went down – all men. And the common cup. My first extended preaching engagement was in the East Church – I was the guy from the wrong side, I never had any problems.'

Choosing a church

> 'The West Church service was at 12, and we didn't want that. We had a visit from people from both churches, they were recruiting round the new houses. We decided to go to the nearer one at 11 o'clock.

> 'People were very friendly but as time wore on and more new people joined the church the original people felt a bit threatened because it hadn't been Church of Scotland for all that long and they wanted to keep it the way it was.'

A man from the village who had been away for a time chose not to go back to the Memorial Hall:

> 'I went to the Baptist's in Johnstone. Worse was to come. I decided to give up religion altogether and joined the Church of Scotland!'

Women elders

> 'Some churches resisted ordaining women elders. In our church we saw the first woman elder. It was so uncommon then, now they are almost all women.'

By 2000 not only were there women elders, divorced ministers and women ministers, but the Church of Scotland was tiptoeing around the issue of gay ministers. It was slowly reflecting the diversity of the nation's population.

The disillusionment of two world wars, increasing access to secondary, higher and tertiary education, the demise of much of the old order, the social changes of the sixties, all combined to put the churches on the defensive. As society had changed radically in a hundred years, so had the churches.

Chapter 13
Organisations

'It was a glorious fortnight, wall to wall sunshine.'

SLOWLY lengthening leisure time and the need for constructive spare time activities made the formation of informal and formal social organisations increasingly possible. Despite the fact that coming out of the Victorian age, children were to be seen and not heard, visionary individuals realised that specific activities, initially only for boys, would develop them physically, socially and morally. The first of these in Scotland was Captain William Alexander Smith who established the Boys Brigade in 1883, which combined cleanliness, fitness, discipline and Christianity in its progamme.

Boys Brigade

A BB presence in Kilbarchan was noted in the *Renfrewshire Gazette* in 1905, with the news that the Boys Brigade was drilling in an old weaving shop under the control of Captain Robert Ramsay. Official records of the organisation show that the 1st Kilbarchan Company began in 1934. David Carlin, who was in the Cubs before he joined the BB, provides an account of its early days:

> 'I used to play [football] for the school on a Saturday morning and for the BB in the afternoons. That shows how fit we were. Beith was the best team. Our team was made up of 12-14 year olds and the others were 18-19. Men against boys.
>
> 'I was in the BB for three years. They met in the parish hall in Church Street. The three Lightbodys were in charge – one did the drill, one did something else and Adam was a

Boys Brigade, 1937. Outside the West Church

kind of sergeant major. The BB did help with discipline and marching, when I went into the army.

'There was a boxing match, and a boy, Iain Nelson, from Low Barholm, was against me and gave me a hammering. I lost the place and melted him. We were ill-matched. [I remember] we learned first aid – I still remember the tibia and fibula!'

Drew Connell [late 1940s] was involved in the BB for many years. Like David Carlin he had been in the Cubs, as there were no Lifeboys [the junior section of the BBs].

'When I was twelve I joined the Boys Brigade. Johnny Lightbody was in charge and Jim Lightbody and Adam Lightbody. They were all officers. Forty or fifty in the Boys Brigade at that time. I stayed up till I was thirty two. My brother John was asked to start the Lifeboys. When I came out of the army I used to do the drill.'

Jeff Webster [late 1950s]

'I wasn't a Lifeboy. I joined the BB for the football team and ended up staying and becoming an officer. Adam Lightbody ran it. His nickname was The Coob because when he called the boys to attention he shouted not 'Company' but 'Coobnee'. We shortened it to Coob, and he never ever knew!

Lifeboys. Established after the Second War: in the East Church hall

'In football one year we were so successful we were called The Legend! The BB was good. The Kirk Session once got us to clean up the ground round the old Kirk, it was completely overgrown. We found this grave with HS on it and the date. Next week in the Gazette it said "Kirk Session discover Habbie Simpson", so we got no credit at all!'

Iain Ritchie ran the wayfaring class, all about the countryside:

'We learned all about flowers and used to go hiking. There was one joint BB/Scout weekend up at Ladymuir, and the Scouts – they were too twee for me – they wanted to sing "Ging, gang gooley" and we wanted to sing "Roll me over". As you do. We played football, Scouts against the BB. I won't tell you how it ended. It was not good.

'We hiked up. The first thing the Scouts did was dig latrines. "What's latrines?" We did that and then we played their kind of games and they played our kind of games. We did integrate a wee bit but it never happened again.

'It wasn't helped by the fact that when the Guides got their new Guide hut, they opened it with a dance: instead of inviting the Scouts they invited the BB.'

After the joint Scout BB camp:

'We started off a hike at the Laverock Stone. We had to take map references from there back to Ladymuir. I was with Gordon [Doc] Brown who tripped up over something in the middle of nowhere. It was a railway line! We followed it to a wee hut and in it there's a wee engine and carriages. We put two and two together – it was for the grouse shooting.'

The track was built by Lithgow's to create employment during the Depression.

'First Aid was taught by Joe Barratt. All the boys wanted to be first to answer Joe's first question, which was to ask what they would do faced with a particular form of injury, to which the reply was to treat the patient for shock. That would absolve them from successive questions.

'Once I replied, "Treat for shock!" Joe asked, "How do you treat for shock?" Floored! That was me! We passed our badges and forgot all about it. I took a sailing class because I'd once been on a yacht and it ran for weeks. Big John [his older brother] had a sailing book and I would read it up. I was very authoritative. We never did it practically.'

Social events to raise funds were held in the church hall. The music for the dances was provided by records as they could not afford to hire a band. Once the novelty wore off the numbers attending fell away. To recover support a Continental Evening was planned, which involved creating the right ambiance in the church hall. The card tables were to be appropriately decorated.

'Ian and I had to go round the pubs for old wine bottles, preferably Mateus Rosé, to stick a candle in, in the middle of the church hall, all wood, tinder dry, ask no questions! 'Ian Miller was a travel agent at A.T. May's and he gave us posters for exotic places and they went all round the walls. Turn off the lights, light the candles on about fifty tables and then the Slipperine on the floor [which makes floors slippery, and is still on the market]. We had a ball sliding on it before they all came in. They were a success for about a year. The parades were good, you'd go into Paisley and there would be about eighty companies – a huge turnout.'

Scouts

In 1908 Baden-Powell published *Scouting for Boys* which inspired both the Boy Scouts and the Girl Guides. These opened up new and often lasting friendships, shared outdoor experiences, new skills and pastimes, to a myriad of young people from different backgrounds. As they rapidly became international organisations they raised and expanded the horizons of many. Importantly, it enabled them to develop their personalities outwith the immediate supervision of their parents!

Within a year of the launching of the Scout movement, six boys met in Sunnyside, Church Street, to found the 1st Kilbarchan Troop. Amongst the originals were Donnie Crawford and David Cummings.

David Carlin described the Scout hall in the early 1930s as being through a lane off Steeple Street. It was in an old building, the upstairs being where they met and the ground floor vacant. He thought it had maybe been an old weaving shed. The remains of it can be seen in the wall separating it from the Old West Manse and the Scout Hall. Both John and David were in the Cubs.

Ian Trushell had a long association with the Kilbarchan Scout Group, one of the largest in Renfrewshire.

Ian [1950s]:

> 'There were six patrols and my Patrol Leader was Ian Davidson. The next door patrol was Gavin Scott. I was an Owl. It was rough and ready, when you came out at the end of the night you were filthy, stoured beyond words. Great fun.

> 'We had camps at East Barneigh. One weekend it was blowing a gale and one of the ridge poles on the tent broke. We had a trench fire lined with stones and someone put an aluminium dixie full of water on to this trench fire and it smelted and all the water went into the fire.

> 'There was a trek cart, of course. Tyred wheels, a flat board with sides, with a central spar with a T-shaped bar, and sometimes there were ropes on to the front, with guys pulling as well and we all set off with it laden with camping gear.'

Ian told how the Scouts, with Walter Murray had pulled the

trek cart from Kilbarchan to Gilmour Street Station, Paisley, for some reason the particular connection did not stop at Johnstone. When they got the trek cart to the station their scheduled train went through without stopping!

The leader Bill Provan decided camps should be every two years. The Scouts camped in the Lake District, Millport, Tobermory, Oban and Cullen.

'My first camp was at Tobermory in a joint camp with Johnstone. We were there for a fortnight and by the time we got to the second week everybody wanted to go home. They had a parents' day on Saturday and some of the parents would take their wee boy out for high tea and the boys just became homesick.

'1968 – It was a glorious fortnight, wall to wall sunshine, nobody wanted to cook, so we ate salads for two weeks. We'd run tabs with the butcher and the grocer, and the grocer said you can have a 5% discount or a bottle of whisky and Walter chose the discount.

Walter used the discount and the surplus camping funds to take the boys to the Great Western Hotel.

'The boys rose to it and had a lovely high tea, back to camp and that night it poured with rain and the tents were soaking wet. There was so much money left from that camp that there was a camp reunion, which began camp reunions in the Steeple Hall.'

Bill Provan left and the leaders decided on week long camps. Everybody was comfortable with that.

'A wee Scout would only pick up a hot dixie lid once. He'd make one mistake.

'Bracken was particularly dangerous. The world record was forty minutes after arriving at camp to the doctor's surgery. A wee boy had been told to collect bracken so he pulled it and it ripped his hand open.

'The worst was at a patrol camp west of the Kilmacolm–

Lochwinnoch road. A Scout was chopping wood and the axe skited and went in just above the ankle bone and he had a deep wound, so deep you could see the artery pulsating. The farmer drove him to the RAH.'

Learning the hard way, or why Scouts no longer have sheath knives or axes.

'In the days before ring pulls one Scout had a can of cola, pulled out his sheath knife to stab it open and stuck it straight into the palm of his hand. We're in the middle of nowhere and Bobby Gardner says to me, "You'd better hike back with him to the hospital".'

'In Ambleside there was a big tree. We wanted to see a famous mountaineer shop so we all took off our rucksacks and laid them at the bottom of the tree and off we went. Someone happened to look back and there was a policeman carrying a rucksack into the bus station. We all went back and asked what he was doing. "Boys, you don't leave your rucksacks in the middle of the street." Why not?'

On January 2nd 1968, a small group, who were, incidentally, Scout leaders, led by Jim Robinson, an experienced mountaineer, climbed Stob a'Choire Odhair near Bridge of Orchy. The snow was soft and wet and hard going but the views were wonderful.

'Decided to go down by another route and as soon as we stepped into the gully we realised that the snow was hard as it was in the shadow. An enormous slab took off with six of us, somersaulting backwards and you don't know which way up you are and it seems to go on forever. Two guys had been killed two weeks before and I remember thinking, "Here we go again." Eventually came to a halt. I realised I was near the surface and stuck my head up, looked around, and there was nobody, then other wee heads started to appear. We all got up. It was stupidity.'

No one told their parents and the rucksacks, ice axes and hats lost in the avalanche were collected in the Spring. And the enormous size of the exposed boulders which they had all avoided was revealed.

Scouts at camp, Kirkton, by Deskford, Cullen 1970

Graeme Dickie [1970s]:

'There were two cub packs and David Storrie was Akela. The highlight was the Tuck Shop at the end of the night. And then you would go home through the back of the Scout Hall, cross the burn, then down through Churchill Place where we'd challenge each other to run through the gardens and jump over the hedges. Along Station Road as well. You'd have your Cub hat, your sweets in hand, jumping over all the hedges!

'The Scouts. I enjoyed it. I enjoyed the summer camps, I was always away on my birthday. You got staked out and all the food scraps thrown over you. It wasn't just getting the dumps. It was quite mediaeval. Then on to the Venture Scouts under Forbes Jardine. After that I took a warrant out as a Scout leader, for ten years.

'I was towards the end of my time in the Venture Scouts. The Soviet youth movement wanted to get more western influences for the youngsters over there. Ten people from

Seventy fifth anniversary of Kilbarchan Scouts, 1984

Renfrewshire and ten from Newcastle. Stansted to Moscow. We're at Stansted and we still didn't have the correct visa. We had to sign disclaimers so that if we landed in Moscow without the visas it was our problem! We had to wait about Moscow airport until we got the paperwork that allowed us to continue. A young Russian woman, Alana, was our interpreter. We all changed ten or twenty pounds. A week later we were all trying to spend ten pounds, there was very little to buy, and anything there was to buy was just pennies. In Moscow we went to see Lenin's tomb, that was an experience. Some of these other things you'd learn in modern studies in school – we'd see them, park the car and take the windscreen wipers and mirrors off and lock them inside because the spares were so hard to come by!

'We went by overnight train to Leningrad. We had taken some Scottish presents, like whisky – there wasn't quite so much whisky left by the end of that journey! We did a wee bit of a touristy thing in Leningrad and went on to a youth camp at Yalta in the Crimea, almost like a summer camp for kids. We took a wee wander and went into a shop like the local Co-op, which had only three items. This guy was selling bread out of the back of the car so we bought some and some butter and we were eating it in the hotel reception area when Alana came in and said, "That's lard, that's cooking fat you're eating".

'Several months later, there was an exchange but it wasn't the people we'd met out there. We had a guest each. We had Damirgul, with gold teeth: the family keep the wealth on them, in case they've got to flee. I had the perception that the parents of the people who came over all had positions of responsibility. From 1990, when we were there, the whole landscape has changed.'

Guides

The Guide movement was launched in 1910. In 1920 Girl Guides met for the first time in the home of Mrs. McRoberts at Lismore [now Lismore Gardens], Tandlehill Road. The meeting took place in the sun parlour. Brownies were established in 1926 and Rangers ten years later. In the late 1940s all the Guide organisations met in the Steeple Hall, then moved to the hall underneath the Congregational Church, which stood on the site of the present Guide Centre. The church was demolished in 1958. Mr. Leggat, Glentyan House, gifted the site to the Guides. A timber-framed and clad hall was built and opened on 21st February 1959, and lasted, although showing signs of age and vandalism, until the twenty first century.

Happy memories exist of Jen Muir taking the Brownies in the Baptist Church Hall, and leading them up a spiral staircase into the church at Christmas time, to sing carols.

Mabel:

'I joined the Brownies. I was only there about three weeks when the Brown Owl was taken away to the army and there weren't Brownies until after the war. I loved Brownies and I loved the Guides. On a Monday I came straight home from school and that hat got pressed with a damp cloth. You got points if your hat was nice. I never starched it.'

1930s A group of happy Guides, taken in the garden behind the old Glentyan Laundry, Merchant's Close

Helen:

'I think there was more content in the badges. It wasn't so easy to get through as it became. Things had to be done properly. We got a camper's badge and we went country dancing.'

Guides never camped before April. Kilbarchan Guides were able to qualify for their camper's badge in the grounds of Glentyan House. Helen said that they camped near the loch and that it was full of weeds at the time. 'We cooked, dug latrines and had a grease pit.' It was the first weekend of April.

Mabel:

'We were frozen! Lying at night with our berets pulled on. Mrs. Hunter was there at the time and I remember her coming down in the morning and saying how sorry she was because she'd liked to have come down and invited us into the house, but then we'd have failed the badge.'

Eliza:

'I was in the Guides for a bit, it was good fun and I knew all the people. We went camping, locally, Glentyan several times and to South Newton. A friend said, "Fancy leaving your house to lie in a park".

'While we were Rangers we went to the chalet in Switzerland. [Our chalet was opened in 1932 as a Guide Centre.] It was a long journey, train to London, crossed the Channel, stayed overnight in Paris, then several changes of train before we got to Adelboden. It was 1953. That was really something. "You're going abroad to Switzerland"!

'We went back with the Trefoil Guild in 1976, almost all from Kilbarchan. Flew to London and another flight, it was so different. The chalet seemed miniature. We slept on palliases the first time, it seemed an awfully long time ago.

'The Trefoil Guild tries to do things that are a wee bit adventurous. We all go out to the theatre at Christmas. People who have not been Guides can join. Christine Erwin's mum was very involved.'

Christine Erwin:

'I wasn't allowed to join the Brownies until the hut was opened. They had been in the Steeple, the school, and the beaming shed in New Street.'

Once Christine joined she never left and remained wholly committed to the movement.

Led by enthusiastic volunteers, generations of young people have expanded their skills and experience and enjoyed confidence building success, whilst having a lot of fun with friends. Many involved, the leaders and the led, would have done a day's work before they turned up to participate. The debt owed to the leaders for the experience they gave the youngsters is immeasurable.

Chapter 14

More Organisations

'You look lovely and fresh, hen!'

THE TWO oldest organisations in Kilbarchan are Lodge Saint Barchan 156, established in 1784, with its hall in New Street. Previously it met in the upper floor of the Masonic Arms at the Cross. It is part of an international fraternity. The other is Kilbarchan General Society, founded in 1765, the last of the purely local self-help organisations that once thrived in a different historical era. The General Society persisted, and has a room in the Steeple Halls, the name of which allegedly stemmed from the fact that women from the countryside rested in it between morning and afternoon worship. It is *The Ladies Room*, which strangers find a puzzling prospect when scheduled to meet there!

Kilbarchan Steeple is a prominent landmark, facing the Weaver's Cottage at the west end of Steeple Street, at the Cross. Originally built as a meal market it has been used as a school, a location for a fire engine and as council offices. A niche on the Steeple houses a statue of Habbie Simpson.

> 'The Masons have 6 or 7 lairs in the Kilbarchan Cemetery which they bought when it opened, and they have not been used. The Masons used to give out coal to some of their members over the years. The Eastern Star also donated when there was need.'

Four flats were built by the Masons in Church Street in 1907.

> 'My father was a Mason and he told me I'm not telling you to join and it won't do you any harm. . . It doesn't do you any harm at all, it does you more good.'

Sandy Graham:

> All the old societies, 1st, 2nd, 3rd, 4th, 5th, 6th and 7th were here in Kilbarchan and they all did the same. You paid something every week. If you were off ill and you weren't working they'd give you something and if you died they'd give you something towards your funeral.'

Other village organisations that had fulfilled similar functions included a Coffin Society, the Rechabites, the Ancient Order of Foresters, and the Independent Order of Good Templars, which promoted teetotalism. The development of the Welfare State, starting with National Insurance before World War I marked the beginning of the end for many of these bodies.

Drew Connell, General Society:

> 'It was the social security for the weavers if they were in trouble. The General Society has a kind of camaraderie. It has changed dramatically over the last thirty or forty years because at that time we used to rely on War Bonds and that kind of thing to get our money. Our money is raised from functions, for example, a Sportsman's Dinner. We made three or four thousand a year.'

Before the Steeple Halls were modernised in the early 1970s the stairway from the upstairs landing led straight to the door out to the square.

> 'One time we had a Burns supper and a guest was that fu' he came right down the stairs and ended up in the Royal Alexandra Hospital. That was his one and only Burns supper.'

Pat Porteous was in charge of the bank.

> 'Pat was great. He used to say, "Ye canny take the breeks off a Hielan' man." I used to go down and Pat would ask, "You in here for the General Society's chain? You know where it is, in the safe," and I'd go in and get it! Latterly, when Pat retired you had to sign for it.'

The Masonic Hall was the only hall in the village then and the General Society's dance was always there.

General Society Committee. 1989

Back: Norman McEwing,
John Leslie Deans,
John Rawlins,
Archie Campbell,
Walter Clelland Meikle,
Ian Lauder,
Tommy Denholm

Front: Drew Connell,
Bobby Murdoch (Preses)
Ian Grieve, John Connell

'At a dance Pat had his black patent shoes and tails and the hard front, which started to roll up as the night went on and as he's dancing around one of the soles came loose, but he carried on. One of the nights Lil [Pat's wife] was at the dance and she had on a long velvet dress and someone said, "You look very nice." Lil said, "I didn't have a dress to come so I just took the curtains down and made them into a dress." They were well matched. Of their time.'

The Rural/SWRI

The Scottish Womens' Rural Institute was founded in 1917. The Rural gave women some of the freedom that menfolk had traditionally enjoyed, to meet, talk, learn and enjoy themselves, free of male constraint.

In rural areas there were few opportunities for women to enjoy exchanging ideas, debating, and taking collective decisions and action. 'For Home and Country' became their motto.

Kilbarchan Rural was unique in the area because it had its own accommodation, which stood at the top of a slope near the junction of Station Road and Station Wynd. Prior to the housing, sidings from the railway ran into a goods yard, where there was a goods shed with a platform and a roof which overhung a siding. Other parts of the area were used for allotments and latterly, before the housing, as a council dump.

Elspeth Robertson, speaking of the Rural hut:

> 'It was old, from the First World War, a hospital, and so many communities bought these after the war – that was the rural hut.'

Elspeth indicated items gifted to her mother by the Rural:

> 'That coffee table there was her present when she retired. And there's another present upstairs that they gave her as well. And it says so on it. Very precious, these things.'

The Rural was loved, enjoyed and vital to its members Its activities were described with affectionate enthusiasm by Ethel Hamilton:

> 'I still go to Brookfield Rural. Kilbarchan Rural had their own hut and it was Mrs. Marshall of Burntshields and Mrs. Hunter of Glentyan who provided the money to build the hut. It was a big hut.
>
> 'I went mostly for companionship. You learned to do different things, crafts and cookery and there were speakers. Mr. Kerr [minister of the West Church] was the only one that could fill that hall, he was so humorous. He kept books in the church covering what went on a hundred years ago and he could tell stories about all the people. Had us in stitches.
>
> 'We had coffee mornings and jumble sales, which raised a lot of money for good causes.'

Many women would have been glad to have done more, but they were restricted by the social conventions of their time.

> 'We played host once to a rural from Northern Ireland. We gave them supper and they would tour and come back for

supper. The Federation used to have their meeting here. We had lottery funding for central heating and what was left went for carpeting. Everyone who had a sewing machine made curtains. They hadn't had enough money to reinsure the building. And then it was burned down.'

'I miss all the people. But six of us meet every week – in each other's houses. And a lunch now and again.'

The Civic Society

There were two separate organisations in the village in the 1960s, the Tenants' Association and the Residents' Association. Membership of both combined Habbies with newcomers. Each worked for the common good, one representing the needs of tenants and the other trying to improve physical conditions in the village.

Colin Campbell:

'Willie Holmes recruited for the Residents' Association, which was a mixture of Habbies and Interloupers. Discussion normally focused on planning issues and the appearance of the village.'

The Residents' Association changed to become Kilbarchan Civic Society. Until the 1975 reform of local governmnent [regionalisation] the society had a good working relationship with Renfrewshire Council. The Civic Society met in Dr. Gibson's surgery in Steeple Street, then in his new surgery at the bottom of Ewing Street.

An annual art show, held upstairs in the Steeple, was the Civic Society's ongoing social event and fundraiser for many years. It focused the interest of art collectors in the West of Scotland on the village and its well-known artists. It began as a one-off in a West of Scotland attempt to help Clyde resorts to retain their holiday trade, which was moving to warmer countries. It was named Clyde Fair International: attempts to retain the event failed, but the Art Show thrived!

The artists' colony in Kilbarchan, Mary and Willie Armour, Bill Birnie and his wife Cynthia Wall and Tom and June Shanks all agreed to exhibit. The exhibition was so successful that the show ran annually for many years, with other artists, jewellers and sculptors contributing. Works were in high demand and the opening night attracted an eager queue, cheque books to hand.

Barn Green was designed to remove traffic from the steep and narrow confines of Ewing Street and Steeple Street, where double deck buses had great difficulty navigating the tight curve at the Steeple steps. The plan for the new road cut through along Ewing Street and Steeple Street gardens that ran down to the burn. Once the road was completed, the rear of the shortened gardens was to be separated from the pavement by a three strand wire fence. John Lee of Steeple Street, joined the society and persuaded it to back a stone wall, which stands there today.

This short bypass was not universally popular, but was necessary to improve traffic flow when increased car ownership was crowding roads everywhere. It was a time when planners still believed that there were solutions to the increasing amount of personal transport.

After the grey utilitarianism of the immediate post-war years, environmental awareness grew and campaigns flourished nationally. In 1973 the Civic Society joined Plant a Tree in '73, supported by a nursery in Moray, which provided an exhibition of trees, set in compost, on Steeple Square. The cherry trees at the Steeple were planted to mark the event. Keep Kilbarchan Tidy in 1974 was part of an ongoing nationwide campaign to stop littering and flytipping.

The Civic Society attended a meeting to decide the routes of new pylons through Renfrewshire. All present were very genteel advocates of nimbyism [Not In My Back Yard], one even suggesting that the power line already to the north of the village should be paralleled by the new line!

In 1988 the society was at an enquiry into a plan by Ravenstone Securities to split Glentyan House into flats, build detached houses in its walled garden, and three blocks of three storey flats between Glentyan House and the North Lodge. Renfrew Council, the Civic Society and other objectors won.

In 1974 Renfrewshire County Council was about to disappear and Strathclyde Regional Council was imminent. It was ironic that at a time when people had more leisure time to commit to local interests, that control over major issues, such as education and social work, was removed from Paisley to Glasgow. Both these events and

an oral history of Kilbarchan 1900 – 2000

The Queen meeting older citizens. Steeple Square, 1974

the fact that Andrew Wilson of Kilbarchan was a major player in Planning in Renfrewshire led to a Royal Visit in June 1974. It was the first visit of a monarch in centuries.

The Queen and Prince Philip visited the Civic Society's Art Exhibition and a Kilbarhan Primary School/ Renfrewshire Council exhibition in the Steeple. In a crowded square the Queen met oldest inhabitant, Mrs Martha Murray [94], followed by a visit to the Weaver's Cottage.

The day was sunny. The number of police allocated for the visit was huge. The centre of the village was crowded. The party was behind schedule and the visit to the Art Exhibition was abandoned, but Prince Philip lingered to see it and had to have the term 'Ladies' Room' explained.

Descending the Steeple steps the Queen met Lilias Day characters. She asked Reverend Ian Miller, 'Mulby', who he represented. Memorably he replied: 'I'm Saint Barchan but I think I'm apocryphal.' 'Really.' When Habbie Simpson's 'coming to life' on Lilias Day was explained the response was identical!

The Kilbarchan Pipe Band developed from the Home Guard pipe band. An early post-war group.

(l to r)
Duncan Crawford,
Jim Downie,
John Masson,
Cleland Meikle,
N. Henderson,
James McIntyre,
J. McNally,
John McSkimming,
Angus McLean

A few in the crowd, to their shocked delight, were spoken to by the Queen. As she crossed from the Weaver's Cottage to her car, parked outside the newsagent's in New Street, a voice in the crowd cried out, 'God save the Queen.'

A few paces further on, from the other side of the street, another called, 'Aw, you look lovely and fresh, hen!'

It was all over. A good atmosphere, lots of happy people, best summed up by a mother whose day was made because the Queen had spoken to her son and Prince Philip had looked up at her at a first floor window and smiled and waved.

The old and new institutions tried to cope with social and political change. The village has its perennial sporting, recreational and special interest clubs which have evolved to take advantage of new technologies, demands and skills. Where there have been unique issues groups formed, fought their corners and disappeared when the job was done. In a century of rapid changes, not always of their making, including the mobile phone and the internet revolution, the people of Kilbarchan, like people worldwide, rose to the challenges.

CHAPTER 15
Football

'The beautiful game.'

BY 1900 playing in football teams or just spectating were established and widely popular male activities. Daily toil for demanding bosses meant that the football pitch was the field of dreams for many young men, on which they might achieve fame and even a little fortune. Even if these eluded them, their standing as a footballer, at any level, mattered to the individual and to his friends. Football provided regular exercise and encouraged routine and discipline. It developed individual skills and teamwork, comradeship and loyalty. For so many, players and spectators, it was 'the beautiful game'.

Villagers supported their local team, but many supported the professionals. Many reasons existed for fans' often lifelong and frequently all-consuming loyalty to a team. It might be inherited, a random choice, or an affinity with a winning team. The loyal supporter withstood defeat and relegation, rejoiced in victory and promotion and persisted against all odds. A team's fortunes were followed with near religious devotion: in pubs and workplaces analyses of the last game and predictions for the next were widely discussed. Each minute detail of the highs and lows in a game could be recalled and often might be remembered for years to come. The pink *Evening Times*, on a Saturday, brought the day's latest results, until its demise in August 1992.

Society at the start of the century was highly structured: touching your cap on meeting your 'superiors' was common. The working day was long, foremen and managers were demanding and often quick to sack. Office workers were physically better off than outdoor workers but more closely supervised. Although trade unionism was making inroads, workers were vulnerable to whims or economic downturns. To defy an authority figure at work meant the sack; to defy a policeman, could result in arrest.

The anonymity of the terracing allowed all life's repressions to be vented on the opposing team's players and their supporters. Players could go from hero to zero in seconds and be subjected to fluent abuse. The referee absorbed everyone's resentment of authority!

It was a man's game for most of the century. It was a sign of the times that no one spoke about women's football. The Scottish Football Association was the slowest member of UEFA to authorise women's football.

Often encouraged to be out in the fresh air, boys started early, with pals in car-free streets or in the park; or alone, playing keepie uppie, headers, or kicking a ball against a wall. Teams were informally organised and often characterised by the humiliation of the last person chosen for each team: too fat, too small, too thin, or just the owner of two left feet.

Sunday observance was widespread in Scotland: every shop and pub was closed on Sundays before and after World War II, and playing any game in public would attract comment, condemnation, or both. Before World War II Walter Gardner played football on Sundays, within range and sight of the West Church Manse [Foremont House], near a named row of trees:

> 'As far as I'm aware they were planted by the Church of Scotland, after the Twelve Disciples. Right along the garden wall, in the field. When we finished playing, you would dry your shoes, clean them up and go straight to the Bible Class!'

David Carlin, Pre-war football

> 'I played for the school team at Johnstone High. Played Paisley teams and Barrhead and mostly Renfrewshire. I used to play for the school on a Saturday [morning] and the Boys's Brigade in the afternoon.'

He played for Glentyan before he went to the army:

> 'There were two or three Kilbarchan boys but there were ones from different areas. Glentyan at that time was a very popular team. There was a lot of rivalry at that time between Linwood, Johnstone and Kilbarchan. Later I used to go down on a Saturday and played in the South of Scotland league.'

But there was a serious conflict of interests in a large number of communities where football and pigeon racing flourished and serious choices had to be made: 'You cannae do both things at the same time,' The pigeons won.

After the war David enjoyed: '. . . going to Ibrox, going to the Rangers' games. They had a good team at that time. I saw most of the good teams.'

Drew Connell

> 'I played for the Grove Swifts, they were formed from the Grove [Wheatlands Drive]. They were run by Archie Deans and big Jimmy Blackwood – he ended up sometime manager of Johnstone Burgh. Archie was the son of the famous Erchie Deans, who was the bookie.'

Kilbarchan was fortunate in having two areas open to the public, the public park, and the Bog Park. The Bog Park, surrounded by trees, lay behind the long feus of Ewing Street, separated from them by Kilbarchan Burn. It was and is, part of the lands of Glentyan House, then owned by Mr. Hunter.

Ian Trushell

> 'Mr. Hunter allowed the team to play there to test its viability for a full sized pitch, a smaller pitch, a running track and a Second World War commemoration garden.'

This was prompted by the death of his son, Richard, in Italy, whilst serving with the Scots Guards. It was tested by Glentyan F.C.:

'. . . but the offer of the gift of the Bog Park was refused at a public meeting, on the grounds that the state of the public park suggested that the district council would not maintain it properly.

'A potential asset to football and athletics was lost, but the post-war years were austere and there were more pressing priorities on most people's minds than recreation. It was an opportunity missed, and must have been of infinite sadness to Mr. Hunter that his plan to commemorate his son had been rejected. The people who worked on improving the Bog Park must also have been frustrated. One of the people who fostered the proposal was Bob Pattison.

'Mr Big in Glentyan FC was Bob Pattison, known as Big Bob, because he was of large size. He seemed to be a very charismatic figure. Glentyan was a juvenile club, they ranked below junior clubs. Junior football was notoriously rough.

'Glentyan Thistle were truly amateurs. Willie Irvine was the assistant manager [Parkview]. The captain [in the 1950s] was called Peachy Paterson, who had played for Johnstone Burgh. Bob got all these footballers to come and work on the Bog Park – they improved the ground, and the drainage and built modest terracing.'

Access to Bog Park was by a long feu from Ewing Street to the bridge over the Kilbarchan Burn. [Starting approximately at the entry to the current car park.] A pavilion was built:

'As Bob got more resources or more ambitious, it got bigger. It started out just as a changing room, it was a corrugated iron building and the roof pitch was very shallow. The door was at the Ewing Street end. It was quite unique in the fifties for a juvenile team to have its own changing facilities. Latterly it grew north, east and west.

'Bob's star turn was hot baths. Bob had installed a gymnasium and a changing room. There was a bathroom opposite, with two or three cast iron baths and when the boys came off they sat three on each side, feet in the bath, and sponged themselves down.'

Word of the team and its facilities got around:

> 'The real laugh – girls came to see the boys playing football. A local would say, "Just go in and see the boys!" All the guys are starkers. There'd be a great scream and they'd all pour out.

> 'They reached the final of the Scottish Juvenile Cup in the fifties and a special bus went from Kilbarchan, and my grandpa took me to the cup final, at Cathkin Park, where Third Lanark played. Can't remember the score but I do remember my grandpa taking me to the cup final.'

Drew Connell

> 'They won the Lord Weir Cup, which was the under-18 Scottish Cup. They won it in 1949, 1951 and 1956. At that time they [some players] went to Manchester City and St. Mirren.'

Jack Miller

Jack had to attend the morning service at the Memorial Hall in Steeple Square with his parents and in the afternoon he and his siblings attended its Sunday School. He lived at Locher Terrace, now demolished, and had to come over the high road from Bridge of Weir. Kicking a ball was a popular way of passing time, but it was a Sunday and he was going to church. They would stop at the lodge house at the end of Pannel Farm's Road, where a family named Barclay lived, related to a football manager:

> 'We'd go up to there and he had a ball planked [hidden] round the corner and we kicked the ball all the way to Kilbarchan and hid it where you come into Kilbarchan, then came back up and kicked it back down to Pannell, and then we'd hide the ball there.

> 'I was dead keen, and I played for the Scouts and for Johnstone High. I played centre or right centre. I was the main goal scorer. The BBs poached me. My pal Murray Syme, he was one of my friends, so I changed over to the BBs.

'Football was really big. I had a trial for the Scotland team, the juniors. I had to go to the Racecourse [St.James' Park, Paisley] and I could have had a game with them but my folks had a holiday arranged at the time and that was it!

'Joe Barrat was a good football player. Charlie Hamilton played for the Scotland Schools, he lived in Meadside Avenue.

'We played football on the road, inside the house. In Glentyan Avenue we used to play at the back and there was a family Armstrong, three sons, much older than us. We played, it didn't matter what size you were.'

When Jack's family emigrated to Australia soccer was already worldwide. While Jack was there he, '. . . played all the time I was there, four years. One of the jobs I went for he said, "D'you play football?" I said, "Yes." "Right," he said, "You've got the job." '

Ian Trushell

'I played goalkeeper for the primary school. The head teacher resurrected the school football club and we had new strips. I was all black. I think the strips were gold and black. There were no feet in the stockings [hose tops]. I only played a couple of games but I did play for the John Neilson Institution in first year, quite regularly, at St James' Park. No gloves and if a leather ball hit your hands it stung. The teachers gave up their Saturday mornings until the McCrone strike in the eighties. Mr MacLeod was the teacher.'

There were no showers then at St James' Park, where hundreds of youngsters played every Saturday. Everyone made their way home wet and filthy, but Ian's team always stopped for a pie in Greenock Road. He played for Kilbarchan Scouts:

'I did score a goal once. The Scoutmaster said, "You can wear any strip you like except white." I misunderstood and turned up with a white shirt and the other team were playing in white. I was right in the penalty spot and the Kilbarchan winger crossed from the left and I just met it

Kilbarchan Thistle 1973-1974. The most universally popular pastime of boys and men of the village was football

straight on the forehead and the goalkeeper jumped and it went straight through his hands. The first time I'd ever scored a goal. It was a beauty.'

Shortly after this highlight, Ian retired from football!

Jeff Webster

'The park was just down the road and everybody played in the park. We played football in the spring time, you didn't go down much in the winter. In the summer it was rounders or French cricket. It was great, the boys played, the girls played, the old ones played with the young ones. There was an older guy who lived in Glentyan Avenue, he must have been five or six years older than me. His name was Eric Calder. I've never seen such a footballer! He was fantastic. He'd pass the ball to you, a wee kid. It was brilliant.'

Eric Calder and the bigger boys were, consciously or not, informally passing on their skills to the youngsters.

'Football was very big. I was an outsider because my dad

was born in Edinburgh. My grandpa played for Hearts, so they were all Jambos. He played before the First World War and they sent a huge contingent [to the war]. But my grandpa made it back – John 'Jock' Webster. I supported Hearts, my dad supported Hearts and everybody was Rangers, there were no Celtic [supporters]. They thought I was Celtic because I didn't support Rangers.'

Continuing the family's footballing tradition may have spurred Jeff's enthusiasm. The primary school:

'. . . had a good football team, but we were a wee bit young to play in the Primary Seven team. They filmed Dr. Finlay's Casebook and one of the episodes was about a young football player. The actor didn't know one side of a ball from another. So we provided the legs and he provided the body. The cameraman took our legs and his upper body and he got all the kudos! I never got to see it.

'Everybody who could play football in Kilbarchan chose the Boys Brigade. I got a very rude baptism. My name was read out to play Renfrew, away. The total [collective] age had to be 170 and you got real big seventeen and eighteen year olds. I was eleven, it was miserable, sleet and snow, I'd joined to play football – this was murder! We were beaten 7-1. I was praying for the game to end. Coob [Kilbarchan BB] was refereeing. I said, "How long to go?" He said, "Oh, come on, there's plenty of time to get goals back."

'BB football was the breeding ground for the future. Nowadays they've got kids in organised football from seven or eight and the football is knocked out of them by the time they get to their late teens. If you were good you went to secondary juvenile, Glentyan Thistle. After you were 21, you went either to junior or directly to senior. If you weren't good enough you went to amateur. I just went amateur.

'I played for Johnstone YM for about 25 years. They were second tier. I was asked to join Camphill Former Pupils in the top division and I played for them for four years. I retired when I was forty and the last game was the league decider – we were beaten 5-2!

'When the season finished I was picked to play for Paisley and District Select against an ex-Rangers and Celtic XI for charity, at the Bog Park. Maybe I was selected as I was local! We were playing against all these people we'd watched on the terracing and Davie Wilson was playing. I absolutely loved it!

'Two minutes to go, Billy McNeil – he was the centre half – he knocked lumps out of me, but he did pick me up! He was as hard as nails and he kept saying, "I really shouldn't be here, my hip's not good." Someone passed to me and I was about to slip the ball past Eric Thornton when Billy McNeil tripped me up in the penalty area. The referee gave a penalty. It was four each.

'So I scored. So it was 5-4 against the veterans.

'Davie Wilson got the ball and ran up the left wing and our full back tackled him about twenty yards outside the penalty area. Davie carried on running without the ball, into the penalty area, did a beautiful swallow dive and the referee gave them a penalty – just to be fair and to even it up! Five each!'

'I was very lucky because I wasn't good at football, but I had an eye for goals, and just happened to be in the right place at the right time. I was never a great dribbler, I could pass if I had enough time. Happy days! Not a Jambo any more, I'm a Morton supporter now.'

Eric Borland

The Newtons stayed in Wheatlands Drive. Before they came to Kilbarchan they stayed on Spinner's Row, near the paper mill. There were five boys: the Newtons were all good football players, they all played for different teams. Peter was probably the best, Peter signed for Hibs, also Archie Shedden. Peter was farmed out to Dalry Thistle Juniors and Peter couldn't get a game for Hibs because

Hibs had a great team – the Famous Five, so Peter couldn't break in. Archie Shedden did play for Hibs. He played a few games.'

The Boys Brigade and the Scouts offered qualifications to their members, ran football teams, and camped either in tents or huts, at home and abroad. Before air travel became the norm going abroad was a rare novelty. Eric went to Ostende with the BB:

'We did a bit of touring about to Dunkirk and the Netherlands. It was a great learning curve. It was amazing for village boys. We made friends with the locals: we used to play them at football, you know. When the tide was out you could play football. When we weren't away touring, we played football.'

Like all the football witnesses, Eric summarised his career:

'I played for Kilbarchan Primary, Johnstone High, Johnstone YM, Glentyan Thistle and when Kilbarchan Thistle started I played a few times: we trained in the West Church Hall and in the park on the better nights. Kilbarchan Thistle started off in the Paisley Amateurs Sixth Division and rose to the First Division then joined the Scottish amateurs – top notch. Alan Gordon ran the team at that time.

'My problem was, with Glentyan Thistle and through all my school years, my half cousin, Gordon Cairns was an exceptional goalkeeper. I played second fiddle to him all the way through Kilbarchan Primary and Johnstone High. He was in the first team, but Johnstone High School had two teams. I was in the B team. Then the two of us joined Glentyan Thistle at the same time: I was the reserve and played a couple of games, then Gordon moved on to better things!'

Inevitably, at some time in a footballer's career, reality kicks in. For some it was family life, for others it was work.

'My playing years stopped in 1976. With me being a slater. I was a goalkeeper, right? In those days all the parks had ash and when you're a goalie you're diving about and your knees are getting skint. I was up on a Monday morning and in agony, all because of a game of football. Time to give it up.

'I helped with Kilbarchan Thistle on the committee for quite a few years. I was the Treasurer. They didn't go burst, I couldn't have done that bad a job. Football cards and dances at Greenacres.'

Many former players continued to participate in their clubs' activities. Countless women, mothers, wives and partners gave their time and energy to producing clean strips, raising funds, nursing, sustaining and putting up with the differing fates of the team from week to week.

Team members always carried out essential duties, including laying out the pitch. An aerial photograph (www. nls maps air photo mosaic Scotland 1944-1950) shows, with absolute clarity, the perfectly proportioned lines of the pitch in the Bog Park, where no lines were present in the public park. The laying out of the pitch required skill, and sawdust. Ian Lauder [nicknamed Sawdust] obtained his sawdust for pitch lining from Connel and MacIntyre, joiners of Kilbarchan, whereas Jeff Webster relied on Woodrow's in Bridge of Weir for his supplies!

The enthusiasm with which the football witnesses recalled their triumphs and disasters indicate the importance of the game in village life. At the end of the day, their contemporaries always remember them, at their best, doing what they loved. With pride.

Ten young men under starter's orders, Kilbarchan Public Park, 6th August 1910

Chapter 16
Athletics

'I was running the wrong way!'

GETTING somewhere quickly on foot, and the urge to compete, is one of the world's oldest sports. Kilbarchan runners are up there with the best. There is a tradition of running in the village that has come down the generations. It has just been part of village life: the landscape around it has just about all of the challenges that a runner is ever likely to encounter!

There was athletic activity before the World War I. The photograph opposite shows ten young runners about to set off on the 6th August 1910 in Kilbarchan Park. It also shows a highly organised meeting.

The two men on the right are mustering the group, one ready with the starting pistol. The central characters are a mixed group of young men, some with shoes, some without, whether through choice or necessity. They may be wearing the strips of the different local, or not so local, clubs. A group of male spectators of all ages is present. Newspapers may have informed the bystanders of the meeting, or they may have heard about it locally. They may be there specially to support their brother, son, or friend. It was an event that merited the presence of a photographer.

This is what generations of young men did, in their spare time. They may have continued to compete and maintained their interest in sport throughout their lives, keeping themselves fit. Or have given up running entirely. They could have been at the peak of their athletic careers, if they had one, in 1914. Their future was to be dominated by war and the 1918-1919 pandemic, Spanish influenza.

This is an archive photograph from the Kilbarchan Amateur Athletic Association website. Runners, non-runners and those just interested, can research the club history from the warmth and comfort of their home! It shows how times have changed, and how the Kilbarchan club has become such a success, for male and female, and all ages.

The Kilbarchan Harriers tentatively came together around 1920 and became the Kilbarchan Amateur Athletic Club officially in 1924. Amongst the founder members were Nat Hayes and David Cummings.

The story of the club is told by a founder member, Arthur Smith, who played a leading role in the development of one of the top clubs in Scotland:

> 'They've formed and disbanded over a period of time and round about 1955 they seemed to just fall apart. Re-formed in 1963 and disbanded in 1964! One or two incidents like that. Lack of interest or nobody wanted to take on the responsibility.'

Arthur was one of a group that met in the Trust Inn:

> 'We went to the pub on a Friday night and someone said there was a notice in the newsagent's saying that there was a meeting to discuss the possibility of re-forming the Harriers. Malcolm Rees, who stayed in MacLay Avenue did a bit of running on his own. I used to play tennis and golf, getting my handicap down. I decided I had to do something to keep myself fit, do a bit of running in the winter time. . . five years later I'd given up golf all together!

> 'Elsie Gibson from MacKenzie Drive was the main driving force in 1974. She was looking for something for her boys to do. She worked at Myles Rafferty's camping shop in Paisley. Myles was a member of Paisley Harriers and suggested trying to re-form the old Kilbarchan running club.'

In November 1974, Malcolm Rees and Arthur went to a meeting in The Steeple along with others from the Friday night group, including Alex Ritchie, Norrie Howitt and Robert Barr.

> 'We were the ones that had an interest and did some running. From the old club, keen to see a revival, came George Anderson, Willie Johnstone and his brother and Gardner

Masson, who had been in the club in 1963, as a boy. Matt Turnbull too, was present. About 15 of us went along and decided to give it a go.

'Malcolm Rees was elected chairman, and I was vice-chairman. Myra Rees was secretary: she took the minutes which were neither signed nor dated!

'Les Menelly, who stays in Hunter Place, he was a Shettleston Harrier then a Kilbarchan Harrier. He was involved in the club around 1963/64.'

Some athletes are fit and plan to maintain their fitness or improve it. Some enjoy pushing themselves to their limits, in isolation. Others thrive on team activities and competition. All know that there is no gain without an element of pain. Some are in pain to begin with and find sport relieves it. Norrie Howitt was one of the originals, with a bad back:

> 'When I was young I must have knocked a disc out of my spine and I went to a bone setter. He'd been in America and wrestled with James Cagney – he had a photograph of himself and James Cagney up on the wall. He gave me a lot of abuse, asked me if I'd had it x-rayed. No. The foreman sent me, he played for Motherwell. I'd been off a week and still wasn't any better. I went to see this man, who had a wee block of wood and a hammer on my back and said, "It's out, right enough" and fiddled about and put it back again. Then asked, "Got anything else?" An arch on my foot, so he grabbed my foot and it was like a rifle going off, it cracked. "There you are. That'll be a pound!" '

He was asked if he wanted to go out for a run:

> 'I must have said I'll come for a run. I hadn't run for donkey's years. I could hardly walk up the road my back was so bad. I could actually go and run yet, when I stopped, I could hardly walk again. Over the years it improved with swinging a steel bar about, to try and stretch my spine.

Arthur Smith:

> 'Donnie Crawford worked for the Council and opened the

pavilion in the park for us on the first night. It is said that he was not a bad athlete in his time. They did try to start an elite club in the West of Scotland and he was part of that.

'The first run was from the park to Brookfield, Victoria Drive and Albert Road and back up to the park again. Most of us were walking a wee bit and jogging a wee bit.'

At the finish one of the runners reached for his cigarettes. He did not run again!

'Willie Johnston had suggested it as that was the previous club run. That became a regular time trial until we abandoned it: it was dangerous on the roads, at night time. Just over two miles.

'We had the Quarrelton time trial, which is running through Kilbarchan on the main road, up Quarrelton Road, back along the Beith Road, back down Cochranemill Road and up the main road.

'We had road racing and cross country competitions and ran in other areas such as Balloch Park. Elsie Gibson was the driving force, backed up by Myles Rafferty, who was very keen. She organised buses and transport to competitions. Once the club was established that was her job done. Her husband Jimmy said, "This is another of your daft ideas that won't last".'

Arthur took part in fifteen marathons. Norrie was eventually persuaded. Norrie:

'I used to go quite long runs then someone said that there was a marathon in Greenock, so we all trained for it. We all finished it as well. That was the first Greenock Marathon.'

That was in 1991. Kilbarchan took third place in the team event. Norrie ran the Glasgow Marathon a couple of times. In one of them he found himself running towards a crowd of runners in Pollock Park.

'I was running the wrong way!'

Arthur:

'The Cross Country competitions met at the pavilion, went to different places: usually through the fields towards Marshall Moor where there was a trig point. That was one of the areas we would regularly go to. We eventually had a cross country race from Kilbarchan Park up to the trig point at Marshall Moor and back. We abandoned that as well because it was too dangerous.

'Being in winter, and if the weather closed in, we didn't know who was out there or who they were, because there wasn't a specific route. It's not a marked route. No stewards, no Health and Safety, you had to go out or come back through the woods or the opposite.

'Most people tended to go the same way and followed each other, but there was always somebody who thought they knew a faster route, a short cut somewhere. But eventually we abandoned that, it was too dangerous. Seriously, we were worried at one point and after about ten years began stipulating that people had to take a mobile phone with them, just in case something happened and we knew where they were.

'We did lose one or two people for a while, which alarmed us a bit. One or two locals lost their way coming back into Kilbarchan and finished up in Johnstone. Things like that happened. At that point the majority of members didn't come from Kilbarchan, they came from Johnstone or Paisley.'

'The original club vests are rumoured to have been bottle green. The combination of yellow and black was chosen because yellow was visible from a distance, and one stripe was selected as having more stripes than one was costlier.

The facilities at the park were unsatisfactory. The club moved to Johnstone High School to use the track. The club held talks with Renfrew Council, to obtain its support so that it could develop, particularly as an activity for youngsters. The council agreed and the club began an association with the Linwood Sports Centre (now replaced by the On-X Sports Centre). The club is home to males and females of all ages and stages and traditionally made a deliberate effort to encourage young people:

> 'We had school invitation races. Used to have them in September every year The response was usually minimal from schools. We relied more on word of mouth, by young members of the club bringing their pals along.
>
> 'Although the club initially concentrated on road running and cross country running, with access to more versatile facilities its scope widened to include track and field events. Competition motivates and Kilbarchan AAC has taken part in all the main Scottish Leagues. Members have competed at national level, succeeding in Scottish Championships. Some juniors and seniors have been selected for Scotland in the Home Internationals and a few for Great Britain.'

By 2000 the club was one of the best in Scotland, a tribute to the enthusiasm and dedication of its volunteer leaders and coaches.

Watching a running event has changed so much from physical attendance like the photo in 1910 in the public park. Live televised events brought the sport to a new audience. More people got involved in running on a mass scale. The impact of watching coverage of the marathon encouraged thousands to get involved. The People's Marathon created opportunities for people to do something physical, to raise awareness, and much needed funds, for charities and recognised groups in need. It brought people together, it encouraged even the most non-sporty people to make a personal commitment of time and energy, to get out there and do their personal best!

David Cummings was an earlier local, and international, hero in athletics in Scotland. He was born at 43 Finlay's Land, Bridge of Weir on 7th May 1894 to David and Agnes Cummings. [This part of Bridge of Weir was then in Kilbarchan Parish, which, technically, makes him a Habbie!] In 1901 the family was at 33 Church St, and in 1911 was at 1 Church Street. David was listed in the census as an apprentice plumber.

Arthur Smith knew David:

> 'He was very instrumental in the foundation of the Harriers round about 1920 or thereabouts. Quite a gentle guy, he didn't talk a lot about himself, as far as I knew him, but he

was very keen to see the club progress and any time the club went defunct he was always getting involved in trying to get it started again, by involving other people. His brother George had been a runner as well with Bellahouston Harriers but he was killed at Loos, 25th September 1915. David Cummings gave the David Cummings Trophy and the George Cummings Trophy, to use as we saw fit. One was for one of these dangerous routes, running round the roads. The George Cummings trophy is for the Annual Road Relays that we now have in Houston.

'There were 65 men in the track events at the 1924 Paris Olympics. David Cummings and two others were in the 3,000 metres steeplechase. All participants at these Olympics who were not recipients of a gold, silver or bronze medal, received a Participant's Medal.'

When the Scouts organised a seventy-fifth anniversary dinner in 1984 an article was sent to the *Renfrewshire Gazette* asking any former Scouts to contact Ian Trushell. He received a call from David Cummings saying, 'I was one of the original six Scouts [who first met in 1909 at Sunnyside, Church Street] and I'd like to come to the reunion.'

Ian Trushell:

'It was upstairs in the Steeple. His son brought him. I can still see him, he had grey flannels, a royal blue blazer and on the breast pocket was embroidered 1924 Paris Olympiad. He had two sticks, "I can't stay long, I've got to go and present the prizes at the Harriers." Asked if he had the medal, he brought it out, wrapped in a hanky. It was a big medal. He said, "Aye, I aye carry the medal. My wife says I've aye to carry the medal because if I ever fell into the sea it would hold me down"!'

A modest man of humour, determination and loyalty, Kilbarchan's twentieth century Olympian.

Derek and Callum Hawkins, young men with family and club associations with the village since the 1990s, have followed that dream.

Chapter 17

Dancing and 'the dancin'

'The women stood at one side, the men on the other.'

DANCING was a source of exercise for everyone who took part, which could be taken lightly, for fun, or seriously, to achieve excellence and win competitions. Or it could just create opportunities to meet new people.

It was a talking point with fond memories. Whether it was in the living room, a village hall, a dance hall or at a wedding, dancing brought people together. People learned to dance in various ways, from the example of others, from friends, from formal lessons or at school. Many remembered the primary school dance, where the choosing of partners quickly separated those who had an aptitude for dancing and those who had none; memories which could encourage, or put some off for life.

The choice of dancing lessons for adults within the century varied from the more genteel, to freedom of self expression in all its forms. This chapter highlights people in the village who enjoyed dancing throughout their lives, beginning with, unusually, country dancing. It got women out of the house, away from their men, and kept people fit in the days long before going to the gym was possible.

Cathie McDermott:

'I started country dancing 60 years ago. They had country dancing classes in the school hall, big classes. They weren't very good with learners; they were such good dancers and seemed to look down on learners.'

'Mary Armour was involved, also June Shanks. Mary was very nice, she was a good dancer. There were just women in the classes. There was also another couples' class in the Steeple hall. You had to have a man, any man would do!'

'There were three country dancing classes, in the school, the Steeple and one in the church hall. I'm not sure when it started, but it was up and running over 60 years ago.'

She has a photograph or her country dancing class taken by Stephan Gut.

'Most of the ladies had children. It was a night out, it was nice and cheery, and everyone enjoyed it. It was often the one night out a week, a Tuesday night. I didn't compete. Some of the dancers in the school did. Margaret Metcalfe was the tutor there. They sometimes put a set into a competition. Our class used a record player for music. The classes in the school hall had an accordionist.

'It was a way of keeping fit. There were country dancing classes for children; the West church had them for women, pre-war. Molly McCarley, Margaret Metcalf and Mrs. Buchanan also took the classes.'

Helen Miller:

'Country dancing classes were also for couples. Walter Gardner and his wife Dorothy were one of the founder members of the couples Country Dancing class run by Mrs. Park in the Steeple. My cousin Walter Chalmers and his wife and Andy Knowles and his wife went along. Ronnie Begg, Jim Wilson and the Tytlers came along later on.

'They were all married couples. It took place on a Monday night in the 1950s. It was good fun. We danced to records. Mrs. Park was a good teacher. There was no tea, we just kept dancing. No competition, it was a night out.'

Helen Miller also went along to the classes as an adult.

'Mrs. Park also had mixed classes for husband and wife for

many years. Jack had two left feet, but with women's lib, I went along on my own.'

Les Lambert set up the country dancing a lot later:

'Mrs. Park and Les liked things to be done properly. They were keen on warm-ups, the change of step, the travelling step aimed at lifting feet, being light and off your feet.'

Helen went to country dancing classes at the Thorn school in Johnstone. They competed in the Greenock Festival. Later Helen began to teach country dancing.

The village was well equipped with halls which could accommodate people. The Steeple Hall, the Church Halls [no drink], the Scout Hall, the Guide Hut, Templars Hall, the Masonic Hall were all transformed for great social gatherings. Some had their own bars, some had licences for the night, some 'bring your own bottle' and many with no alcohol at all.

Mabel Murray:

'My dad played the accordion. I was at the Templar's Hall as a baby, wrapped in a blanket and laid at his feet, when my mum was up dancing.'

Many met lifelong partners at a dance. Lottie Dow met her future husband Willie:

'across a crowded room'. . .'Some Enchanted Evening'.

Folk took pride in being good dancers, learning the steps, having fun, and if it seemed a good idea, getting up close and personal. Folk didn't get paid much, but saved enough for transport to and from the dancing and a drink. 'You got paid wallies.' [Scots: wally money – broken pieces of china used as toy money]

In the neighbouring village of Bridge of Weir, the Cargill Hall was a popular place, especially for the local farming community. Agnes Currie met her future husband Andrew at the Cargill Hall:

'I went with other girls from the village. . . Nancy Lee and others, six of us went. We walked over the back road. We sat round the sides, boys at one, girls at the other, the same

as the school dance. The dance had to be finished by 12 on
Saturday nights. They were good dances. The farmers'
dances were held once a month. One brother had a car and
we all used to pile in.'

In Bridge of Weir there was a camp behind the Cargill Hall and Bridge of Weir station. During the 1939-45 war it had housed displaced persons and after the war ended it was a transit camp for people who had been internees in enemy countries. In the post-war wind down of the British Empire people from Israel and India were sent to Bridge of Weir. According to the *Third Statistical Account. County of Renfrew* page 239 [published 1962] 'most of these unfortunate people rested for a month or two, found their feet and departed.'

Alex Murphy:

'The displaced people came after the war and lived in
wooden huts behind the Cargill Hall. The huts had long
rooms, with a toilet and kitchen. There was a beautiful
woman. She was unusual looking. We had never seen
beauty like it in the village. Asian. Her looks, black hair,
her make up. She looked like the painting of the green/blue
woman. [Chinese Lady painted by Vladimir Tretchikoff was
an iconic print, seen in many 1950s living rooms.]
I didn't dance her, I couldn't get near her!

'The Displaced Persons [DPs] had great difficulty. There was
no one to integrate us and bring us all together. When I went
over and danced, it was very awkward, she didn't speak. It
needed someone to go into their company, bring them out and
deliberately mix them, so that they could talk more.

'One of the DPs served his time in Lang's [Engineering
Works, Johnstone] so they were there for a while. He didn't
play football, so didn't socialise much.'

With better transport links, town and city became a big draw. Taking the bus was the easiest. Lottie Dow:

'We spread our wings and went to the Templars Hall, the
Town Hall, and upstairs in the Paisley Co. We went to

Glasgow, Barrowlands, Wilson's jiving in Cathcart Road. It was a dive. Downstairs you got orange, lemonade and a biscuit. We got the bus to Clyde Street and got the tram. The bus home, leaving at the back o' ten. The bus back to Cartside and then walk home. We also went to The F&F in Partick, now Carleton Bingo Hall. Sunday night was 'Go as you Please'. It was like The X Factor. I was in the audience.

'We went to a wee café next door that had a jukebox. We put our money into the machine to hear Sammy David Jnr. We would try to write down the words to sing "Shu Shu Bop".'

Alex Murphy also went to Glasgow:

'I went to Barrowland, the best dancehall there was, it had a sprung floor. I danced this girl, I told her I lived in Paisley, as most didn't know where Kilbarchan was. I offered to take her home, she said I would get lost; she would see me to the bus stop in Clyde Street. When waiting for her at the bottom of the stairs, three or four shadowy figures appeared and shouted, "That's him," one said, "That's no' him," and left. I chose not to wait, jumped doon the stairs and ran away. The lassie's still there!

'I went to The Plaza at Eglinton Toll, where I met my wife. We used to dance round the papier-mache fountain, complete with goldfish, in the centre of the hall. Until I was thrown out for paddlin' and trying to catch the fish.'

Some went to the coast. Agnes and her friends went to Largs.

'We also went to The Moorings in Largs, going in the bus from Milliken Park corner. Robert had a car. We would persuade him to take them down, five plus the driver, sometimes two cars went. We sometimes got a lift back. We all knew each other. The Moorings played modern, Jazz, swing and 1950s pop tunes. The Marine and Curling Hall was a posh affair. A special thing, all dressed in tails and long dresses.

'At the dancin' you could get a pass out. You could go and

get a drink, but no drink in the hall. There were bouncers. They were very strict. There were ones patrolling the dance floor for those who danced too close. Even the last waltz was suitably chaste in the era before the 1960s. There was no alcohol. Orange juice and tea. Likely drink, round the back or at the toilets. Hot orange. . . that was really racy.

'Bands played, mainly accordions and drums, a ceilidh band, which also played the tunes of the day.'

Drink did not necessarily involve alcohol.

Lottie Dow:

'We got a double nougat, or a cup of tea and a Blue Riband biscuit. There was nae vodka and coke.'

To copy movie and music star idols, influenced by advertising on billboards everywhere, cigarettes were part of the night, and added to the atmosphere in more ways than one. Dance halls were filled with smoke, cinema goers watched the screen through swirling clouds, being upstairs in a tram or bus saturated clothes with tobacco smoke, cafés, restaurants and bars were smoke-filled.

'I smoked like a chimney, as most folk did.'

Wherever the dance was, there was protocol. Alex Murphy:

'When at the dancing, the women stood on one side, the men on the other. If she says no, she didn't dance with anyone else, that was the protocol. If she didn't like you, she danced away from you, if she liked you, you danced face to face!'

Late at night, walking back to the village was for most the only way home. From Bridge of Weir the route led past past the tannery. This involved crossing the Locher Brig, and walking up the steep and dark 'Pinnel bend'. Stories would be told of the Locher Brig ghost, making a scary end to the evening out. Only for the brave, encouraging a sprint to safety to the lights of the village.

Late night busses from Glasgow and Paisley stopped in Johnstone. This could involve a half hour walk to the top of the ill lit village. For many this was a trudge uphill all the way on a dark night in changeable Scottish weather.

Lottie Dow:

'I had white sandshoes for the jiving, having taken my outdoor stilettoes off in there. When the bus got to Cartside, I put them back on again to walk home. My mother told me "you shouldnae be walkin' that road".'

Lottie didn't like passing the paper mill. Young women, at night, alone, then as now, often felt vulnerable. One dark night on the lonely road she saw a car coming towards her.

'I was shaking from head to foot, but it was my friend, Andrew Russell.'

For a young man, apart from the weather, their attitudes were different. Alex Murphy:

'To get to and from the dancing I got the bus from Kilbarchan to Clyde Street, on the way back the last bus to Kilbarchan was at 11pm. There was an all-night bus that left at one o'clock but only went to Johnstone. The 12-o'clock bus went to Young's Bus Station in Johnstone and I walked home from there.

'One night the police stopped me, put me in the van and took me to the station which then was in Collier Street in Johnstone, next to the Masonic Hall. I was put in an identity parade with five others. When it was over I was given half a crown. I asked for a lift home, but was refused!'

Although there was dancing in Glasgow on Sundays, traditional Sabbath habits died harder in the village, as in most rural places. Not until the late sixties would social events be tentatively planned for Sundays. Thereafter the end of widespread religious observance and the rise of retail therapy eliminated the old restrictions, and sporting and social engagements were scheduled for whatever day of the week suited folk best!

Chapter 18

Hatches, Matches and Despatches

'I was born on the floor.'

This was said by a woman born in the late 1930s. Childbirth practices changed radically. The same woman then told of her own experience of childbirth.

> 'My son was born on the floor, with two doctors.
> Mr Barr, the top expert, Dr Houston, Mamie, and my
> friend, who was also heavily pregnant, were all in the room,
> with my husband standin' at the close.'

The now seemingly incredible location of the birth, i.e. the floor, was probably far more common than it first reads. The likelihood was that this was planned, traditional, and easier for all concerned. It is also probably enough information other than that both mother and baby were fine and healthy.

As if there were not enough people present during this time, another offered assistance.

> 'The neighbour put her head round the door: "Do you want
> Tom to come in? He's done first aid"!'

The time frame of the births shows also a change. In the 1930s it was likely to be a female or females, experienced women, professional midwives, or a male doctor who were in attendance at the birth.

The presence of an expert obstetrician would have been unlikely in the 1930s. The difference was due to a revolutionary reform of health care. In 1942 the Beveridge Report stated, 'Medical treatment covering all requirements will be provided for all citizens by a national health service.' The National Health Service was established in July 1948. Free to all at the point of need. Poverty no longer prevented the sick seeking medical care, as it had often done before 1948.

> 'In the first half of the century, few men would be seen pushing a pram, let alone beside a pram.'

Men, the husband or the father of the child, were elsewhere. Very few men, up until the 1960s, unless they were in the medical profession, would have much of a clue of the realities of childbirth. They simply would not be there, nor would they be expected to be there. Most probably followed the norm that had prevailed for generations and kept out of the way.

Many birth certificates which show children recorded by registrars in the village as being born in the house, there is the signature of the father, with the word 'present' stated. The probability was that he was outside the door, in the close, in the garden, anywhere but in the room. Men were unlikely ever to be present at the birth, supporting their partner, witnessing the birth, or physically involved in any way, until the late twentieth century!

In the first half of the century, few men would be seen pushing a pram, let alone beside a pram. Even as late as the 1970s, older men would be standing at the front of the close shaking their heads in disapproval at the sight of a man walking down the Barholm pushing a pram, with no woman to be seen.

Although many would be experienced mothers themselves, for women, much may have still depended on tradition and old beliefs rather than proven fact. Many women may never have spoken of, or had the opportunity to speak of, their personal experience of childbirth. The very real dangers of childbirth were ever present. The loss of a child, the loss of the mother, often both, could leave families grieving, when grief could not be spoken of. The trauma of a difficult birth could have physiological as well as psychological consequences throughout a mother's life.

They 'just had to get on with it.'

The building of the maternity hospitals, and access to the new NHS enabled women to be in a place of expertise and comfort and cleanliness, away from the home, being able to rest, before returning to family life. The movement into hospitals with the benefit of pain relief, urgent medical care and after-care, saved many lives, both of the mother and the child.

This example from the 1960s was a young married woman who had her first baby in one of the old 'room and kitchen' housing in the village, without access to a bath.

> 'It was a Sunday when I walked up the park. I knew that I was goin'. I went up to my mother's for a bath that morning. My mother told me, "now don't you be gaun' anywhere, 'cause you're definitely goin' to go"!'

By the 1960s home births in the village were becoming increasingly rare.

In the first half of the century the tradition of large families persisted until contraception became more acceptable. Additions to families put parents under extreme financial pressure: a drawer might house a new baby and children were clothed in garments previously worn by older siblings. There were no luxuries. Families improvised and friends relied on one another's help.

> 'A pram and cot would go round the family. There was a pram and a cot. If you heard a baby was on the way, that would be the pram and cot taken up for a while.'

Increased prosperity meant that buying and gifting new cots, prams and every item needed by an expected baby became the custom, for many, but not all. Those who had the space had a nursery, a far cry from earlier times, and a mere dream for most.

It was known that some women with unwanted pregnancies in the 1950s would give birth in Glasgow. The stigma attached to this was not uncommon.

> 'These were women who didn't have a husband. They were sent up to Rotten Row to deliver, the doctor would send them up.'

At the beginning of the century families were large. It took until the 1960s with the development of the pill to provide women with a working contraceptive that gave them choice. Abortion laws changed in 1967. For many this was, and still is, upsetting, and against their religion. This was, and continues to be, a sensitive subject of much

> 'Additions to families put parents under extreme financial pressure: a drawer might house a new baby.'

debate on many levels. The twentieth century, for the first time ever in history, gave women the right to choose. Change in attitudes saw complete acceptance of the freedom of couples to live together and choose not to get married. Financial support for single families helped many.

The 1960s saw a new drug to cure morning sickness during pregnancy. Thalidomide had adverse effects, with which many individuals and families had to live throughout their lives.

> 'Names – first born son after father, first daughter after mother, then grandparents etc.'

Like families everywhere, parents could now, as far as possible, 'plan' their family and smaller families became the norm.

By the end of the twentieth century the expectation was that all babies should be born in hospital, with access to a medical system with the professional expertise and equipment available to deliver a baby as safely as possible.

As was tradition at the beginning of the century, children's names were, in most places in the country, in strict order.

Sandy Graham: 'It was Daniel or Alexander.'

First born son after father, first daughter after mother, then grandparents etc. Although sometimes confusing, this predictable pattern is useful for those tracing ancestors. Failure to comply with the strict order could result in much offence taken by family members, the fall-outs from which could last for years!

By the 1960s parents were choosing for themselves, still possibly causing offence and upset, but more likely to be met with a 'whit?', a shake of the head, or both. More and more exotic names appeared. Film stars – Tyrone, songs – Charmaine, celebrities – Kylie, gave some indication of the time of birth and age of child. By the end of the century Gaelic names became popular, Ruairidh, Eilidh [how do you pronounce it, then how do you spell it?] All with a variation of spellings which further confused family, teachers, and later employers.

By the end of the century all has changed so much. The families of the twenty first century are in a much better financial, social and healthier state to have the best start in life.

Apart from marriages in church or at home, at which a minister was present, in Scotland, marriage could also be by agreement before witnesses and by a promise of marriage. Both were abolished at the start of 1940. There might be a lack of evidence in census documents or marriage registration records, but in the eyes of friends and relatives and the couple, they were married!

Church weddings became big affairs, with much expense and rivalry. Almost every Saturday afternoon in the summer there was a wedding. Word would get around the village, some would congregate outside the church, or homes, to catch sight of the bridal party, for the sheer entertainment of commenting on the proceedings, and the outfits worn! The children gathering in anticipation of the 'scramble' when the best man threw handfuls of copper coins on to the street as the cars moved away.

For many women the dream wedding could only have been a dream. In reality, the loss of so many men during both World Wars impacted heavily. Many women who lost sweethearts never married.

Marriage itself changed dramatically by the 1960s. Couples chose to live life without the need for a certificate. By the end of the century there was no longer the need to be married at all. Divorce laws came in, giving freedom and choice to both parties for the first time. No longer was marriage 'until death do you part'.

The Victorians had the mourning period and the funeral business down to a fine art, with the undertakers taking care of all of the practicalities of death.

> 'Many believed that the dead were looking down on the living, until recently.'

The churchyard was the place for most burials. The Old Parish Church is built on an early Christian site, where almost all would have been buried. What is now Kilbarchan Parish Church was built in 1787, with the layout of a graveyard soon after. Lairs could be purchased, with lair holder certificates produced, passing down the generations.

Graves were built on top of graves. At the Old Parish Church, the pressure on the high graveyard wall at the side of the road in

Church Street, caused its near collapse. It took until recently to rectify. A team of archaeologists worked with the Council to repair the situation. The work required the full deconstruction and reinforcement and reconstruction of a large section. The remains of 66 individuals were exhumed and re-interred. Permission was given for examination and the findings recorded. It provided a unique insight into the people of the past and their customs.

New, well ordered, and managed, Burial Grounds became commonplace throughout the country. A burial ground was begun on the edge of the village. There was no longer the need or desire to be buried close to the church. The new Crematorium in Paisley opened in 1938 and its use increased throughout the century.

Every churchyard would have a communal, unmarked burial area. These were most likely for the poor from the village. Many families were unable to afford the expense of a gravestone. It was a huge expense from the family budget to provide this. Occasionally a gravestone was paid for by workmates. Examples from around the 1930s in Kilbarchan Cemetery include those from colleagues at Linwood Paper Mill and Kilbarchan Primary School.

The village, as in most other villages, had its own Coffin Society. Members could save up for their own, or family members' funerals. Many saved money in an organised, or unorganised way, in a formal or informal way, in any way as best they could 'tae see me oot'.

> 'As a hearse passes by, curtains in the street were drawn. People stood at the side of the roads and the men took their hats off to pay their respects.'

Death was most likely to occur at home, few would make it into hospital. End of life care, as it later became known, would most likely to be at home. Many of the older homes had no private rooms, and sleeping in a built-in bed recess was commonplace. This was in the living room, with normal life going on all around in the same room. No inside toilet, hot water, bath, or washing machine. The care of the dying was usually kept in the family. People did the best they could, often under very difficult circumstances, often living with their own health issues. Families were expected to help. Wives to nurse husbands, adult children to nurse elderly parents.

When death came, the people of the village quickly found out.

Sometimes this became obvious in an unusual manner.

> 'Jimmy Nelson the undertaker lived at Yardshead. He
> would be seen walking down the street with the
> strauchenin' board to measure the length and breadth of
> the coffin, you knew someone had died.'

Often linen was used, kept in the family, especially for the purpose of wrapping the dead.

> 'After the coffin had arrived, the dead were wrapped in a
> strauchenin' sheet.'

The Strauchenin', or strachein', Scots for straightening, fulfilled that practical purpose. The body was wrapped in the linen after death before being dressed and placed in a coffin. It is likely that this would have been done by a family member, probably the older women, the main carers.

The strauchenin' sheet could not be used for any other purpose Even when it would have been of use in other ways.

> 'We had a family one. I was going to make it into table
> napkins, but the family were against it! It was beautiful linen!'

The dead were kept in the house, sometimes for days.

> 'You were meant to look in the coffin.'

If possible, a room would be recommissioned for the purpose, usually the 'good room' or a bedroom.

> 'You could be taken into the house to see inside the coffin.'

It was almost expected that neighbours visited the deceased as a mark of respect. For one family who lived in one of the older houses for generations the same room was used.

> 'A family member who was superstitious used to hate that
> room. He thought that there was a presence.'

With a stiff upper lift, reserved, Scottish culture, where women could cry, and 'real' men did not, people rarely publicly showed their grief. In a nation scarred by loss in two world wars, where news of death away from home was common, with graves, if any, in far off lands, it is little wonder people did not talk about loss. Once again, they just had to get on with it.

By the end of the century much changed in attitutudes towards bereavement. The development of hospices, support from home and counselling services helped many. It became easier to talk, and easier to access professional support, during difficult times.

After the formation of the National Health Service things changed. More access to healthcare professionals and increased hospital beds, units and transport, meant that those from the village had more options available. The pressure is eased from the family and home. People have the freedom to express their feelings, in a way never before known.

Chapter 19
Gardens

> 'There was a lovely garden at Todholes. Had fruit trees and bricked pathways, stretched about 100 yards with a drystane dyke around it.'

THESE are the words of David Carlin speaking about the garden of his home on the edge of the village, as a child in the 1920s. Liza MacKenzie also remembers her garden in the 1940s.

> 'There were all sorts in the garden. We got a lot of food from it. My grandfather was a very good gardener. He was really interested, to the end.'

Like many old villages, the older houses had few front gardens, most were at the back. Many are surprised by the extent of the gardens, particularly in the Barholm, as they cannot be seen by passers-by. These houses were previously lived in by a number of families each of which had their own area of ground and a shared drying green and washhouse. Many of these houses, by the end of the century, had became single homes with their own private garden.

Some people had allotments, which were well tended, at what are now Cedar Court and Rock Drive. The building of tenements in Barholm and Milliken Road in the early twentieth century included a communal washing green. The social housing in places like Milliken Drive and Wheatlands Drive incorporated large gardens, hedged for privacy with drying greens and space for a shed. The flats in the Fulton Crescent area offered new residents verandas and communal drying areas. Some larger houses had private walled gardens. All the gardens needed maintenance.

David Carlin talked of his parents using their garden in the 1930s:

'She [mother] could turn her hands to different things. Making jam; strawberry and apple. Some would pickle, some would bottle. We also had gooseberries, blackcurrants, red currants and rhubarb. We had a pear tree and apple trees. Good cabbage, cauliflower, Brussels sprouts, potatoes, onions and peas. Every year we did sweet peas.

'Fine stems of rhubarb with a poke [Scots: bag] of sugar.

> **'My father liked the garden. He spent most of his time with the hens.'**

'My father liked the garden. He spent most of his time with the hens, and he was good at weeding. The garden got the sun from morning till night. It was sheltered by a wall. They had a border where his mother grew the flowers. It was nice when it was all done and the grass cut.

'One year they would have dahlias; big, wee, pom poms, the next year, chrysanths.'

He and his brother John would tend the same garden.

'It was a lot of hard work, along with the pigeons, hens and that. It kept you out of mischief most of the time.'

Many of the old gardens were worked for generations. Knowledge was passed on through experience, observation and patience. With those fortunate enough to have a garden, they were well used, well worked, and for many, a source of great pride. Routines were passed on, traditions kept, until war changed everything.

Gardens were no longer for the individual and their family, but needed by the nation.

Myra Goldie:

'I was was old enough to understand rationing. We knew that there wasn't the food, but we never went hungry. . . we had cheuch [Scots: tough, also teugh] chickens to eat!'

They got fresh eggs. Once the hens were past laying, at a certain stage, they wrung their necks.

'The hens and bees had to be registered; they came every week to register the eggs. There were 12 people in the building; the rationing allowed one egg a week, each. You'd to watch. The rest went away in a van. Aunt Jean was in charge of the eggs; it was all properly done by the government.

'There's a difference between shop eggs and fresh hen eggs.'

Rearing chicks was a well organised routine. They were, invariably, well maintained.

> **'If the hens didn't lay, they got their necks wrung.'**

'The chicks were hatched in the bathroom, in an incubator at the window. They would be watched. After 2-3 days, they went out into the first hut. They were put into a round thing with a blanket in it to keep it cosy. It had a paraffin heater in the middle. The kids used to watch the wee chickens emerging from their shells.

'When the chicks were a bit older, they went into the black shed after the washing green, and then on to the main shed nearer the burn.

'There were galvanised bins to preserve the eggs. A water glass was used. It preserved them throughout the winter. They were used for baking or cooking, but not for eating, they were disguised as something else.

'If the hens didn't lay, they got their necks wrung.'

Years later, as an adult, her father would come to her house, two doors away, with an old hen under his arm, saying, 'there's something for your tea!' Her father wrung its neck, but she was left to deal with it afterwards. To feather and gut it. . . 'You were lucky if there was an egg inside it.'

'The hens were put in at night. The wings were clipped. They had a cockerel, big Jock, he flew at you, even the adults were afraid of big Jock.

'We got sugar for the bees for winter feeding, they [the government] didn't take the honey, we were allowed that.'

Myra's family had at least a dozen beehives. Her father took the hives up to the heather in Muirsheil in July, where they stayed until October. 'There's a difference in the [heather] honey. We were fed on honey.' They also sold it.

Her family were members, probably founder members, of Kilbarchan Beekeepers Association, one of the top associations in Scotland which has carried on well into the twenty-first century. Ian Craig, renowned beekeeper, would have learned much of his skills from Myra's father and beekeepers like him in the village.

> **'Everyone grew veg. They had soup every day. Granny's broth, that was a meal. They knew what a parsnip was; city people wouldn't.'**

Myra's description of three of the older houses in the village, is probably typical of village life in many areas of Scotland for generations.

'There was a shed beside the washhouse. Everything was in that shed, children were not allowed in. Some things were dangerous. There were lathes and tools. More likely that it was a sanctuary for the men in the family.

'We had fruit trees, pear trees. We picked the fruit. Each pear was wrapped in a sock and put in a drawer. We had big green apples, which were sour. They were cooked.

'We used to climb on the pear trees. There was also a rowan tree. By the path up to the hut, they grew marigolds, which were the only flower that was grown; there would have been a reason for that, known to keep aphids away.'

In addition to the eggs, honey, pears and vegetables in her family's garden,

'. . . they had gooseberries, blackcurrants and raspberries. The neighbours had apples and plums. Lots were shared amongst the neighbours.

'My dad and uncle Willie got permission to put a bridge across the burn into the old Bowling Green. They would scythe the hay and had chickens there. They made haystacks. My sister fell into nettles and dock leaves were rubbed on to stop the sting.'

There was satisfaction and pride in work well done. The smell of fresh air from clothing that had been hung out on a washing line, the sight of well-ordered, clean washing blowing on the line, were things known to past generations. Women had a pride in these kinds of jobs well done. Most of the older houses in the village had a wash house with a boiler in the corner, underfed by coal. It was communal, with each family having an allocated day. It was hard work, invariably done by women. With large families, older female children were expected to help out.

Helen Dooris:

> 'My father grew lots of vegetables. The garden where I grew up had chickens, ducks and pigeons. People used their gardens. Everyone grew veg. They had soup every day. Granny's broth, that was a meal. They knew what a parsnip was; city people wouldn't.'

Mabel started her married life in a flat in Ewing Street. She was there when her son Douglas was born in the late 1950s.

> 'Annie McCarley, my neighbour and I did the washing together. Whites, nappies etc. We did the boil wash together. I loved the smell of the washing house. Buckets could be used to fill the boiler or a hose from a nearby spigot.'

Helen Dooris:

> 'We were bathed in the boiler house. It was either that or the front of the fire. I chose the front of the fire, as I hated the smell of the boiler house. My granny went out and lit the boiler every Monday.'

There were seasonal activities in the school playground. The next was an autumn highlight! A raid on fruit trees in gardens was a common occurrence, more for the excitement than for the fruit!

> 'People were sitting in their room with the lights on. The man came out and shouted. We ran up behind Low Barholm, High Barholm, over, through and under hedges, to exit at Station Road, then walked along the Well Strand to come out at the Spoot Well. As we casually strolled back down High Barholm, we heard ambulance sirens. When

'The smell of fresh air from clothing that had been hung out on a washing line, the sight of well-ordered, clean washing blowing on the line, were things known to past generations.'

one of us had run away, he had climbed over the wrought iron house gates. His foot had caught on the spikes and he had fallen and split his head open. The owners of the house helped him. Our pal had a scar for a while, but was still ok. It didn't put us off, and spooling continued in other areas in the village.

> 'A raid on fruit trees in gardens was a common occurrence, more for the excitement than for the fruit!'

'We were caught once by the village bobby, PC Munro, known as Big Marilyn. The usual "what have you been up to?. . . I know who you are. . . where you live. . . know your faither". . . then as you turned away, you got a boot up the backside. It was not a fatal kick.

'The most scary part was the thought of him coming to the house to see my father. I shuddered to think what would happen. My parents were very religious, Memorial Hall. It was a terrible thing if the police came to your door.'

Gardens by the end of the century had changed:

'Young folks today are too busy.'

The regular routines of the wash day, hanging clothes on the line, constantly checking the weather to avoid using the winter dyke round the fire to dry clothes, were no longer needed with the introduction of washing machines and tumble dryers.

The sounds of the garden, of children playing, the chat and banter of neighbours as they worked, often together in the shared gardens, by the end of the century were not often heard. The sight and sounds of the hens, pigeons and bees – all of which needed daily feeding and maintenance – made the gardens busy places.

The land was used differently by 2000. The new buildings in the village had smaller gardens, many with driveways and garages taking up the space. Flats were built with verandas, some with no garden at all. There were more people working and travelling away from home, more distractions and other interests. The use of the computer, videos, PlayStations and other home-based activities replaced the traditional outdoor play for children.

Electrical and petrol tools changed the sounds of the garden. Wash houses were unused or demolished. The washing greens themselves were transformed into paved patios. Front garden flowerbeds were turned into driveways. With smaller families in more private gardens, plastic outdoor toys, swings and trampolines, replaced the traditional ball, skipping ropes and hide and seek: the garden changed to make room for them. Paving and later decking replaced the need to cut the grass, or to have any plants at all.

Gardens became less busy and less used. The economic need for fertile gardens and their cultivation passed with the availability of better wages and cheaper food. There grew more emphasis on them being private, safe, low maintenance and secluded spaces in which to relax.

Many enjoyed their garden, others thought it a chore. A lot depended on era, age and fitness. At their best they kept people active outdoors, communicating and interacting with one other. Gardens were much more than a patch of ground.

> 'Gardens by the end of the century had changed: 'Young folks today are too busy.'

Chapter 20

Pigeons

Doocot, Dookit, Dooket: Dovecot. Doo-dove or pigeon

JOHN and David Carlin have lived in Mount Pleasant, Shuttle Street for most of their lives, over ninety years. Pigeons, or locally doos, have been their lifetime passion. They built doocots, maintained them, built new ones, nurtured and freed the birds daily to swoop and soar encircling the trees around their home. The Carlins were not the only people in the village to keep pigeons for most of their lives, but by 2000 theirs were almost the last. For many, keeping pigeons was a way of life. John and David were the prime example of a long, highly organised, and hugely popular, tradition in Scotland. They were the last of Kilbarchan's doo men.

> John: 'We started when we were five years old. My uncle used to keep them, in Belford, Northumberland. He worked in a quarry. He had to give them up when he married.'

> David: 'He sent some one time and we kept a few. They were out, guess which ones the cat got! Most of the big pigeon men were miners. The pigeon game started with the miners who were down below all day. They wanted fresh air at the weekends. The pigeons started to go back the way, when all the pits shut down. Away back you had to make your own entertainment. You had to choose between pigeons and sport.

> 'We got [some of] our first pigeons from Ayrshire. Our father came from Kilmarnock and there's pigeon men down there.'

The Birds

'The birds that I've had over the years have been the best that I can afford.'

David watched the pigeons closely. His car was parked strategically, facing the pigeon hut, to offer him shelter and comfort on wet days whilst watching the birds in action!

'There's one there! No, it's gone! I paid one thousand three hundred. It never filled an egg, it was barren. A chap who died, a school teacher in Wales [sold it]. It was only a year old when it came here. You don't race them – he didn't know that when he died. It never sired a youngster. £1300 for that one, one at £900 and two at £600. Males and females.

'I bought two pairs in 1947 or '48 when I came out of the services. I paid £6 for that. In today's prices that's nothing, but see in 1947, £6 was a lot of money. Your wages then were only about £4 or £5 a week. In fact it was £3 or £4 a week at that time.

'You know when they are match fit. You know the condition of their bodies, you know – they're up flying all the time, up and down, up and down. The condition of their feathers, shiny. . . two or three days on eggs, others fourteen days on eggs and others just, when they go to race, see that night, you slip a young one underneath them, in below them.

Falcons

Peregrine falcons kill pigeons and other medium-sized birds.

David: 'A peregrine catches a pigeon and takes it back to its youngsters. They decimate the pigeons even in the races. At some places in England they congregate and attack them when they come out. A lot of the boys get them back all injured.

'The peregrines, if they see some pigeons flying, thirty or forty, they set their sights on one and they go straight for the one bird and they disperse the lot. Instead of the flight for home they're all over the country in panic. They split up in wee groups and they'll go here there and everywhere. It spoils their flight. It's finished the pigeon racing, I would say so.

'See during the war, the peregrines, they shot them, as the carrier pigeons got used on aircraft, and they got rid of all the peregrines. After the war for a number of years they got free.

'People still shot them and the effect of pesticides killed them. Since the 1960s they have been protected by law. This has disadvantaged pigeons and annoyed their owners. Even birds training, round and round above their lofts were vulnerable.'

John: 'A peregrine took one of the best birds we had here.'

David: 'There were fifty birds out there, flying one day. This bird had won the Cheltenham race twice. . . this peregrine dived on the fifty birds and picked out the good one and killed it. See the ones with the white flight feathers, they see them first, pick it out and they dive at 120 miles per hour. They keep their eye on that bird, they don't bother about the other forty nine. The fright they get, they just disperse. If they get away from a peregrine a pigeon will dive into a wood where the peregrine can't get it.'

Despite the losses, cherishing and training the pigeons was rewarding.

David: 'You've got to spend a lot of money and time. The big national races, in France and that. They have prize money, the nationals, a thousand pounds. We've won a thousand pounds quite a few times.'

Fanciers and punters alike may have dreamed of a big win. The planning and debate of what they might buy was all part of the appeal. The lucky winners would be the subject of conversation, speculation, and great envy.

One of the most enviable items to own in the 1950s would be

something that few people had and many highly coveted. Ideally it would be expensive and a classic. . . 'a guid motor'!

More practically, for John and David, a car was a means of transporting their pigeons.

Transport

David on buying the first car:

> 'The first car we got was a Standard Companion [1954-1959]. A shooting brake. We went up to the Kelvin Hall – they used to have the Motor Show there. This car was on the stand. We can get the basket in the back and it's still comfortable.

> 'Pat Porteous was the banker. We hadn't a lot of cash at the time. I went to the bank but the bank was shut. I went to Pat. Pat used to come in here, he used to go fishing. We used to know him well. I chapped his door and said, "I'm going up to the Motor Show: Any chance of getting £500?" "Five hundred quid?" He says, "Aye." He just went through the back and gave me five hundred quid and the bank wasn't even open! Cash!

> 'The chap on the stand said, "You'll never get a car like this in your life. This has been specially doctored up for the Glasgow stand." A chrome engine, it was. So we got it. It was black with white windows. It lasted about ten years. Then it was a Morris 1000 and later we just got vans.'

John: 'Mother used to like pigeons in a sense because, see if you got a run, away down to Sanquhar or Dumfries, she would come.'

'The Airedale went too. . . I used to take my mother in the motor, and the dog. It always sat at the front beside me and my mother had to go into the back!'

In France, Reims, Rennes, and Nantes were regular race points for races. The National race of the year was the Reims Gold Medal, which took place annually on the weekend closest to the longest day, in late June. The pigeons went to Glasgow in a transporter to meet up with other clubs at Queen Street Station. They also used to take them on the bus and later by car to Glasgow, before they were taken to France.

Starting points closer to Kilbarchan were dictated by a route originally established by the former Glasgow and South Western Railway, that went through Kilmarnock to Dumfries. The closure of the Kilbarchan–Lochwinnoch loop in Dr. Beeching's cost cutting in June 1966 ended that direct rail link for the fanciers. But before the final closure, the railway had said, 'We'll still do your pigeons for you. We'll make money and you'll get the same treatment but you'll have to go to the same race points.' Agreement could not be reached.

> David: 'When we burst up with the railways we had to organise our transport ourselves. Lorries were used instead.'

Until then, on Friday evenings, a procession of individuals pushing or pulling trollies containing pigeon baskets, made their way along Station Road to store their birds in the old goods shed.

The birds, said David:

> '. . . used to get the 7.30 train in the morning from Kilbarchan which used to go to Crosshouse, Mauchline, Cumnock and Sanquar, the Dumfries train. They used to make a lot of money off it.

> 'Used to come down and the porter was on. He used to come off that train in the morning, "Get your pigeons on here." That was a fiddle, that. . . all the pigeons were in the Goods Shed in Kilbarchan. Used to take all your birds up to the station. You used to take the baskets from the goods shed and you walked along and across the line and up into the station with the baskets. You put the basket on the scales – 30, 35 or 36 lbs and they priced it. You stood with your foot in below the basket – that maybe took £10 off the basket!'

Followed by an aside, about his other obsession:

'I used to go to the football – listen to this – used to get the train from Kilbarchan to Kilmarnock Station and I'd walk to Rugby Park, four or five hundred yards. Three-quarters of an hour from the house here and I was in Rugby Park.'

Many villages and towns had club huts, the last of which was in a small space on the site of Spring Grove House, flanked by flats.

John: 'There used to be 55 members in Kilbarchan. And we're the only ones that's left.'

David: 'See when the hut was built. It went up in the sixties. The ground was just a piece of waste ground. It was Renfrewshire County Council who gave the ground to the Pigeon Club to keep the young boys off the streets. Now they're charging rates and they've had to put £60 on to the membership to pay the rates. We built it ourselves. They did [fundraising] nights to raise money.'

David: 'There's a lot of work to it. When we joined the club the first thing they said was "you have to stick to the rules" not like they do now when they change them halfway through the season. In the club you had to fight your way to the top. When they started at first they had a boys' club and they took the pigeons

'Rings are new every year. All registered in our name. If you were using one of someone else's you'd be disqualified right away.

'All the birds are liberated at the same time, going to different lofts. They give you the time and the wind direction and when they arrive you take their ring and the owner enters the time of arrival.'

John: 'The pigeon game is a dying game now. . .'

The Nationals

Midsummer was the highlight in the pigeon calendar.

David: 'See the Nationals, everyone in Kilbarchan, even the poorest fancier, sent to the Nationals. The Nationals is always flown on the longest day of the year. The summer nights are brilliant and warm and the fanciers and the punters used to wait in the village until 11-12 o'clock in case they got a bird, and then they used to go for a walk round the Cut and came down around 3 or 4 in the morning. They never went to their beds.'

Starting at The Cross, the walk took the men up Shuttle Street and Forehouse Road, with a left turn at Lawmarnock, then down and up the steep little valley that gave the walk its name, past Meikle Burntshields, Burntshields House, Overton Farm, down the Dam Brae to Church Street, returning to the Cross.

'I slept out there one night. I was out there at 12 o'clock but the race wasn't due to finish until about 3 or 4 in the morning. So I thought I'll sleep out there in the hut.
3 o'clock in the morning up and back into my bed. Cold.

'There was a National with 7000 birds coming from Rennes and Nantes. Ten minutes to five in the morning is when I clocked it.

'I remember one morning we had pigeons at Nantes. I got up at 5 o'clock, you never saw rain like it in your life, thunderstorms – no pigeons could fly in that. I came back in and shaved and psyched myself up . My mother wasn't so good at the time and used to get up in the night sometimes and go to the door to get some fresh air. She'd seen a pigeon up on the loft at 5 and didn't go out. When I went out at twenty to seven it was sitting on the eaves. And it was still well on in the race.

'Other people would sit in their house and look out their back window, like that view there – "we've got to go out there to see them". That commitment to "go out there and see them" typifies the enthusiasm that the sport generated.

When up to fifty five men were involved, with hundreds of birds, it was a financial burden, a labour of love and on a good day, for owners and punters, a source of cash.

At one time, much available garden space was used to house pigeons. Men learned woodworking skills in building the huts, often working together. Children played in and around them, pocket money was earned in cleaning them. Wives and daughters fed and watered the pigeons. Their needs were part of the family budget. It was one of the great topics of discussion, it was the interest, focus and escape for so many. So great was the commitment of people to their pigeons, that their loss could be devastating. This knowledge gave an additional edge to the old Kilbarchan curse, told by Jack Miller:

'Ah hope all your pigeons die an' you cannae sell your doocot.'

Listen Closely

Glasgow and South West Railway train, halted at Kilbarchan station, on its way to Glasgow

Paisley and District tram at the final terminus at the Co-op. The original terminus was at the Trust Inn, but village opinion persuaded the company to lay extra track

Chapter 21
By Road and Rail

'All the Kilbarchan folk went into "their" compartment.'

IN 1900 road transport was dominated by the horse. Almost all the goods from railway goods yards and city warehouses to retail outlets were pulled by horses. Private two-wheeled gigs, bakers' vans, Co-op vans, milk carts, brewers' drays, flatbed four-wheeled coal wagons, charabancs and farm machinery depended on horses.

The heaviest work was dominated by the Clydesdale. The ownership, maintenance and feeding of horses was a vital part of the lives of owners, farriers, blacksmiths and saddlers. Keeping horses fed created a vast movement of fodder, which had to be dispersed to stables and sheds throughout the country.

Kilbarchan Co-op's horses were stabled in back premises off Ewing Street, still visible from Well Road. Private houses would have both a stable and a coach house. The Bull Inn had a pend to allow horses off the street – it was a drinking place for both men and beasts.

But change was under way. The *Renfrewshire Gazette* reported that the annual horse market, which took place at the broadest part of Church Street on 20th December 1902, St. Barchan's Day, had witnessed dwindling trade. The road revolution had begun. Small numbers of motor cars were being sold to the better off. Albion in Glasgow built cars from 1900 to 1915, but concentrated on lorries from 1909 onwards.

Horse-drawn and mechanized vehicles overlapped until after

World War II and up to that point into the 1950s the village relied on both for supplies. In the 1920s Dan Trushell recalled, in summer holidays, rising early to join a Kilbarchan Co-op driver in a horse-drawn journey from Kilbarchan to the Scottish Co-operative Wholesale Society's warehouse at Morrison Street, Glasgow. They would have breakfast when they arrived, load up, and return with a van load for the village Co-ops.

Railway access to Kilbarchan began in 1840 when the Glasgow, Paisley, Kilmarnock and Ayr Railway Company opened Cochrane Mill Station, which, in 1854 name changed to Milliken Park. The company later became the Glasgow and South Western Railway. To relieve traffic on the main line to Ayr, in 1905, it opened a loop line from Johnstone North to Kilbarchan, Lochwinnoch and Kilbirnie to rejoin the main line at Brownhill Junction, north of Dalry.

> 'Villagers had two railway stations to choose from, or three, if Bridge of Weir was included, all within what in these far off days, were regarded as easy walking distances.'

Villagers had two railway stations to choose from, or three, if Bridge of Weir was included, all within what in these far off days, were regarded as easy walking distances. People were able to go further to work, it was easier to keep in touch with families, and mass transport, which is what rail introduced, enabled new friendships to be formed amongst regular travellers.

Christine Erwin, talked about her mother's parents in Kilbarchan in the 1900s:

> 'She [her mother] used to talk about how, when her folks were young they would walk over to Bridge of Weir to get the train to Glasgow. That line must have been there well before the Loop Line.'

Christine Erwin, speaking of her maternal grandfather:

> 'He commuted to the Fish Market in Glasgow after he returned from the war.'

Jan Keir spoke of her husband Ian's youth, when he stood at one of the two exits from the platform:

> 'From Ian's father's day [1920s and 1930s] they all went by the train and Ian used to say that when he was a wee boy he went out to meet the train. He'd stand at the opposite side of the road from the subway and all you saw was the bowler hats coming down the subway, all the bankers. . .'

Jan married in 1960 and came to live in the village:

> 'One person I loved to get on the train was Jessie Mitchell. She had a very good job – I think you'd call her a paralegal, a legal secretary and she was so funny. She really was, an unconscious comedian. And one or two others. Once my children came along I visited her mother in Coatdyke, Coatbridge, with a change of trains in Glasgow. There was no provision then for big prams or bicycles in the passenger coaches. I put the pram into the guard's van.'

Georgina Stephen, who lived near the station:

> 'I could wait to hear the train coming and run up the tunnel to catch it. It was fantastic. It was the old clatter of steam trains. Everyone had their own compartments: all the Kilbarchan folk went into "their" compartment and it was the same coming back at night. There was Mr. MacKinnon from Lochwinnoch and there was me and Jenny Muir and Margaret Connell, Ian Park and David Sharp. If a stranger came in, the conversation dried up! Albert Haines worked at the station. Albert did everything. You were hardly on the train when he was shutting the doors.'

Before he left the railways to craft furniture and frame paintings in the village, her husband John worked for British Rail:

> 'It was handy for me, because I was starting at 9 o'clock at Paisley Gilmour Street and you got the train here at ten to nine.'

Accidents in the early days of railways had led to the development of methods which, if adhered to, guaranteed safe journeys. The key individual in this exercise was the signal man. The relief signal man had wider experience of the local network than most others.

Ian Trushell:

> 'Charlie Mooney was a relief signalman. Charlie was on Kilbarchan regularly. At lunch time Charlie's wife would take his piece down and give Charlie his dinner. You went down Station Road, turned right up Potts' Lane and Mrs. Mooney

'I could wait to hear the train coming and run up the tunnel to catch it. It was fantastic. It was the old clatter of steam trains.'

would stand at the fence and Charlie would come out of the signal box and take it. The signal box had a coal fire, so he could heat things up and make tea. It was up one floor.

'One day he said, "Would you like to come down to the box, it'll be quiet, don't tell anyone." So I went with Mrs. Mooney and crossed the track to get to the signal box. That was very naughty. "Don't touch anything," he said. "I'll give you a shot."

> 'Until the Clean Air Acts of 1956 and 1968 the air was heavy with smoke and soot.'

The line between each signal box was closely controlled. Nothing could leave Lochwinnoch without the Kilbarchan signalman's permission and nothing could leave Kilbarchan without Cart Junction's permission. Warning bells from one to another had to be acknowledged. Ian was allowed to reply to the bell from Lochwinnoch:

'After it finished the telephone from Lochwinnoch rang: "I'm getting some funny signals." Charlie said. "Aye, I've got a learner in the box." He let me pull back the home signal and the starter signal.'

Until the Clean Air Acts of 1956 and 1968 the air was heavy with smoke and soot. Industry was largely coal-fired – railway engines were powered by it and electricity was mainly coal-generated. Every home had at least one fire burning for most of the year, to heat water and part of one room. Domestic fires were often banked up with slow burning coal dross or coal briquettes, increasing smoke emission. Mists or fogs were common. The combination of smoke and fog created an almost impenetrable atmosphere which affected the health of people with lung conditions and made it almost impossible to see the way ahead:

'Charlie told me the story about the train that pitched up at Kilbarchan and the driver stopped outside the signal box and said, "Where am I?" "Kilbarchan," replied the signalman. The driver said, "Ah shoulnae be here. Ah'm meant to be on the direct line tae Glasgow. Ah thought there was something wrong at Brownhill Junction." The signalman at Dalry had put him on the Kilbarchan line instead of the main line.'

The end of the trains

British Rail was losing money and travel by road seemed more convenient. Dr. Beeching produced a report in 1963 which slashed 5,000 miles of track from the United Kingdom railway network. One of the selling features for the new homes in Kilbarchan had been its station, which closed just as they were all finally occupied.

The track was used for occasional goods traffic until 1972, after which it was lifted. In the 1980s young adults in the Youth Training Scheme carried out the transformation of the rail bed into a gravel cycle track, which was later tarmacked. It is now part of Sustrans National Cycle Network.

Nan Chittick:

'When the station went on fire Margaret next door came out and we stood away up the garden and watched it in flames.'

> 'In the 1980s young adults in the Youth Training Scheme carried out the transformation of the rail bed into a gravel cycle track.'

Trams had an even shorter lifetime in Kilbarchan than the trains. The Paisley and District Tramways Company was set up in 1903 and expanded routes in Renfrewshire. On 5th July 1906 a line to Kilbarchan was officially opened. It initially ended at the Trust Inn, which is what the company planned, and was later extended to what became known as 'The Terminus' at the main Co-operative building, which is where Kilbarchan people had wanted it in the first place. From Johnstone to Kilbarchan it was a single line track, with passing places. The trams were open-topped, unlike Glasgow trams. The fare from Kilbarchan to Renfrew Ferry was just 4d.

In a brief memoir Dan Trushell recorded that the trams were known as Murphy's, a tribute to the General Manager, a Dublin man, who established the network, which ran all the way to Rouken Glen.

Walter Gardner had a clear memory of travelling on the tram: he liked to sit upstairs as it gave him a view of places not normally visible to a five year old on his feet. On Fridays or Saturdays a specially illuminated tram briefly visited the village. The trams ended two months before his sixth birthday.

Georgina Stephen, post war:

'I remember the tram lines, standing at the door when I was three or four, quite vivid to me. Single track. The hooks for the wires at the terminus are on the Co and the building opposite it.'

Myra Goldie had no recollection of having travelled by tram, as she was only two years old when they stopped, however:

'I was in them, I was taken from Kilbarchan to Paisley to see my gran – I was told. When the tram tracks were lifted, people went and got the causeys [granite setts in which the rails had been set]. We've got a wee wall out there made of causeys. A lot of the houses down Low Barholm have paths made of them, if you look.'

The Paisley and District Tramway Company was taken over by Glasgow Corporation Tramways in 1923. In 1932 the trams had their four wheel bogies updated to standard Glasgow bogies: when they were used on the Kilbarchan line, they derailed at the passing places. It was too expensive to relay the track, so the service ended on 30th April 1932.

Walter Gardner:

'When the trams stopped a Corporation bus replaced it. There was a Young's bus service which was great. It started from the terminus and I think you could get right through to Glasgow.'

In the middle of what was exclusively Young's domain, the Corporation bus ran until the mid-1950s. Western buses took over when services were nationalised and in 1988 buses were privatised. Arriva emerged as the local provider.

There was a time keeping device outside No.12 Low Barholm, used by the Glasgow Corporation bus crew. It was known locally by the name of its American inventor as 'the Bundy'.

The legendary Glasgow clippies, when asking people to remove themselves from the vehicle, would say 'C'mon, get aff.' During the 1939-45 war this confused visiting Allied service personnel. The atmosphere on a bus often reflected the attitude of the conductor, usually a woman – the clippie.

Jan Howitt:

'The Western drivers and clippies were most rude, nothing

like the Glasgow ones, nothing like them at all. You were struggling on with the kids and carry cots. In Glasgow it was, "C'mon hen, I'll help you with that" and the same getting off. It was very different. There were some regulars and you could stand at Paisley Road West with your hand out and they'd just go past you. They were so unhelpful compared to Glaswegians. I think they knew that we were the new people, house buyers.'

Jeff Webster:

'I got a Western SMT bus every twenty minutes, on the dot. Brilliant. When I came home at night I used to jump off at the corner off the back of the bus. You held on to the bar and as it slowed down to go round the corner, you could step off the bus, and if it went a little quicker you had to be on your toes!

'Grace was the conductress, she became a driver: she was absolutely great. Going back from Paisley Grammar, the buses were four o'clock and twenty past. You never got the four o'clock bus so I would just walk up to the Cross [Paisley Cross] but loads of other kids, going to Johnstone or Elderslie would get on the bus and if it was busy some Kilbarchan kids wouldn't get on.

'Grace would say, "Kilbarchan first." You wouldn't get that now. Grace was absolutely brilliant. When I was fourteen the Harriers had a record hop in the Steeple Hall and I asked this girl from Elderslie if she'd like to go, first ever date, so I went in to Johnstone, met her at the top of the Thorn, got the bus to Kilbarchan and of course, who was the conductress? Grace. "Two returns to Kilbarchan, please." I was just on the cusp of paying full fare. She said, "That'll be the full fare." I gave her the money and she gave me the change for a half fare!'

Colin Campbell:

'Dan Trushell told me that on a trip home one dark and very foggy evening from Paisley the bus driver could not see where he was going. Dan sat on the mudguard beside the bonnet, navigated and shouted instructions to the driver through his open window.'

Personal transport was normal by 2000, but the older people recalled the early days of cars, when they presented substantial maintenance challenges to their few owners. Myra [1930s]:

'There was one man had a car all my young days, Mary Gibson's brother Wattie. He was the only person that had a car right down here. And it definitely wouldn't have passed an MOT, tied up with rope and string and things. He and my dad went through to Edinburgh to pay the feu duty. They went away in this car.'

Ian Trushell [1950s]:

'Glentyan Avenue. The post-war baby boom. The street was jumping with kids. There was one car across the street, Uncle Jimmy across the road, Jimmy Ford, he was a mechanic at the quarry and nobody else had a car. There were endless games of football on the street and if a car came along we just stood aside and watched. If anyone hit Uncle Jimmy's car we all beat it. He was out shouting at us.'

> **'Unless someone was well enough paid to have a garage to maintain their car, people did it themselves.'**

Unless someone was well enough paid to have a garage to maintain their car, people did it themselves. Cars were cherished. Garages had inspection pits or cars were precariously raised off the ground on jacks or wooden blocks to carry out maintenance. A whole range of new skills were required to keep cars on the road. Until the 1970s cars were not sold with underseal, which could be applied for a price, or rust set in.

Service intervals were frequent, new cars were limited to the speeds they could travel in each gear. After a thousand miles they had to return to the garage to have adjustments made. Service intervals were short. Until MOTs were introduced in 1960 many unsafe cars were on the roads, potentially endangering the drivers and other road users. Fixed fly deflectors at the front or front-facing, open-ended door handles or lack of safety belts were amongst injury inflicting flaws long since eliminated. As the century ended legislation had made cars safer, but the freedom that motorists had enjoyed when they were fewer had been destroyed by the sheer volume of traffic in urban areas and motorways.

Informal transport – 1950s

Carts, friendly van drivers, or car owners were a source of unofficial transport. People might be invited to pile on and make the best of it. The following became unimaginable on both health and safety and child care grounds 50 years later!

Ian Trushell:

'The Council had a man who came and cut the grass, it was a big machine with cutters that went side to side, lethal. He lived in Lochwinnoch and had a tractor with a flat trailer. He would load the cutter onto the trailer with planks. The kids would all clamber up and he'd take us off down Church Street and up the Dam Brae, maybe a dozen, were on it. We were dropped off at Clochoderick and we walked back. I was terrified. I was maybe eight. I thought I was lost and when we got to the top of the Dampton [Pad], just above the lake, and a guy lifted me up on to the wall and I could see Glentyan Avenue, I felt better.'

'Carts, friendly van drivers, or car owners were a source of unofficial transport.'

Increasing disposable income, more efficient manufacturing methods, progress in the air as a result of the wars, revolutionised both private and public transport. The quiet and empty streets of the village, once the preserve of pedestrians, horses and occasional cars, filled with parked cars and heavy traffic shortcutting, typical of traffic problems caused by progress everywhere.

Shops in New Street. Co-op van parked near the top Co-op. The Pullar's of Perth advertisement on the left was widespread throughout Scotland for many years

CHAPTER 22
Work

'Your uncle has spoken for you.'

PATTERNS of work were revolutionised during the course of the twentieth century. Through it all, villagers had to adapt to changing demands and practices. The freedom of choice that people enjoyed by the year 2000 contrasts so strongly with working life in 1900, it can barely be imagined. Convention, as understood by society at large, expected people to marry, raise a family and maintain and feed a household. Pay was low as the supply of labour outstripped demand. Many were trapped in challenging and underpaid work. Real choice was only available to the economically secure.

Living in a small, crowded community, where lives were scrutinised by friends and neighbours, made unconventional life choices unlikely. Working in the local community, with local employers and small businesses, with minimal employee rights, no access to Trade Unions and uniformly minimal wages, people were restricted. It took courage to challenge the the old order!

In two world wars women experienced jobs that had previously been exclusively male, but any hope that such opportunities would continue after the wars vanished when the men returned. That took until the 1960s, when choice became a possibility for many women and the concept of working couples or single parents, with childminding or nursery facilities available, increasingly became the norm.

Bad health affected people at every stage. Three censuses in Scotland show that the death rate in children under the age of one fell from eleven per hundred in 1901, through just under four in a hundred in 1951 to 0.5 per hundred in 2001. There was justifiable fear of diseases for which there was no cure. Tuberculosis [TB] was a scourge until BCG vaccination began in schools in 1953. Prior to that TB interrupted a victim's education or jobs and separated them from their families and friends, leaving some in a weakened condition and others dead.

Irene Gibson [1940s]:

'When I was in my mid-teens I had tuberculosis and I was in Johnstone Infectious Diseases Hospital. I wasn't well for a long time before I was diagnosed. You were put in bed for a year, with the windows wide open, and one part of it was all open. The trains used to go along and tooted and we waved out to them. I was only there for a short time but it WAS cold. They were trying out things to stop it. My lung collapsed and I had a lot of fluid. They took the fluid off for quite a long time. Propped up for draining. More than a pint from my pleural cavity, but I felt great afterwards.

'There was both fear and stigma associated with TB. For parents or spouses TB in the family was a matter of major concern and demanded optimism and the support of friends. People had a strange attitude – quite a lot of people kept well out of my way. I wasn't home until I was all clear.

'At different points in my life my mother would say, when I needed a chest X Ray "Don't announce it." That was years after they'd said to me, don't come back. When I got engaged to David my mother said, "Have you told him about it?" Yes! My mother would have a roaring fire on and the windows wide open. My mother never got over it.'

Irene was lucky. She was cured and able to further her education.

'I went to college to do shorthand and typing, in Gilmour Street in Paisley, there was a place up at the top of a building. Then I went to work with Galloway's the butcher at their head office in the Gorbals, in Clelland Street. The owner himself, the managing director, interviewed me. Going in I loved the look of the place it was all wood panelled and I thought, I'd love to work here. And I did, for a long time, and worked for him, latterly. The empire was still being built and when I left they had 50 or 60 retail shops and two factories and it also had farms. He had borrowed fifty pounds from his Auntie Mae and set up a shop in Dumbarton Road in Glasgow. He paid her back in six months. He made sure that every new lady, even if she was only buying a marrow bone for soup, was going to come back again, and he was nice to them and talked to them, to make sure they came back to his shop. It certainly worked for him. He ended up with his Rolls-Royce.

'I married in 1963 and worked on for a wee while, much to my father-in-law's disgust.'

Another village girl who attended college and secured a job in Glasgow was Myra Goldie, who went to Skerry's College in Bath Street, by the 8 or 8.15 train from Kilbarchan Station. 'I used to keep a lipstick in my handbag, put it on, but took it off before I went home!'

At the end of the year, her mother said that she was to apply for J&P Coates in Paisley because their wages were good, there were paid holidays and a good pension.

'I didn't want to do it but I worked in the Counting House there, in the shorthand typing pool, as they called it, for a year and a half. Went to night school in Paisley to a wee man up a close in the High Street, two or three of us, to keep up our skills and one night he said, "I've a friend who is looking for a secretary up at Rotten Row [maternity hospital]. Would you be interested?" So I went up on the Saturday morning and worked for Dr. Girvan.

'It was very different. I was up there for ten years and enjoyed every minute of it. I didn't go down to the mortuary but I got all the bits and pieces from the mortuary, put them in jars. I enjoyed the lab, there were lots of people. I helped the pathologist and did all his shorthand typing – and any of the chiefs in the wards, I did their work too. You had your main meal in the middle of the day, it was taken off your wages, 1/6d a day, and Friday it was steamed fish and boiled carrot. I think there was some white sauce on it. It was the nurses' dining room and these poor nurses, I don't know how they survived.'

Myra stopped working when she had a family.

Helen Dooris [1940s], worked in two factories:

'I went into Reid Gear. That was a very easy job, because Mr. Reid lived in Kilbarchan – if somebody from Kilbarchan applied, that's fine! He lived up Tandlehill Road. I did office work and then I left there. Then I moved to Kilbarchan, Merchant's Close. They made oil storage tanks. Sheet metal, for the likes of restaurants, that needed ventilation. The amount of stuff that went on in that workshop!

'The office was just a thing that they put up inside, no ventilation, rats. I came in one day there was a terrible smell, it was two dead rats under the floor. I worked there from 1966 to 1977 until they moved to Port Glasgow and I went with them.'

Eliza MacKenzie [1950s] worked in a factory and university:

'I went to The Glasgow and West of Scotland College in Pitt Street. It was shorthand typing, and that kind of thing, and I quite enjoyed it. Most of my life it was Babcocks. I was there until I was over fifty. It was really decimated. I ended up at Paisley University. It was quite different.'

Helen Miller [1960s]:

'I applied to go to Logan and Johnstone Nursing School out about Glasgow Green. I was 16. You weren't allowed to start nursing until you were seventeen and a half. I didn't like it, it was just school all over again. I persuaded my parents to let me change. I got a job at Scotscraig School in Thornley Park. It was the Eadie family in Paisley that donated it and also the land for Corseford. I was there when they moved from Paisley. I was a nursery assistant, then I became a classroom assistant. That was up until I had the boys. There was no question of staying on, you just came home and looked after your children.

'Away back in the 1980s a friend, Mirrlee, showed me an advert, "This is the job for you." Over at Corseford, a house mother, but it was residential. I didn't want to be residential. I did get the job so they changed it and it wasn't residential. After a wee while I went to James Watt College in Greenock to do an HNC and an HND in supporting special learning needs. I became the administrator for the residential unit until I retired, and I loved it.'

Mabel Murray [1940s] chose working in shops:

'I wanted shop work. I liked being with people. Paisley Co-op, down Causeyside Street, I was in the children's department. It was long working hours. Opened at 8.30 every day and until 6 on a Saturday. There and back by bus.'

Nan Chittick, as her family grew older [1970s]:

'I worked in a wee shop in Johnstone first. Margaret MacKendrick worked for Dr. Gibson and she told me about the job in the Fish Shop. Two days plus Saturday morning and Mabel did the other two days and the Saturday morning. I enjoyed it, you get to know people. Then I moved to school meals and I enjoyed that too. Cochrane Castle first, then I was sent to Bridge of Weir Primary. If our numbers were low I was sent to another school. The cook in Linwood said, "Every time you pass that pot, anybody, give it a stir – there's tablet in it!" Then I went to Gryffe sometimes, where I did nothing but make Empire biscuits!'

Lottie Dow [1950s] worked in a mill and in the Carpetfields:

'You signed on at the broo and they sent you to a job. I was sent to Clark's Mill [Mile End, Paisley] and my mother said "Don't come in here an say you're going into the cotton mill, because you're no going into the cotton mill." You know how years ago, if you worked in a cotton mill, you ended up getting ill because of the cotton in the air. I went to the mill at Mile End. I was spinning cotton. I was in it four months. I'd tried to get into the Carpetfield, but I couldn't get in. I was never well. I don't know whether it was the noise of the machines or the cotton flying about; I used to take terrible headaches.

'I had been sent home and really wasn't well and I heard my mother talking at the door and saying, "She'll be there, don't worry." She came through and said, "That was Bertie Miller, you've to go up to the Carpetfields tomorrow morning, Saturday, and get an interview. Your Uncle Duncan, [my mother's brother in law] has spoken for you."

'So I went up on Saturday and was interviewed and I got a wee test. I worked at the darnin' when the carpets came off the loom they came up to your flat and you'd pull it through with the pile down and you repaired it or you could get it face up and some of the pile would be missing and you filled that in with wool, you darned that. Carpets that had been bought for big houses and function suites years ago, they would be brought in and some smelled to high heaven. They smelled terrible. They steamed them after they had been repaired. Happy days there, we used to have a good laugh. I was up there until I was expecting.'

Helen Miller, the library [1960s], talking about her mother, Mrs. Reid:

'The lady there, from Paisley, whose husband had died, was part time in Kilbarchan and the office in Paisley were offering her a full-time position, because she would be the breadwinner then, bringing up her family. She said to my mum, "Would you not consider this because this position would be ideal for you?" My mum had been a librarian before the war, in Kirkcaldy. My mum got the job and had to persuade my father that it would be a good idea to go out and work: 3 o'clock in the afternoon till 5, then 6 to 8. Three days a week. It was a big issue but my mother won! She made great friends there, I got lovely letters from people when she died.

'There was an anthracite boiler and although my father

didn't work for them he would come down at night and while mum was locking up he would stoke the boiler to get it through to the next day! It was a very good thing for mum. She worked there for thirty years.'

Helen McCaig worked in the library:

'Mrs Reid? Oh, aye, a stalwart, that's for sure. The things she couldnae do, weren't worth doin'. She was really good. We were a good team. We did it properly, a lovely wee library.

'There were characters. On a Saturday afternoon it was Mrs. Finn, Jean Anderson and Cathy McDermott. Mrs. Finn always had a wee Tupperware and in it there'd be two wee cakes for the staff. Mrs. Taylor from Dalhousie would always bring a wee box with something for us.

'One day a local Lord came in and ordered a book, "I'm going to like this. . . wait till I phone HQ. . . and tell them a Lord is lookin' for a book"!'

By 2000 women might work full time or part time, go straight from school into a job or pursue further or higher education, change careers, decide if and when to have children, and with whom to have them, have the right to child and health care, maternity leave and nursery provision for their children. Equal pay was available to some. A total contrast from the limitations upon women a hundred years earlier, not all of which have been eliminated.

Until the 1950s, when boys left school at 14 or 15, time was passed in low paid jobs, whilst they sought apprenticeships. Without an apprenticeship a lifetime of unskilled, semi-skilled or labouring lay ahead.

Helen McCaig [1920s]:

'Bill's grandpa had a horse and cart and worked at the pend, for Curries. He collected the goods from the station to deliver to the Co-ops in Kilbarchan and Johnstone. There were lots of Co-ops. The goods probably came from the SCWS in Morrison Street, Glasgow.'

Alex Murphy's dad [Alex's dad was a foreman dyer in the 1920s]:

'My mother and father were very Labour people. My father was the foreman, at 22, in a dye works in Paisley and when the General Strike [1926] came he walked out and the men walked out as well. They blamed him as the foreman for taking the men out and he was banned from all dye works in the whole of Britain until 1952. [Until then] he worked at anything at all. He was a very good worker. He always got a job.

'He went back to the dye works and when he retired, the manager came out and asked him if he would go back – blue is a hard colour – he could match colours and this boy came out and asked him to go back to mix the colours. But he'd had enough.'

Walter Gardner's dad [1920s]:

'My father was a joiner. He used to walk to Kilmacolm to his work [six miles]. Later on he worked in a lace factory in Johnstone, near the site of Morrison's [Finlayson, Bousfield and Co]. I had an older brother who was killed: he fell off a ladder in Hillington, at the start of a Glasgow Fair. He was twenty years older than me.'

Ian Trushell discussing his grandpa [1920s and 1930s]:

'Grandpa Trushell worked in the calico mill print works as the cashier across the road [now the tannery]. I think it was a Thursday he had to go to Kilbarchan Clydesdale Bank branch to pick up the wages and he used to say he was armed with a Gladstone bag to carry the cash and a whistle in case he was robbed. Who was going to respond to a whistle on the Bridge of Weir road? Everyone knew that wee Bobby was going for the wages.'

John and David Carlin both left school at 14, John in 1938 and David in 1940. John worked in Reid Gear, Linwood, all his working life. David went to work in Jack and Anderson's, which opened in 1915 and closed in 1953. It was on the left of the road at Waterside Terrace, just past the electricity sub-station. It employed about 40 people.

David [1940s]:

'It was a wee cotton mill, opposite Harrison's yard, next to the laundry. I was a cotton boy, helping the workers with the cops for the cotton. They gave you a shillin' if you were good! The coal for their boiler was dumped in their yard. [Once] it had been raining all night and next morning there were tracks from the coal dump to a nearby neighbour who had helped himself!'

His father had worked at Edmiston Brown in Glasgow from the beginning of the Gyproc business. David started his electrician's apprenticeship there. The firm carried out electrical work at Pressed Steel, Linwood at the start of the war. He was called up in 1944 and served overseas. On his demob he toyed with signing up as a regular soldier but returned to Edmiston Brown.

'I heard from a friend that there was a vacancy coming in electrical in Smith and McLaurin's. I waited for that. Although the money was better up in the city, it was compensated for by saving the fares. It took you an hour or two in the morning to go up there and the same back at night. It gave me more time for myself.'

Smith and McLaurin is a long established paper mill at Cartside, just outside the village. David was put in charge of maintenance in the mill.

David recollected a fire, about thirty years ago:

'You never saw anything like it in your life. It was gutted from top to bottom. We worked right through the weekend to keep the production going and managed to salvage some of the paper. The old part, where the fire was, got everything they wanted brand new.

'We supplied all the print works in Glasgow. The vans went up every day. See, when trade was bad, they never laid anyone off. They painted the flats.'

Stoddart's Carpets of Elderslie were big employers.

'A lot from Kilbarchan worked in the Carpetfield

[Stoddart's]. Our Ronald worked there. They had a store in Paisley that he looked after. Most of the people in Kilbarchan worked in Smith and McLaurin's, the Carpetfield or Patons [shoe laces].

At the small holdings at Nether Johnstone:

'They used to come from Cartside, the strawberry pickers and the smallholder walked up and down the drills to make sure they were doing their work all right and they told me at that time, see the toilet, he'd say, "Just dae it where you are." He didn't want them to skive! They were happy with what they got, money and a basket of strawberries.

Walter Gardner [1940s]:

'My first job was at Loudon's where I served my time. Six months before my apprenticeship would have ended I was called up [conscripted to the armed forces in 1944].'

Walter trained at Canterbury, then as an anti-aircraft gunner in Wiltshire, before attending an engineering course in Wakefield. He did not go overseas and was demobbed in 1948. Walter went back to Loudon's and in 1950 moved to Remington in Hillington and subsequently worked for Rootes in Linwood, Roche in Dalry and Fairclough's in Renfrew.

Alex Murphy [1940s onwards]:

Alex left farm work when he was 16 [1949]: his mother said he had to come home and serve his time.

'My father spoke to a man in the pub who was in the joinery business who said he could probably give me a job as a joiner. I went down in the morning and lo and behold, the son of the man who owned it was a school teacher, a joiner and he had taught me and he and I didn't get on. The father gave me the job but the son didn't!

'I went into Lang's and the timekeeper shouted, What are you doing? I'm looking for a job. He and my mother were young together and went to the dancing. D'you know Jess

Murphy? So he gave me a job and I became an engineer. They sent me to school in Oakshaw. After five years I left there and met a man gardening in the allotments in the old canal basin [in Johnstone], and he's working for the government at Bishopton. So I worked for the Inspectorate of Armaments. Royal Ordnance Factory, Bishopton was a great place for people who had learning difficulties, the government paid x amount of money to hire them – the jobs were window cleaning, walls, doors and that was good, because the place was spotless. But came the closedown these were the first jobs that went. They were working, they were earning. They were happy.'

Jack Miller [1960s onwards]:

'I just left school straight into work, 15 years old. When we left somebody came and said Pressed Steel needed people. I worked there for a year in the office. They were finishing off aircraft panels. I was in an office up high, you looked right down on rows of presses. My job was to go down and get time sheets, how many hours on each job.

After that I went to start a trade at 17 and I worked for a joiner in Kilmacolm. Never finished it. My father died, my sister was already in Australia and talked my mother into going there. Train to London and six weeks on the ship. Dad was 52, he was an engineer that worked in Kincaid's in Greenock. Asbestosis.'

Norrie Howitt [1960s]:

'I was in Coates up in Glasgow in the head office in St. Vincent Street. I used to go by train but that didn't last long! I'd always wanted a job in Glasgow where you'd be wearing a suit. If you were working on a Saturday you could wear a sports jacket!

'I went for a medical up to George Square for a job with the council water department and the doctor said, You want to work for the water department, is that the best you can do for yourself? Plenty of work but never any money to do it. I took a degree in the Open University in my spare time! I had trained as an electrical engineer and I wanted to keep up to date.'

Lottie Dow on her father Archie [1940s onwards]:

'To trade he was a fitter engineer and he eventually worked in the quarry but he took TB and that was it, he wasn't working. But he was a bookies runner. He was the only one. He used to go up to the quarry to collect bets.'

Until May 1st 1961, when betting in the UK was legalised, a network of illegal businesses, entitled 'turf accountants' or 'commission agents' had been tolerated in major centres. Runners in factories or communities collected bets and delivered winnings.

David Carlin:

'They all congregated at the Cross on a Saturday morning. Archie Deans was a terrible man for the bookies! Archie used to stand at the Cross and get all their lines for the horses and dogs. They hadn't much money at that time and they used to do a tanner or a bob-tanner doubles. The big policemen came up, most of them at that time were Highlanders, "Morning boys". Then he'd go round the corner and Archie would follow him and then the copper would put his line on with Archie! Then he'd walk back down, nobody saw him doing the business!'

Drew Connell:

'The famous Erchie Deans was the bookie, the Kilbarchan bookies' runner. He used to stand in Maggie Fulton's close in Parkview and get all the guys coming from the quarry. Every day he was up there and everyone knew where to get him. My father would send me up when I was an apprentice for the guys who worked there – the Grand National or the Derby. He could tell you to the halfpenny how much he owed you, he could do all the betting.'

Mima Borland:

'The majority of the people gambled. In fact we had Archie Deans, the bookies runner, if you didn't get him at both the park gates, you got him at the pub; if you didn't get him at the pub you got him at the Cross, you got him down at the monument. Father told me one day to take a line, "Take it up to Archie." I said, "There's no money in it." "Just take the line to Archie, get up that road and get the bet on for me." I didn't realise he had money lying with the bookie. I found him at the Cross just opposite the Weaver's Cottage.

'My dad went to work for Dr. Gibson for a year in 1964. Dr. Gibson bought the cottage [Beltrees Cottage, previously the telephone exchange] and got my dad in to do it up and said, "Arthur, I really don't know what to do with this place." And my dad said, "It would make a great bookies, Dr.Gibson!" "I don't think so, Arthur, I don't think so!" '

Until 1960, at age 18 all fit males were liable for two years national service. In 1960 Alex Murphy joined the RAF:

'I was put on a charge on the second day, second night and third morning. I was taken in before the old man [his officer].

'Kit issue consisted of two of everything. I was balancing it all and I tumbled my best blue and he [the NCO / Non Commissioned Officer] said I'd lost it. He charged me. The second was in the parade ground. This fella with an English voice shouted – I'd been in the BB and knew how to march – some went right and some went left and I said, Pardon? Another charge. I realised later that you did something, that you didn't just stop!'

In 1957 after training in the Royal Engineers, for Drew Connell, there were overseas options:

'I volunteered for Hong Kong or Germany and ended up at Whitehaugh Barracks in Paisley. We went away with the Territorials, building bridges.

'I was in charge of four trucks, including a ten ton Leyland Hippo, with eight gears. I had to teach another man to drive it.

'. . . going through East Kilbride I said turn to the left at this wee roundabout and he went to turn up a wee dark road. He went straight over a grass roundabout – great big tyres – back to the workshop cleaned it and painted it. I enjoyed it. It got me away from my mother and father's apron strings because I'd gone straight from school to work for my father and I'd never been out in the wide world.'

Arthur Smith was called up to the armed forces in 1953, when he was in an insurance office:

'When you look back it was an experience that probably did me a lot of good because I was a wee quiet reserved boy. The standard of the National Service officers was appalling, as long as you went to a certain school, and had a certain education and an accent you were in. Some of the regular NCOs were just about as bad, all bitter and twisted. Oswestry for my basic training – you had to run for a mile in full kit carrying a rifle and I proved to be quite good at that so I was immediately in the regimental cross country team. Anyone play rugby? Cricket? Got you away on one or two trips. It took two years out of my life but it took me out of that insurance office.'

To pay the rent and have food on the table work was always essential. Having links to people already employed provided avenues to securing jobs. The century began with labour intensive jobs which were radically changed by mechanisation. Higher and increasingly more accessible standards of general education prepared people to meet the challenges of a rapidly changing world.

Shorthand, carbon paper, stencils and spirit duplicators transformed office work and then further changes came about through ballpoint pens, tape and digital recorders, video conferencing, e-mail, mobile phones, computers and personal laptops.

Factory jobs reduced in the face of automation, mass production, computer assisted design and robotics. Only a few of the businesses named in this chapter persist. The death of heavy industry in the West of Scotland, the export of jobs to cheaper labour sources and takeovers, destroyed many skilled and semi-skilled jobs. Jobs in local shops lost out to retail parks, supermarkets and buying on the internet. Raising the school leaving age, opening new colleges and universities, a vast hospitality and travel industry and the motor trade created employment.

Despite vigorous protests, including a protest march and the invasion of a Renfrewshire Council meeting, the village library closed in 1998 and was replaced by a mobile library. Health and safety and workers' rights improved. An increasing commitment to pre-school education, social care for all categories and ages, and an expanding National Health Service opened opportunities that had not previously existed.

Baker's advertisement

CHAPTER 23

Shops

'The Co-op also delivered by horse and cart.'

'The big retailer in the village was, as in most communities, the Co-operative.'

A VISITOR to the village at the beginning of the twenty first century could see that there are very few shops. Like all villages in close proximity to a town, city and retail park, technological progress had changed shopping over the past century. The independent retailers, specialist shops, old crafts and trades people of the village had almost all gone.

Shops were crucial to community life. Early postcards show the variety and numbers of them at The Cross and New Street. Some shops sold similar goods. Often there was no need to go from the bottom of the village to the top, or vice versa. Many people didn't need to mix with those from the opposite end of the village; few needed, wanted, or could afford to venture further than the village for everyday supplies.

The big retailer in the village was, as in most communities, the Co-operative. Offering everything, benefitting its members, from cradle to grave. The first co-operative was begun by weavers in Fenwick, not far from Kilbarchan, in 1761, well before the Rochdale Pioneers in 1844. Many other villages followed suit. The largest Co-op was built in the early twentieth century and is at the centre of the village. In line with all other co-operatives management was in the hands of a local committee.

The main Co-op in the village had three shops in one building with housing above. From left to right it had a small butchers, or fleshers shop, a large drapery shop, and a small dairy. They also had what was became known as the 'top Co', in New Street, with public halls above, which sold groceries and a 'low Co' in Low Barholm, another large grocery store. Throughout the century these changed physically, with the final demolition of the top Co and sale of the low Co, to the amalgamation of the main buildings to make a supermarket.

Myra Goldie:

'The Co-op – there was the butcher's, now the pharmacy, still has the original ceiling, the walls had been tiles with pictures of cows. Through the back a lovely big roaring fire on one side and a cow hanging up on the other, waiting to be cut up!

'There was a close, then the draper's, a close, the dairy, which would be in the middle of the current shop, and a dairy at the end. Miss Boyd was in charge of the drapery, stayed upstairs. It is said that she came to Kilbarchan during WW I; her fiancé was from the village. He was killed, but she remained for the rest of her life.

'She sold everything, including shoes. If she didn't have it, she gave you a line to take to the Co in Glasgow, at Morrison Street. Wholesale. She was a character.'

> 'People walked to the shops, bought locally and supported local businesses.'

Shopkeepers relied on deliveries by horse and cart, the railway, and lorries. The village itself was a bustling, busy place, where people walked to the shops, bought locally and supported local businesses. Money was earned locally and spent locally, invariably in cash.

Borrowing from the local bank could be a last resort, when borrowing from a pal or a relative may have been more common. People saved for things that they wanted, using a variety of means, a tin on the mantelpiece or Christmas Clubs. Catalogues were especially popular where the latest fashions and home furnishings could be paid up by weekly instalments.

Many shops offered 'tick', where goods could be paid at a mutually agreed time. Tick was common in the villages, although it was not like many model villages, like New Lanark where weekly earnings were spent in the village shop, owned by the company.

For independent local shops, it was either sink or swim. Peter Barr set up his business in High Barholm, which eventually left the family, but retained the name until the 1980s. It changed from the top quality Grocer, Wine and Spirit Merchant to a self-service store. Peter Barr's was one of the oldest shops in the village. They had huge counters, with many workers.

Barr's had a big wooden counter, cheese cutter, ham machine, butter pats and fresh butter, Belfast ham and a selection of meats. On the right side they sold alcohol and had a coffee grinder! Mr. and Mrs. Innes worked there, as did Mrs. Newton. It was a good-going shop.

Before self-service, customers had to ask for the items they wanted, which, in some cases must have put people off. People knew what each other liked. There was little anonymity, everybody knew your business. Choice was limited, especially during the war years and rationing.

> 'Before self-service, customers had to ask for the items they wanted, which, in some cases must have put people off.'

Willie Sunshine used to go to Barr's. Willie Sunshine was a well-known character who lived around the village, reputedly sometimes washing in the trough on Forehouse Road, working on farms and sleeping in farm buildings or in the open in the better weather. He wore thick glasses like the bottoms of lemonade bottles and a coat tied with string. His Sunshine nickname originated from a brief career in Prohibition America, where he had allegedly been involved in moonshine – illicit alcohol.

Meat supplies, slaughtered at the back of the butcher's before World War II, were replaced by meat from a local central abattoir. Cobblers, where shoes were actually repaired, not merely replaced and segs, laces and shoe polish were sold, were common.

Haberdashery shops sold wide choices of thread, buttons, needles, ribbons, and fabrics for dressmaking, as so many people made and repaired their own clothes. 'Make do and mend' was commonplace. These skills became increasingly rare in a developing, largely disposable, cheap and plastic world.

There were two favourite smaller specialist shops, the one earliest to open, selling the sweet, the savoury and the staple of most households, bread.

> 'They sold macaroon cakes, doughnuts, snowballs, potato scones, crumpets, pies; they were famous for their pies.'

David Carlin:

'On the corner was Hamilton the bakers. He was a good baker; his rolls and pies were brilliant. Through the pend was the bakehouse. As boys we used to get the rolls, still hot in the bags, good with butter in them. One penny a roll before the war, they were real rolls then. Willock Smith the baker got up at 4 in the morning. On a Saturday he'd go for a walk to a football game in Ayrshire, back at night. I used to watch him carry the baker's boards on top of his head. He kept pigeons too, carrying the pigeons to the station on the top of his head!'

Ethel Hamilton's husband Bert was the baker and his father before him.

Ethel:

'The bakehouse was in Church Street, through the first pend opposite the church. The charcoal for the ovens was kept there. The horse and cart would come and dump it in the pend. There was a walkway between that and the back door of the shop, which was where the chiropodist is now.

'They sold macaroon cakes, doughnuts, snowballs, potato scones, crumpets, pies; they were famous for their pies. Old Geordie Hamilton used to make and decorate wedding cakes. They did purveying a lot in the Masonic Hall.

'Work was hard for the bakers. 5am start, Friday night an all nighter. Bert would work on Friday morning, purvey at functions at night and work again on Saturday. This trade continued into the 1970s. Being fairly near the school, it was a popular place. Pupils were not allowed out of the school grounds.'

The sweetie shop, throughout the generations, was a favourite. From the big jars came a penny's worth, a quarter pound of, one or two of, all methods of measurement now largely lost. Decimalisation and pre-packaging in particular changed the purchase of sweeties forever. As did health and safety laws! Although it was likely to be more efficient to shove a bare hand into a jar and empty sweets on to scales, having just handled money, or something equally insanitary, and complete the job by blowing open a paper bag to wrap the sweets. Times changed!

Mrs. Painter's, Annie McCleerie, Beaton's, Brunetti's, Burridge's, Barnaby's, Mrs. Malone's were a few of the names mentioned by those who had fondly remembered sweet shops.

Christine Erwin:

> 'I stopped at the Cyclists' Rest to buy barley sugar sticks or rhubarb rock. There were plenty of sweetie shops in the village. . . next door to Mrs. Parks in Low Barholm, The Cyclists' Rest, Alexander's in High Barholm, Mrs. Malone's in High Barholm, Burridge's on Ewing Street, Barnaby's at the Steeple steps.'

Shops offered delivery services. David Carlin [1930s and 1940s]:

> 'Alex Orr, the fruiterer, with only one arm, went round the village with a fruit cart. Up to the war. There were butcher's and fish deliveries by bike.'

Irene Gibson [1930s and 1940s]:

> 'As a child, lots of vans and carts came round. Milk was delivered by Jack Smith of Auchencloich. Flem Craig was also around with two big churns with taps. The old women would take out jugs to him.

> 'A lorry came from Beith with paraffin oil for heating. Willie Henderson sold fruit "apples, eggs and ingins". Ripe bananas! Coal was delivered from Barr's of Bridge of Weir. The Co-op also delivered coal by horse and cart.'

Deliveries of produce arrived early every morning, with fresh items sold by the end of the day. The product was guaranteed to be gone by the end of the day. Although they had limited stock, shopkeepers knew their customers and could purchase enough, with minimal wastage.

Refrigeration was basic or non-existent. Lighting in shops, to which we pay little notice to today, was badly needed. There was little storage space in houses, with no refrigeration in the early days. Milk was delivered and purchased daily.

> 'Mrs. Painter's, Annie McCleerie, Beaton's, Brunetti's, Burridge's, Barnaby's, Mrs. Malone's were a few of the names mentioned by those who had fondly remembered sweet shops.'

Large front windows maximised light and provided much space for display. Window dressing became an art form. People looked in shop windows. In the passing, walking to work, or for the bus, people could see in the window. It was in the shopkeeper's interest to put items on display.

By the end of the century few cared about what was in the window. They parked their cars, did their shopping and drove off again without paying much attention. In some cases shop fronts were covered over as more space was needed inside the shop. Space was needed for refrigeration, freezers and drinks machines.

> 'By the end of the century few cared about what was in the [shop] window.'

Women usually did the shopping. It was what society expected. Children ran errands for family, friends and neighbours, whether they wanted to or not!

People had their favourite shops. The flavours and tastes differed, as each shop had their own trade secret recipes, the mysteries of which were perhaps best not known! Scotch pies, rhubarb tarts were not uniform, pre-packed and with long shelf lives. Reputation was everything. It was in the shopkeeper's interest to keep a good stock, to listen and be friendly to their customers, in the days before this became known as 'marketing'.

Days of the week affected shopping, people knew the best times, when the pies would be hot and the delivery days. Shops opened at certain times, closed for lunch and were never open on a Sunday. Wednesday was Kilbarchan's half day. All of that was part of the everyday shopping experience of the village.

Hairdressers and barbers were always social hubs in the village, with businesses surviving when others closed. A visit to the hairdresser or barber enabled people to meet, find social support, exchange news, and have personal attention in a comfortable place. It was a relaxing, companionable place to go from crowded homes. A visit to the hairdresser was much more than a new haircut!

Another meeting place, the pub also changed. The drinking rooms of the past were often converted front rooms, selling alcohol. At the beginning of the century the more formalised Public House had emerged. Licensing Acts controlled standards and measurements. The Trust Inn and the Glenleven, the two long established pubs, changed with the times. From the bar with sawdust on the floor, with a separate Lounge and an Off Sales, they became open plan.

Bar food, juke box, live music, quiz nights and TV sports' channels took over.

The village, like most villages, had a chip shop. Helen Dooris' family owned this: 'They had a fish and chip shop, mum was in among the potatoes.'

There was a chippy at what is now Bobbins. There was also a chip shop called The Hub, where the old Police Station is now in New Street. It was a hut arrangement – 'from the Pub to the Hub'.

Some of the village shops provided a real experience! Alexander's Newsagent in High Barholm in the 1970s was a typical example.

Myra Goldie:

'Shoe lasts. For repairing shoes, boots, and football boots. Segs were put on heels and toes. Segs were bought in Alexander's shop across the road; you could buy anything there, including Kirby grips and hairnets.'

Helen McCaig worked in Alexander's at this time:

'When the Sunday papers were delivered to the shop, you could hardly lift them. They were dropped off in the morning in the close. Alexander's had a brass click on the door. The counter was on the left. There were five steps in the middle to go upstairs.'

'They sold paraffin. I didn't like getting that. "If anyone asks, say, I'm no here"! Paraffin was kept in the back shop, with the flat above! It was sold by the gallon. They had everything on strings, pencils, rubbers, hairnets, shoelaces [brown and black, nae white for yer saunnies (Scots: sandshoes)]. You had to duck under the strings when you were working. Betty got her wig caught in the thing going upstairs. It was such good fun, you know, really good.

'A woman came in. "Can I have a wee pan?" So I went and brought a pan loaf. She said, "A cannae bile ma eggs in that!" They sold pan loaves as well as cooking pans!

'A man came in with his case from the potteries in England.

> 'Alexander's shop across the road; you could buy anything there, including Kirby grips and hairnets.'

Classic stuff. Not the Betterware man! Someone in the shop was looking for a present for a friend. Bought a beautiful crystal ashtray. Everybody smoked in those days.

'They sold money savings banks in the shape of the old threepenny bit. There must be some still floatin' about this village somewhere.

'The shop was packed out, full of stuff. Glass cabinets, brass scales that were cleaned and polished. They also sold potatoes. Santa was upstairs. Bill had to step in as Santa once, but a wee boy knew that it wasn't Santa; it was Mr. McCaig dressed up. Maybe his beard didnae fit, I don't know.

'People would come in and pay the papers very week. Each had a number in a big book, with a wee tear-off slip. They had their own boys to deliver the papers. One had a wee dog. He had to do a double run on a Sunday, as there were so many, and the papers were so big. After the first run, the dog went home. The dog said to himself, "I've had enough, I ain't doin' another round"!

'The *Citizen* was green, The *Times* was pink. It had the football, and swimming results. A gentleman in Easwald Bank came in every Saturday, a man of few words. He would sit on the back step waiting on the papers with the football results to come in.'

Tobacco and cigarettes were huge sellers in many of the shops. Children were interested in cigarette cards, which became collector's items. Smoking was common amongst adults, whether it was fags or pipes. Some teenagers thought that smoking gave them an adult image. Health research in the 1950s, education and pressure by lobbyists later in the century began to break the habit.

David Carlin [1930s]:

'There were a lot of smokers then. John and I used to stand at the wall and ask them if they had any cigarette cards which had pictures of footballers, film stars and so on.'

During the war, and for a time afterward, cigarettes were hard to come by. It helped if you kept in with the shop owner, which David did...

> '... she was selective as to who she gave cigarettes... sometimes the cigarettes ran out. She would say that she wanted to speak to me in the back shop. She had kept cigarettes for me. I smoked Passing Cloud, also Players Navy Cut. Posh.'

A character in the 1930s ran a hosiery shop. Selling stockings, socks and underwear in a village was a sign of the times! However it was not the sale of such items that she was remembered for...

> 'She used to put on a line, Archie used to go in there to get her line. She put money on two horses in the one race in case one fell.'

Miss Margaret Gray had a Milliner's and Dressmaker's shop in High Barholm in 1917. The latest styles would have been recreated in her home in the back shop, probably using a treadle sewing machine. Clothes were not purchased off the peg. Customers could come for a personal fitting, with alterations and adaptations made at the customer's request. This continued until her death, unmarried, at the age of 51. The end of an era. The shop changed with each new owner, and with each new specialism, until by the end of the twentieth century, the business closed. In the 1960s it had evolved into the Fish Shop. Georgina Stephen worked there, as did Nan Chittick, Mabel Murray and Christine MacLeod. Georgina and Christine in conversation about work in the late 1970s:

> 'I remember Miss Allan's fish shop up at The Cross. Miss Allan moved from the Cross, when the shops were knocked down, around 1964. I only came when Andy Thompson took over.' [Georgina's son John was the delivery boy.]

Christine:

> 'The potatoes came in sacks, the first thing I had to do in the morning was to bag them up into 3lb and half stone bags ready for the busy day ahead. Cauliflowers were trimmed with a machete, which was also used to halve the turnips by

battering them off the floor until they split. No health and safety!'

Georgina:

'Little did I think that I'd ever be able to gut a fish – the thought of it! Most of the fish came in filleted but when a whole salmon and cod came in. . . Would you like it gutted? Oh, the mess. Gutting salmon and trout was a regular occurrence, as was going through the haddock, whiting and lemon sole to suit customers' demands for the right size, before wrapping and cash handling!'

Georgina:

'Andy went into Christmas trees that had all to be put out and taken in daily. I used to come out in a rash with the holly! And there were plants outside. People debated, took ages, deciding on the right height and shape of the trees!

'There was such a demand for turkeys at Christmas, there wasn't enough space in the fridges, so they just went in the back shop. They were all just stacked up. It was mobbed at Christmas time, turkeys, Christmas trees, wreaths. There were never any health issues, no one ever came back and complained.'

Christine:

'Jimmy Stewart brought strawberries from his smallholding at the bottom of the village. He did punnets, but also sold loose jam strawberries. Marmalade oranges came in winter. The big blocks of cheese were cut, using a wire. Canadian Red Diamond, or Lockerbie.'

Georgina:

'The ham machines, where the haunle was cau'd [Scots: turned], had to be cleaned at the end of the day. It was all washed and all put back together and someone would come in and ask for two slices of ham, at twenty five past five, so it would have to be redone.'

Christine:

'At the church village coffee mornings people would come down with flasks of milky coffee and home baking for the staff. Regulars were in the shop at certain times of the day, some early, some late! Talkers talked, and talked more. Orders were delivered by John on his bike. Extra fish deliveries on a Tuesday when the fish came in fresh.

'There was an old lady who had her cats in a pram when she came to the shop. She collected fish boxes for firewood. Then there was Mrs. Blair from Blair's farm, she used to get her order. The orders came in on a Thursday and were made up and delivered on a Friday. It was a happy wee shop with Andy.'

Georgina:

'Now everyone gets in their car, comes home and watches their TV. No one knows anyone.'

Having a village shop became uneconomic, so many closed. These shops became incorporated into the houses above or beside them, and in many cases, both.

The movement from the local shop to the supermarket, the building of shopping centres like Linwood and later Braehead, changed shopping habits entirely. The building of the A737 bypass meant easier access to the motorway to town and city by car and people working in the city could shop there. The small shops could not compete.

As a result of increasing acceptance of technology, new methods of shopping evolved and continue to evolve. New artisans can work in their own community, in their own home, anywhere in the nation. They no longer need the shop, where people visit. People can visit their website, from anywhere in the world and purchase what they want, to suit their style, free from tradition and its limitations.

Listen Closely

Mother and children in the Public Park... playing above concrete!

Chapter 24
Childhood Memories

'I had a marble peever and roller skates.'

EVERYONE involved in this book had some great stories. Doing what most children did anywhere. Mostly in a time before television and before the other distractions of later twentieth century life. Childhood in the village sounds idyllic. Most of their recollections required little money. Ingenuity, imagination and willingness to make the best of what they had was evident throughout.

This chapter is a bit different from the others. David, Helen, Mabel, Christine, Mima, Drew, Georgina, Ian M, Ian T, Myra, Moira, Jeff and Eilidh all shared their childhood stories. They are, in no particular date order, snapshots of happy memories.

> 'The street was full of kids after the post-war boom, with 2-3 children in almost every house. There was one car. We played a lot of football in the street, if anyone hit that car, they all ran, PDQ. [Pretty damned quick]!'

> 'At birthday parties [in the 1950s], there was no one-upmanship. The mothers may have got together; no one would up, or outdo anyone. The purvey. We had the same meal at every party; egg and mayonnaise and corned beef with HP sauce. To drink, we had a glass of lemonade, [Krystal Clear], American Cream Soda or Koala Cola from Struthers of Lochwinnoch. They played pass the parcel etc, had no TV, then went outside.'

> 'The sun always shone, and skin peeled on the first exposure to sunlight, there was no sunscreen in those days.'

> 'The spare ground was the children's playground. The girls would dress up and do amateur dramatics.'

'Some children went to great lengths to get something extra to eat. Aunt Bella lived in Number 5. She had gorgeous biscuits, we used to go in and pinch them.'

Some things that are now unusual:

'Fine stems of rhubarb with a poke of sugar.'

'You went to the park and ate wee plants, it looked a bit like watercress. Also gentian root. We dug it up in the park. Lucky we're still living. Sugarally watter – liquorice. The roots were good for cleaning teeth and sweet tasting.'

'Connective tissue. I ate this. I thought this was lovely, but it made my friend feel sick. . . running about with a knuckle bone. My dad scraped every bit of marrow out of the bone into my soup. It's now a delicacy. We were well fed and didn't know it.'

'One of the favourite foods of children and adults, to fill you up and feed large numbers was the cloutie dumplin'. Made for generations. It became something for occasions like birthdays and Ne'erday. It was common to put tiny trinkets, sixpences, a silver threepenny, in the dumplin' mix. These trinkets could be tiny horseshoes, for luck, minute wedding rings, buttons, thimbles, all symbolic. These were wrapped in brown paper. There was great enthusiasm and fun when the dumplin' was given out to see who got what, a form of fortune telling. Looking for the items in the dumplin' would far reduce the choking hazard!'

'During the war, instead of dumplin' they put trinkets in mashed potato. Now if you put a sixpence in a dumplin' they'd go hysterical.'

Some earned a bit of money:

'Spoolin' apples. There were good ones at Mountview. Barr the coal merchant lived there at the time. She was more interested in her rabbits. We used to go over and see the rabbits. We picked dandelions for the rabbits, and she would gie you at tanner. This would be spent on sweeties. Used to buy lollipops with different flavours. These would last about twenty minutes. Sweeties didn't last.'

'I used to clean out the hen hut once a week, my father gave me a penny or 2d.'

'Mrs. Painter had the sweetie shop at The Cross. My friend would buy a bottle of Ginger every week and keep it in the shop. Most days he would take a swig out of the bottle and put a mark on it. Ginger was also called Pop.'

'Betty MacIntyre worked in the Post Office and when we were boys we used to go up and stand around the Post Office and hope that a telegram would come in because you got a tanner [sixpence] to deliver a telegram. Maybe going up for your *Beano* or your *Dandy*, then *Adventure*, *Wizard* and *Hotspur*. I used to get all those comics. We used to go up and stand and wait for them. Later [1950] *The Eagle*, *Dan Dare*.'

'Folk used to sit on the steps of the cottage. Old Miss Christie used to get a pail of water – the steps were all worn away – and shove it down when they're all sitting there, to clear them off the steps!'

Many children knew of, and used, old remedies:

'My sister fell into nettles and dock leaves were rubbed on to stop the sting.'

Some old remedies are no longer applicable as some things just don't happen anymore!

'A lot of folk in Kilbarchan used to go to The Law for a nightly walk, the healthiest spot, for fresh air. In summer the tar on that road used to melt. Our mother used to give us a row for having tarry feet. Butter took off the tar.'

On the go all day, children did as they were told and when it came to bedtime. . .

'We were put to bed early. "It was time you were in bed."

> It was 7 o'clock! While my friends played next door, my mother shut the curtains and me and my sister were in bed. The next generation got to stay up until 8 o'clock! We were told we needed our sleep; we were still growing.'

Some couldn't or wouldn't go to sleep:

> 'I remember lying in bed trying to stay awake until the twenty past nine train would chuff its way up past our house to the station. Obviously meant to be asleep long before then!'

> 'I heard noises coming from the radio station late at night with lots of snap crackle and pop when my dad was listening to a Polish channel.'

Some families had ingenious methods of storage that children loved.

> 'My granny's oven was somewhere to store games, as she always cooked on top of the stove. The Great Universal catalogue was also stored there, and well looked at.'

> 'We didn't venture to the top of the village much, we never really ventured beyond our own area. We used to play ring, bang, skoosh. Ringing doorbells. And running away.'

> 'Some played close by, others ventured further from home, it just depended on where friends and family were and the age and stage of life.'

> 'We used to meet and play at the Bundy clock, at the end gable of Low Barholm.'

> 'I went to school going up Gateside to be with my cousins, and played there a lot.'

> 'When I was about 9 or 10 the wee group would make pieces and walk to Clochoderick Stone. One of the boys fell off and broke his leg.'

> 'I was not allowed a bike in case of accident. I was an only child. My cousins had bikes and I could go a bike fine.'

'There were few cars; we would go away for a whole day. Nobody batted an eyelid.'

'At [what is now] Lewis Crescent there were donkeys or horses, taking carrots to feed them. I played in the Glebe and in the burn. There was a line of trees at the top of the hill, near Toppersfield, where there were also horses and cows. The burn was a great attraction. Beside my house was a fence where I used to do "gymnastics".'

'In winter I played in the snow across the road, there was no need to go to the park.'

'Outside the village, I played in the Locher burn. I used to get slapped aboot when I came home, as my feet were always wet, and my socks shrunk!'

'We played at The Glebe. Our ball went over the wall into the manse gardens. The minister was not too complimentary. We're sayin' "Christian"!'

'Wallace's cave legend. It was thought to go through to Elderslie. I found it over the Milliken wall, over to the left. I knew of people in school who got in and walked to Elderslie! It was probably nothing. Could have been an old seam cut into the hillside. Mythology.'

Cul-de sacs were a safe place to play.

'I would go cycling to Simpson Terrace, which was where the Primary School is now. The houses were pre-fabs, with a turning circle at the end of the cul-de-sac. It was like centrifugal force going round. Often got skint knees.'

'Gateside Place – the lamp post outside was our silent partner for skipping.'

'We played out in the street at Gateside Place. We only played indoors if it was raining heavily. My dad roared a name when it was time to come in. We used to come out of all sorts of places.'

'We played in the woods behind the Bank house, and behind the Hunt's house. Unbelievable, fantastic. We climbed trees, built hides, racing."

We played over the Banker's. Everybody went through our close and over the wall. We didn't go into the graveyard, which was close by, it was not the right thing to do.'

'We built tree houses, went digging, made twig and leaf roofs, survival stuff.'

'We walked up on the park wall. Played kick the can at the old garages. Played in the old school building, which was derelict, as was the house beside it.'

'We were never in. The street was great for skipping, peevers [Scots – hopscotch], I had a marble peever and roller skates. An old annual was used with the skate, with the skate below, we could use the annual and roll down the street. It was a great flat surface. Skipping, could use a huge rope, to ca' the rope, although this was usually done at school.'

'The primary school playground had a mixture of surfaces, some areas flat, some grassed with trees, and an area behind the playground you could throw balls against the wall. We were constantly on the go.'

'Christmas time [at Gateside Place in the 1960s] was unbelievable. We couldn't sleep. We had to tip toe past mum and dad's room. One year we got nurses uniforms [not doctors] and woke up parents to show them what Santa had brought.'

'It was magical. My parents had six children; they tried their best. Mum loved Christmas. They didn't have a big Christmas tree. They had a big Christmas dinner, feeding all these folk, including gran and papa. They sat in the sitting room at the table, which had special tablecloth and cutlery, which only came out on special occasions. All round the table.'

'I played in the street. We played on our bikes a lot. There were a number of children there of similar ages. We played Kerby, ball games, tennis in the street and made up plays for our parents to watch, who were very enthusiastic.'

'The public park was the place where all went to at some stage. There were no cars; we could walk to the park.'

'During the Apprentices' Strike of the 1960s, there were constant games of football. All the engineers from Johnstone were at a loose end. They played on the bit between the diagonal path and Park View.'

'We went to the big hill, sledging. You were brave if you came down the big hill. Someone crashed into a wee boy who was hurt. It was rough.'

'The playground had a whirlygig, a roundabout and two sets of three swings. Kids played there a lot.'

'The families in Gateside used to go to play in the public park; families with a room and kitchen piled out there to the public park. Mr. Dick lived at 10 Gateside, upstairs. He was the park keeper. He could see everything that was going on. He ruled that with an iron fist.'

Going into the Grove estate with impunity:

'The Well Road had an entrance. There was a house just inside. An elderly lady lived there with her even more elderly dug, like the Hound of the Baskervilles; we thought it would tear us apart.'

Nicknames were common:

'Nearly everyone had a nickname, you didn't mind being called by your nickname. Nicknames are not so common now.'

'Snowball Irvine. David's mother asked a girl to tell big Jim to come in for his tea. She called him Mr. Snowball, as she had heard him being called Snowball!'

Many parents paid for private lessons for their children. A great deal of emphasis was placed on the ability to speak 'properly'.

> 'I went to elocution lessons to Jenny Irvine's. I loved it. We put plays on before Christmas. Mum didn't want us to talk broad Scots like dad. I later worked in Paisley, so mum thought she had wasted money.'

> 'Quite a few were sent to elocution lessons, which were also taught at the Grammar School. I took part in the Greenock festival. Dad was my prompt. 2/6 a class, 5 bob a week for two children. Parents paid hard earned cash. BBC, correct, meticulous grammar important.'

> 'The standard BBC voice affected people in those days. It was the big listen, not the big look.'

Some parents went that extra mile to help with homework.

> 'I had a great dad. I got my dad to do lines. Dad did my homework. Fractions. His educational system was completely different. In P6 Mr. McArthur knew – I didn't ask your dad to do homework. Dad had done it and I copied.'

Television changed lives:

> 'We got TV as dad was told that there was horse racing on it. Dad thought Top of the Pops was brilliant, especially when you turned the sound down! Got a record player at 16. Dad sponsored me. I paid it up. A Dansette. No record player coming in here, or the TV is going! No way would my dad do that, as he would have to give up his Saturday racing.'

Parents controlled the television. It was the only screen in the house, so it was family viewing, with the scheduling of programmes setting new timescales at home. Mealtimes, play times and bedtimes were often adapted to suit whatever was on television. The age of the screen changed lives forever.